MECHANICS-
MERCANTILE
LIBRARY.

Arthur F. Mathews '08

D1016222

# Stem Cell Century

# Stem Cell Century

Law and Policy for a
Breakthrough Technology

RUSSELL KOROBKIN

*with Stephen R. Munzer*

Yale University Press   New Haven and London

Designed by Nancy Ovedovitz.
Set in Minion type by Integrated Publishing Solutions.
Printed in the United States of America.

Library of Congress Cataloging-in-Publication Data

Korobkin, Russell.
    Stem cell century : law and policy for a breakthrough technology /
Russell Korobkin with Stephen R. Munzer.
        p.   cm.
    Includes bibliographical references and index.
    ISBN 978-0-300-12292-3 (cloth : alk. paper)
    1. Tissue engineering—Law and legislation—United States.
2. Stem cells—Research—Law and legislation—United States.
I. Munzer, Stephen R.   II. Title.
    KF3827.G4K67  2007
    344.7304′196—dc22                              2007017353

A catalogue record for this book is available from the
British Library.

The paper in this book meets the guidelines for permanence and
durability of the Committee on Production Guidelines for Book
Longevity of the Council on Library Resources.

10 9 8 7 6 5 4 3 2 1

For Jessica,
child of the stem cell century

# Contents

# Preface

In the past several years, the country's increasing fascination with the potential of stem cell research has been mirrored by the publication of a number of books on the subject. None of them is like this one. Some of these books are basic science texts that provide a sound description of the technology behind stem cell research for nonscientists. Others concern the policy and politics of conducting research on stem cells obtained by destroying human embryos.

Although Chapter 1 provides a very brief background in stem cell technology—just enough, I hope, to enable readers to understand the nuances of the policy debates—this is a book about policy, not science. The range of policy issues it considers, however, extends far beyond the battle in Washington, D.C., over funding embryo-related research. This particular debate is a critical part of the story of stem cell research, and it is analyzed in detail in Chapter 2, but it is only one part. The remaining eight chapters of the book critically analyze a raft of additional issues that are of fundamental importance in the nation's quest to fulfill the promise of stem cell research. How we as a nation choose to resolve these important and challenging issues, which receive relatively little attention in the popular media, will shape our era, which I call the "stem cell century."

The theme that runs throughout this book is that legal institutions, not just scientific knowledge, will play a central role in determining whether stem cell technology is able to achieve its tremendous promise. It is thus fitting to describe the way in which academic institutions have been central to the creation of the book.

The UCLA Center for Society and Genetics, as the name suggests, exists to study the interplay between a booming field of scientific inquiry and importance and our broader society. The center seeks to bring together in formal and informal ways faculty and students from the biological, physical, and medical sciences (who inhabit the portion of the university unofficially known as "South Campus") and those from the social sciences and humanities (who reside on "North Campus").

In the summer of 2005, the center was planning a conference that would offer cross-disciplinary perspectives on stem cell research. The center's co-directors, Dr. Ed McCabe and Professor Norton Wise, approached UCLA School of Law dean Michael Schill to seek the law school's involvement. Schill agreed that the law school would co-sponsor the conference and suggested that McCabe and Wise approach Stephen Munzer and me, both law professors, about the possibility of presenting a paper at the conference on relevant legal issues. Ed and Norton asked, and Steve and I agreed.

As is typical of academic types, Steve and I launched into the project vastly underestimating its scope and challenge. I teach health care law, among other subjects, and I have written about the topics of physician-assisted suicide, the regulation of managed care organizations, and rights to health care services. Steve is interested in biotechnology and has taught and written in that general area on occasion. Neither of us, however, could fairly claim expertise in stem cell research or its legal and social implications at the time.

As we immersed ourselves in the subject and expanded our knowledge, we realized that the topics we were exploring would interest not only lawyers and professors interested in law and science but also educated members of the lay public who are intrigued by the most important and challenging policy issues of our time. From that realization sprang this book. It would never have come to be on the strength of our initiative alone. Its existence required the foresight of UCLA to recognize the potential of creating the Center for Society and Genetics and the commitment of both the center and the School of Law to interdisciplinary research. We are forever indebted to both of these institutions and their leaders for their generous intellectual and financial support for this project.

Although we started on this path together initially and continued on it for some while, differences in our substantive views and preferred style of presentation prevented Steve and me from being able to truly collaborate on the final product. Chapter 4, "Stem Cell Patents," is a joint product. Steve offered me helpful comments and editing advice on drafts of other chapters and some research on a few of these chapters, which I gratefully acknowledge. The views expressed in these chapters, however, are my responsibility alone. Steve should not be called to account for any of the errors in fact, analysis, or judgment that may have resulted.

Because the book crosses so many areas of law and policy, both Steve and I are indebted to a large number of colleagues, at UCLA and elsewhere, for sharing with us their knowledge of particular areas and, in many cases, commenting on draft versions of various chapters: Rick Abel, Michael

Darby, Ken Dorschkind, Guoping Fan, Mark Greenberg, Sally
Gibbons, Mark Grady, Anja Karnein, Brent Kious, Doug Lichtman, Ed McCabe, Mariko Nakano-Okuno, Steve Peckman,
Heather Tarleton, Eugene Volokh, Norton Wise, and Lynne
Zucker—all at UCLA; Ian Ayres at Yale University; Carl Coleman at Seton Hall University; Judy Daar at Whittier College of
Law; Rebecca Dresser at Washington University; Einer Elhauge
at Harvard University; Jesse Goldner at St. Louis University;
Michael Heller at Columbia University; Jeffrey Kahn at the
University of Minnesota; Peter Lee at U.C. Davis; Mark Lemley at Stanford University; Arti Rai at Duke University; John
Robertson at the University of Texas; and Richard Saver at the
University of Houston. Thanks are also due to workshop participants at UCLA, Harvard, and the University of Michigan,
as well as students in an intensive one-week course on stem cell
policy that I taught at the University of Houston in January
2007 and students in seminars offered by Steve and me at
UCLA in the spring 2007 semester.

We are also grateful to Michael O'Malley, our editor at
Yale University Press, for his enthusiasm and support for this
project, as well as for his substantive suggestions. Most important, we owe a tremendous debt to UCLA law students Brad
Flood and Yan Leychkis for their outstanding and tireless research assistance over a range of topics; to law student Heather
Danesh, Ph.D. candidate Jessica Richardson, and undergraduate Taera Robbins for their more focused research assistance;
to law students Preston Ascherin, Kuan-Hsun Chen, Gauri
Manglik, and Alyssa Schabloski for their assistance with editing and cite checking; and to faculty assistants Robin Lee,
Karen Mathews, and Sunny Sanchez for their aid in preparing
the manuscript.

In the months immediately preceding publication of this book, I included significant portions of the material in Chapters 2, 3, 6, 7, and 8 in the following law journal articles: *Embryonic Histrionics: A Critical Analysis of the Bush Stem Cell Funding Policy and the Congressional Alternative*, 47 JURIMETRICS JOURNAL 1 (2006); *Stem Cell Research and the Cloning Wars*, 17 STANFORD LAW AND POLICY REVIEW 161 (2007); *Autonomy and Informed Consent in Biomedical Research*, 54 UCLA LAW REVIEW 605 (2007); *Buying and Selling Human Tissues for Biomedical Research*, 49 ARIZONA LAW REVIEW 45 (2007); and *"No Compensation" or "Pro Compensation": Moore v. Regents and Default Rules for Human Tissue Donations*, 40 JOURNAL OF HEALTH LAW 1 (2007). I am grateful to Yale University Press and to the publishers of these journals for their understanding and cooperation in my effort to make as many of the ideas as possible readily available to both the general public, in the form of this book, and to more specialized academic audiences with a professional interest in one or more specific topics.

# 1

# The Promise and the Hype

Hans Keirstead is a professor of anatomy and neurology at the University of California at Irvine who has done something incredible with paralyzed rats. Able to walk only with their forelegs, the rats dragged their torsos, hind legs, and tails behind them. Keirstead coaxed stem cells derived from human embryos into becoming oligodendrocytes, cells that help neurons send impulses throughout the body. He then injected the cells into the rats. The result: the rats miraculously could move their hind legs and tails.[1]

In the fall of 2004, Keirstead campaigned for California's stem cell initiative—Proposition 71—by showing "before" and "after" videos of his rats to various groups of potential voters. He and his work have been featured in a segment of the news magazine *60 Minutes* and an article in the *New Yorker* magazine.[2] Keirstead's primary financial backer, the biotechnology firm Geron, hopes that the Food and Drug Administration (FDA) will soon make its oligodendrocyte preparation the first product derived from human embryonic stem cells approved for use in human clinical trials in the United States.[3]

---

Hwang Mi Soon spent nineteen years in a wheelchair, paralyzed after falling from a bridge at the age of nineteen while running from a would-be attacker. In October 2004, she received a spinal injection of stem cells collected from umbilical cord blood. The next month, with the help of a walker, she stood up and shuffled several steps. Repeating the description used by Soon herself, newspapers around the globe called the results a miracle. The creator of the therapy announced plans for clinical trials and claimed that it would be widely available by 2006.

Within weeks, though, the apparent benefits had completely dissipated. Just months after her first injection, Soon underwent a second stem cell treatment. This one caused an infection and, according to reports, left her in constant pain and unable to sit for more than a couple of hours at a time. "I was like an animal they used for testing," she said the following year. "I don't want there to be another victim." She blamed her condition on "unscrupulous doctors who were more concerned with making their names and earning money by enabling me to walk than the potential risks."[4]

---

Over the past decade, there has been no shortage of scientific experts and political leaders predicting that stem cell research will lead to the most important medical care advances in our lifetimes. Former National Institutes of Health (NIH) director Harold Varmus testified before Congress that "there is almost no realm of medicine that might not be touched by this innovation. . . . It is not too unrealistic to say that this research has the potential to revolutionize the practice of medicine and improve the quality and length of life."[5] The dean of the Harvard University Faculty of Medicine claimed that stem cell therapies "have the potential to do for chronic diseases what antibiotics did for infectious diseases" and hopes that current research will lead to a "penicillin for Parkinson's."[6]

Senator Orrin Hatch (R-Utah) called stem cell research "the most promising research in healthcare perhaps in [the] history of the world."[7] More than two hundred members of Congress signed a letter to President George W. Bush claiming that "stem cells have the potential to be used to treat and better understand deadly and disabling diseases that affect more than 100 million Americans, such as cancer, heart disease, diabetes, Parkinson's, Alzheimer's, multiple sclerosis, spinal cord injury, and many others."[8]

Whether the potential of stem cell research will be achieved, justifying these prophecies, or whether a path strewn with unfulfilled expectations will cause history to regard the stem cell revolution as more hype than substance depends on the intrinsic power of stem cells and the creativity and brilliance of the research scientists who work on the revolution's front lines. But that is only part of the story. The ability of these scientists to deliver improved treatments and cures for a raft of debilitating diseases depends, in turn, on how our government makes the policy choices, designs the laws, and creates the institutions that surround the stem cell research endeavor. This book is about what the critical choices are, how the law ought to be structured, and how institutions should be designed.

The policy issues raised by stem cell research are wide ranging and varied. As a result, this book has an extremely broad scope. Some of these issues garner a fair bit of attention in the popular press, although the media's superficial coverage rarely does justice to the complexity of the questions involved.

Many of the issues receive little attention at all outside of a very small circle of people who study bioethics and scientific research for a living. Dealing with all of the issues in a thoughtful and prudent manner, however, is critical to ensuring that the stem cell revolution leads to the most far-reaching improvements in the treatment of disease that the underlying science is capable of delivering while at the same time not undermining our society's moral fabric.

One set of issues that we as a society must confront in the early years of the stem cell century is whether, in spite of its potential health benefits, ethical considerations should lead us to prohibit or refuse to fund certain types of stem cell research. A second set concerns the regulation of the relationship between researchers and the donors of the biological matter that is the raw material for stem cell research. Of course, embryonic stem cell research has attracted enormous interest in the United States and internationally, not only because of its scientific and medical potential, but also because of its commercial promise. Forecasts of the market for stem cell technologies range from a fairly modest $100 million to a more optimistic $10 billion by 2010.[9] Such financial projections raise a third set of important policy concerns: how the law should allocate intellectual property rights to the innovations that result from stem cell research. Rules of property and contract law not only serve to allocate the financial proceeds of research, but they also create incentives for research that are likely to have a significant impact on what research is undertaken, how much private funding it will attract, and how successful the research will be in leading to new and more effective medical treatments.

The following nine chapters engage this broad range of legal issues implicated by stem cell research and the potential of that research to revolutionize the treatment of disease. Each issue-specific chapter attempts to achieve three interrelated but distinct goals: (1) identify the most important, interesting, and salient legal issues raised by stem cell research; (2) for each legal issue raised, describe the current state of the law. In some instances, the law is clear and this task is straightforward; in others, it is quite unsettled, and a large amount of interpretation is required; (3) offer a critical assessment of the law and proposals for optimal policy.

Chapters 2 and 3 concern the legal relationship between the scientists on the front lines of stem cell research and the government. Chapter 2 addresses the stem cell research controversy that has gained the strongest foothold in the media and the popular imagination: the morality of human embryonic stem cell (hESC) research, whether the U.S. government ought to fund such research, and the consequences of the current funding embargo. Chapter 3 considers the subject of therapeutic cloning, including both the policy issues and constitutional concerns implicated by proposed legislation to prohibit this area of research, which has tremendous but uncertain medical potential.

Chapters 4 and 5 turn to issues relating to intellectual property rights in the fruits of stem cell research. Chapter 4 considers patents. Should people be able to own innovations in stem cell technology to the extent that they can prohibit others from using that technology without permission? A negative answer might stifle basic research, but a positive one might stifle applied research, in addition to having the unsettling consequence of making what exists in one person's body the property of another. Chapter 5 focuses on controversies over whether and how the public ought to benefit from innovations that owe their development to public funding. What payback, if any, should we expect from innovations that blossom from our tax dollars?

Chapters 6–8 shift from the scientists upon whom society relies to innovate in the field to the donors of human tissues, the raw materials on which scientists will increasingly need to rely. Chapter 6 examines the autonomy principle and "informed consent" rules that underlie the legal regulation of scientific research involving human subjects and considers complicated questions in this area of law raised by stem cell research. Chapter 7 takes on the controversial question of whether the embryos, ova, and other human tissues needed to fuel stem cell research should be subject to market transactions rather than merely altruistic donations. Chapter 8 grapples with how the law does and ought to deal with tissue donations when compensation is not mentioned at all by either researcher or donor.

Chapter 9 looks ahead to an era of clinical regenerative medicine in which stem cells are routinely conceived of as therapeutic treatments. It addresses three distinct questions: In what circumstances is it appropriate to use one person's stem cells for the medical benefit of another? To what extent should the origin of stem cells in the human body subject them to different regulatory treatment than other medical products? In what circumstances should the makers of such a new class of products be legally liable for harm that they inadvertently cause? Finally, Chapter 10 concludes with a summary of the book's findings.

While this book is about public policy and law rather than cell biology or medical research, for nonbiologists a brief description of stem cell science and its potential is nevertheless a necessary prelude to analyzing the social issues that are considered in detail in the chapters that follow. It is at this point that we shall begin.

## The Role of Stem Cells in Human Biology

Each human cell contains forty-six chromosomes, half inherited from the mother and half from the father. Together these chromosomes contain the person's entire genome—that is, every one of his or her genes. According to the findings of the Human Genome Project, the genome of each human consists of between twenty thousand and twenty-five thousand genes. Different types of cells have different characteristics and different functions—skin cells, blood cells, bone cells, and brain cells, for example. In order to serve such different functions, different genes are activated, or "expressed," in different types of cells, while the remaining genes in any particular type of cell are inactive. Through gene expression, the cell creates particular proteins that, working together with proteins created by other cells, build and maintain the organism and enable it to function.[10]

When a specialized cell is created, its function is decided and is fixed. In the language of cell biology, such a specialized cell is "fully differentiated" or "terminally differentiated." The genes that are expressed will remain expressed, while the others generally will remain dormant. A stem cell, in contrast, is one that is not fully differentiated. It can divide into two identical copies of itself, but—and here is the important part—it also can divide into one copy of itself and one different, more specialized cell with a different gene expression pattern.[11]

At the earliest stage of development, a sperm cell fertilizes an egg cell and the nuclei of the two gametes fuse, creating a single cell that contains a new genome. This cell, called a zygote after the fertilization process is complete, has the ability to create all the cell types needed to produce a mature version of the organism; from that one cell all of the body's cells will descend. This necessarily means the zygote is completely undifferentiated and possesses maximum potential, earning it the description of being "totipotent."

By the fourth or fifth day after fertilization, a human embryo has matured to a stage at which it is called a blastocyst. At this point, the embryo is made up of approximately 150–200 cells,[12] is approximately 0.1 millimeter across in size, and has yet to implant in the womb. The blastocyst is made up of two types of cells at this point. Some cells have formed an outer wall of the embryo, called the trophectoderm.[13] These cells will develop into the placenta and other membranes necessary to connect the embryo to the uterus and maintain it. An interior group of approximately thirty cells, called the inner cell mass or ICM, will develop into the embryo itself, later to become a fetus.[14]

The ICM contains human embryonic stem cells (hESCs), which are "pluripotent," meaning that they have the ability to create all of the tissues that make up the human body.[15] hESCs usually are not considered totipotent because they do not create the type of cells that form the trophectoderm and are thus unable to create a person on their own.[16] The value of this distinction has been called into some doubt in recent years, however, by research showing that hESCs can be coaxed in vitro into differentiating into trophectoderm cells.[17]

From this time forward, the cells that make up the ICM differentiate in a series of steps.[18] When the embryo reaches the age of about fourteen days, cells begin to cluster in a line, forming what is called the "primitive streak."[19] The embryonic stem cells thus begin a week-long project, called gastrulation, of differentiating into three groups of cells that will make up the ectoderm, mesoderm, and endoderm of the developing organism.[20] Up until this point, the embryo may divide spontaneously in two, creating monozygotic (identical) twins.[21] When gastrulation is complete, the potential of the cells has become somewhat limited. Ectodermal cells, for example, can become nerve or skin cells (among others) but cannot become muscle or bone cells.

By the end of the fourth week of development, the embryo develops what are called primordial germ cells. These are precursors of egg or sperm cells, depending on whether the embryo later develops into a male or female fetus. At their primordial stage, these cells are diploid, meaning that they have twenty-three pairs of chromosomes (forty-six total). Before they can become sperm or egg cells, they will need to go through a process called meiosis, which results in the creation of haploid cells (having only one set of twenty-three chromosomes), suitable for combining with another haploid gamete cell and creating a new genome. Primordial germ cells share the pluripotency of hESCs and are often referred to as human embryonic germ cells (hEGCs).

By the time the human embryo reaches two months of age, its stem cells have differentiated into cells with more particularized functions. At this stage and beyond, cells that have the ability to self-renew and differentiate are usually referred to generally as human adult stem cells (hASCs). This term can be confusing for laypeople because adult stem cells appear long before the organism reaches adulthood and, in fact, even before it is fully gestated.

hASCs have differentiated to the point at which they can produce only one category, or "lineage," of specialized cells.[22]

In some cases, hASCs are "unipotent"—that is, they can produce only one type of specialized cell.[23] In other cases, they are
"multipotent"—that is, they can produce several types of cells
that are usually closely related. For example, one type of stem
cell found in the skin produces only keratinocytes (cells that
produce keratin). Hematopoietic stem cells, in contrast, can
produce nine different types of blood cells. Adult stem cells are
thus less flexible in their potential than embryonic stem cells.
However, like their embryonic cousins, they have the ability
both to reproduce themselves through mitosis—forming additional adult stem cells of the same variety—and to produce
specialized cells. Some types of hASCs produce an even more
differentiated type of stem cells, called progenitors, as an intermediate step toward producing specialized cells.

For an organism to grow, it needs to add to its number
of cells. In addition, cells—not just a few cells, but huge
quantities—die all the time from injury, malfunction, or old
age. Human white blood cells and platelets, for example, live
only for hours or days, while red blood cells live no more than
about four months. The skin you have today will *in its entirety*
die, fall off of your body, and be regenerated from below by
stem cells within one month. These examples are the tip of
the iceberg. An average adult loses and replaces as many as 10
billion cells every day.[24] This means that survival, as well as
growth, requires that the body constantly create new cells, even
after gestation and after the organism has reached physical
maturity.

Some specialized cells can divide and make copies of
themselves but only to a limited extent. Others cannot do even
that. Stem cells, however, retain their ability over time both to
replicate themselves and to produce mature cells. Stem cells
continue to exist in organisms, including humans, throughout

the organisms' lives, waiting at the ready to create replacements for the particular type of cell in which they specialize
whenever the need arises.

## Sources of Stem Cells
### EMBRYONIC STEM CELLS DERIVED FROM
### FERTILIZED EMBRYOS

The process of creating embryonic stem cells begins with the
fertilization of an egg cell with a sperm cell in vitro (that is, in
a laboratory dish), rather than in a woman's fallopian tube.
The resulting zygote is allowed to divide in culture, becoming
two cells, then four, then eight, and so on. By the fourth or fifth
day, the embryo, if it has survived to this point, reaches the
blastocyst stage, the cells having differentiated into those of the
trophectoderm and those of the ICM. At this point, scientists
remove the cells from the ICM, destroying the blastocyst.

In order to make the isolated ICM cells useful for research, they must not only be extracted from the blastocyst but
they must also be kept alive and able to replicate indefinitely—
without differentiating—outside the body. When these criteria are met, the result is referred to as an "hESC line."

Creating any type of viable cell line is a tricky business.
Keeping isolated cells alive in a foreign environment requires
putting them into a man-made solution, known as the
medium, that contains just the right combination of nutrients.
In 1981, scientists reported success in creating mouse ESC lines
that were both kept alive and prevented from differentiating.[25]
The task proved more difficult in primates. It was not until
1994 that James Thomson, who had learned to harvest stem
cells from mouse embryos as a graduate student, and his colleagues at the University of Wisconsin were able to develop the

techniques and nutrient mixture that would enable monkey stem cells to live and replicate in vitro for more than a year with no ill effects. Four years later, in the November 6, 1998, issue of *Science,* Thomson and his colleagues published positive results of their attempts to use the same technique with human stem cells. At once, the subject of *human* embryonic stem cell research moved from theory into reality.[26]

Thomson later explained that after he published the results of his primate stem cell work, he expected other labs to apply the principles to humans quickly and create hESC lines. When that did not happen, he decided to try it himself. A local clinic donated embryos created as part of the in vitro fertilization (IVF) process but never implanted into the uterus of a woman attempting to become pregnant. Making use of these embryos as a source of stem cells proved difficult at first. IVF clinical practice is to implant an embryo into the womb about three days after fertilization, but the ICM is insufficiently developed at this point to be harvested. Thomson needed the embryos to live in vitro for two more days, but the medium developed for IVF could not keep them alive this long. When further experimentation with the nutrient mix solved this problem, Thomson was able to create a stable hESC line—according to him, on the first try.[27]

Thomson's achievement created an enormous amount of excitement in the scientific community. *Science* called it the most important innovation of 1998. It also created controversy because extracting hESCs, at least given the current technology, kills the blastocyst. To most who believe that a blastocyst has the same moral value as a human being, the practice is obviously unacceptable. To those who think a blastocyst has less moral value than a human being but greater moral value than

other human tissues, the trade-offs necessitated by hESC research can create a moral quandary. Chapter 2 analyzes the
hESC controversy in detail, including the Bush administration's policy of limiting federal funding for hESC research and
the congressional alternative.

### EMBRYONIC STEM CELLS
### CREATED THROUGH SCNT

A potential alternative source of hESCs is somatic cell nuclear
transfer (SCNT). Rather than beginning the process with an
embryo created by fertilization—that is, a sperm cell combining with an egg cell and thus mixing the genomes of two
adults—SCNT can create embryos using one egg cell and one
adult cell, which, in theory, can come from any part of the
donor's body. The nucleus of the egg cell is removed and replaced with the nucleus of the somatic cell. The result is an egg
that is genetically almost identical to that of the adult cell
donor (the egg retains a tiny bit of its original mitochondrial
DNA outside of the nucleus).[28]

The trick, at this point, is to stimulate the egg in a way
that causes the genes in the transplanted nucleus to express as
if the cell were a zygote rather than an adult cell. If this feat is
accomplished, the embryo begins the process of cell division.[29]
After about five days, the embryo reaches the blastocyst stage,
and the ICM can be harvested and its cells used to create an
hESC line, just as if it had been created through fertilization.[30]
Because the same initial technology is used as that which
would lead to the creation of a human clone, SCNT technology is often referred to as "therapeutic cloning" or "research
cloning"—as distinct from "reproductive cloning," a term that

implies the gestation of the embryo in a womb and the creation of a baby that is genetically identical to the somatic cell donor.

Animal cloning technology was developed in leopard frogs and is about half a century old, but until the 1990s scientists could create clones only by replacing an egg's nucleus with a cell from an embryo. That is, the technique just did not work with a fully differentiated adult cell. In essence, once a cell reached this level of development, scientists could insert its nucleus into an enucleated egg, but they could not figure out how to trick the genes into believing they inhabited a zygote and acting accordingly. In 1996, however, Ian Wilmut and his team from the Roslin Institute in Scotland produced a clone using a cell from a six-year-old sheep, apparently solving the problem of reprogramming.[31] The birth of "Dolly" created tremendous excitement about the therapeutic potential of stem cell science because it suggested the possibility of one day creating human blastocysts, followed by hESC lines, with the same genomes as adult humans.

The promise of creating such hESC lines is exciting because it suggests the possibility of individualized stem cell therapies—that is, cellular material to be used for medical treatment could genetically match the cells of a particular patient and would thus address the problem of immune system rejection, an important stumbling block for any cellular treatments. Bone marrow and organ transplants, skin grafts, and the like, which require placing cells from one individual into the body of another, have always faced this problem. Proteins on cell surfaces called human leukocyte antigens (HLA) alert the body's immune system to the presence of foreign cells. Because foreign cells could be harmful viruses or bacteria, the immune system of the host responds by attacking (and killing) the cells of the donor. The donor tissue can also sense that the cells of the host are foreign to it and attack those cells. This side effect of transplants is known as graft–versus–host disease (GVHD).

In modern practice, physicians attempt to match transplant donors and recipients with similar HLA profiles; the practice reduces the rejection problem but does not solve it entirely. Recipients of organ transplants also must take immunosuppressive drugs, which produce side effects and render the patient more vulnerable to infections. If stem cell treatments can be developed using only cells that match those of the patient, the tissues would be a perfect HLA match, and the problem of rejection could potentially be avoided without the need for high doses of dangerous drugs.[32]

Although the use of SCNT to create individually tailored stem cell treatments would solve the problem of tissue rejection, it would create a different problem. If a patient's disease is caused by an inherited genetic mutation, attempts to replace dead or malfunctioning cells with stem cells derived from the same genome might simply replicate the problem. This concern might be resolved with new technology that can repair gene defects in hESCs before using them to create a cell line that will be used for treatment, however. This process has been demonstrated successfully in mice.[33]

In 2004, South Korean scientist Hwang Woo-suk announced that he had used the SCNT process to create thirty human embryos that were the clones of an adult cell and that he had created an hESC line from one of them. The following year, Hwang claimed to have improved his laboratory's efficiency and created eleven hESC lines from cloned cells. Scientists around the world were impressed with the hard work and technical skill demonstrated by the South Koreans in beating the world to this development, but they were not particularly surprised by the reported results. After the birth of Dolly the sheep, most scientists believed that the application of SCNT technology to a human cell was only a matter of time. By late 2005, however, rumors began to circulate that Hwang's data and photographs, published in *Science,* might have been forged. After several months of investigations, South Korean officials determined that Hwang's results were a complete hoax.[34]

With the Hwang claims debunked, therapeutic cloning of human cells remains a future possibility rather than a current reality. Most scientists in the field continue to believe that the feat will be accomplished, however, and probably sooner rather than later. The race to perfect this technology remains controversial, both because of the close relationship between cloning for research purposes and cloning for the purpose of producing a human being and because therapeutic cloning itself involves creating embryos that will then be destroyed. Chapter 3 examines the politics, policy, and constitutional issues of therapeutic cloning.

## EMBRYONIC GERM CELLS

In the mid-1990s, when the race was on to create cell lines from hESCs, John Gearhart of Johns Hopkins University looked to fetal tissue as a possible source of pluripotent stem cells. His inspiration came from mouse research, which had shown that primordial germ cells in mouse fetuses, when harvested and cultured, could be made to develop into every type of cell in a mature mouse.

Using five-to-nine-week-old embryonic or fetal tissue supplied by an abortion clinic, Gearhart's team was able to harvest early cells from what would have become the fetus's testes or ovaries—cells that would have eventually become sperm or egg cells. As was the case with the development of hESC lines, the main obstacle to using these primordial germ cells for research purposes was figuring out what nutrients were required to prepare a medium that would keep cells alive and undifferentiated in vitro. When that problem was solved, Gearhart's team was able to create hEGC lines with similar potential to hESC lines. The team's report was published in the November 10, 1998, issue of the *Proceedings of the National Academy of Sciences,* only four days after Thomson's Wisconsin group published news of its success with hESCs in *Science.*[35]

To date, scientists have had more difficulty working with hEGCs than hESCs. One major problem is that the former are difficult to obtain: they must be harvested from aborted embryos at precisely the right stage of development. A second problem is that scientists have had far more difficulty coaxing hEGCs to proliferate continuously in culture without differentiating.[36] For these reasons, hEGCs are considered by most scientists to be a less promising source of biomedical innovation than hESCs.

## ADULT STEM CELLS

Unlike embryonic stem cells, which must be harvested from embryos, adult stem cells can be extracted from human beings without destroying the host. Adult stem cells reside in many tissues throughout the body, but they exist in relatively small numbers.

One unanswered question is whether adult stem cells exist in every part of the body. Most scientists believe that the body does not have adult stem cells with the ability to produce every type of specialized cell. An example is the pancreatic beta cell, which produces the insulin necessary for the body to process sugars correctly. Type 1 diabetes is caused by the body's immune cells attacking and killing most of its own beta cells. Pancreatic stem cells could potentially be used to regenerate the missing beta cells, curing the disease, but such stem cells have never been found and are thought not to exist.[37] Proving the nonexistence of something, of course, is quite difficult, and scientists might someday discover that pancreatic stem cells do exist. Until a surprise discovery in the late 1990s, scientists believed that nerve cells did not regenerate and that therefore neural stem cells could not possibly exist.[38] And it was not until 2000 that stem cells that create retinal cells were discovered in human eyes.[39]

## Why Stem Cell Research Is a Twenty-first Century Revolution

Most diseases that cause death and disability, at least in the developed world, are degenerative conditions that result from cell malfunction or death. Some, such as Huntington's disease, cystic fibrosis, and sickle cell anemia, are attributable entirely to an inherited genetic mutation—if you have the mutation, you will contract the disease. Others are likely the result of inherited genetic mutations interacting with environmental factors. Still others are the consequence of genetic mutations that arise after birth, often also in concert with environmental factors. Whatever the underlying etiology, the proximate cause of illness in any of these cases is the failure of certain cells to perform tasks necessary to keep the body functioning normally. Other disabilities result from injuries caused by external traumas (such as car accidents) or disease mechanisms (such as strokes) that cause widespread cell death, which, in turn, prevents normal physical functioning.

Stem cell research offers hope for curing this entire range of conditions in at least three different ways. First, by studying the mechanisms by which stem cells differentiate to create and repair the body's structures, researchers hope to better understand the process of disease formation. For example, because cancer cells create a protein that is found in stem cells but not ordinarily in fully differentiated cells, some scientists believe that all forms of cancer might be the result of stem cells proliferating out of control. By coaxing stem cells to differentiate in different ways and following the resulting changes in gene expression, scientists could improve their understanding of tumor formation, which could enable the development of new treatment strategies.

Second, if scientists can prompt stem cells to differentiate and develop in ways that mimic the progression of diseases, they can then test the efficacy and toxicity of pharmaceuticals and other medical treatments on these cells. For example, stem cells could be prompted to differentiate into large quantities of cardiac cells, and new chemical compounds could be applied to those cells to see if the compounds were dangerous to them. Stem cells could be prompted to differentiate into diseased cardiac cells, and the same chemical compounds could be tested to see if they would halt or reverse the progression of the disease. Using stem cells as test subjects in this way has the promise of reducing the cost and the time needed to bring to market new therapies for diseases as well as reducing the risks to participants in clinical trials.

Third and most significant is the potential of stem cells to cure diseases directly. This possibility, often called regenerative medicine, is the Holy Grail of stem cell research. If its promise is fulfilled, stem cell research will revolutionize, rather than merely improve, the way the medical profession treats disease.

Currently, degenerative diseases are usually treated with efforts to remove, destroy, or fix errant or damaged cells with surgery, chemical compounds, or radiation. In theory, however, stem cells, prompted to differentiate into healthy mature cells, can be used to replace diseased or dead cells and thus restore proper functioning. In other words, medical science could harness the body's natural healing powers to cure disease rather than relying on blunt external force that fights against the body's biology. One approach is to inject stem cells into the diseased area of a body and allow them to repopulate it with healthy cells. Another is to prompt stem cells to grow replacement cells or tissues outside of the diseased body and then surgically replace the diseased tissues with the specially constructed replacements.[40] For example, cardiac cells destroyed by a heart attack could be grown with stem cells and used to repair the heart, or stem cells could be used to grow an entire liver that could be transplanted into a patient with liver failure.

In theory, stem cells potentially could be used to treat almost any type of disease. In the near term, the best candidates are diseases that are caused by damage to or death of a particular type of cell. Type 1 diabetes and Parkinson's disease are mentioned frequently because the former results from the lack of pancreatic beta cells and the latter from the deterioration of neurons that produce dopamine.

It seems almost certain that stem cell research will, to a greater or lesser extent, provide the first two of the benefits scientists foresee: a greater understanding of cell development and a source of material for testing new pharmaceuticals. For these two benefits alone, the game is worth the candle. But it is the third potential benefit—a new paradigm for the treatment of disease—that makes the term "stem cell research" generate great excitement in the United States and around the world. The achievement of this goal is certainly possible, and probably even likely in time, but it is by no means certain, even if scientists can garner the large amounts of research funding and human tissues that will be necessary.

Scientists need to understand far better how cells operate and how they mutate and malfunction. They need to learn how to manipulate stem cells into working the way they do on their own inside the body, a subject that is still poorly understood. They need to figure out precisely where and how to apply stem cell treatments to a patient so that the cells provide the regeneration necessary to cure disease; moreover, they need to learn how to make the cells conduct their repairs in a diseased environment while ensuring that the therapy will not cause new problems for the host, such as tumors. If and when the science is mastered, production difficulties will also need to be overcome. For widespread clinical application, scientists and engineers will need to find ways to generate billions of stem cells and their progeny—not just a small number of cells in a Petri dish—and to do so in a cost-effective way. The stem cell revolution could founder on any of these shoals.

## hESCs versus hASCs

The question of whether hESC research is morally proper divides public and political opinion in the United States. As noted, because blastocysts are destroyed when their ICMs are harvested, most people who believe that blastocysts have equivalent moral worth to persons oppose this field of research, while many people who believe blastocysts have significant moral worth—even if not as much as persons—feel conflicted.[41] Research on adult stem cells, in contrast, is almost completely uncontroversial: nearly everyone with an educated opinion favors it. Because of the stark difference in the level of controversy surrounding the two research paths, the issue of whether hESC research is necessary to achieve the potential of stem cell medicine is significant. If it is not, common sense suggests that science pursue solely the path of hASC research.

Opponents of hESC research point out that it has yet to lead to a single therapeutic treatment, while many treatments using hASCs have already been developed and are in clinical use. The best known of these is the bone marrow transplant used to treat leukemias. Chemotherapy or radiation is first used to destroy the cancerous cells in the patient's blood. Unfortunately, however, chemotherapy and radiation do not discriminate: they destroy the healthy blood cells and the stem cells that produce those blood cells as well. Bone marrow is then transfused back into the patient to regenerate the cells necessary to keep the patient alive. The procedure works because bone marrow is rich in hematopoietic stem cells, a type of hASC. With a better understanding of the function of hematopoietic stem cells, scientists have created more efficient methods of providing the benefits of bone marrow transplants. Today physicians can harvest hematopoietic stem cells directly from a donor's blood for transplant to a patient, while leaving behind the other cells that lack therapeutic value.[42]

Most accounts in the popular media of why hASCs lack the therapeutic potential of hESCs state that the pluripotency of the latter allow them to differentiate into all of the body's cell types, whereas the former can create only one type (or possibly several related types) of mature cells.[43] This is an incomplete and unsatisfying defense of hESC research because there is no obvious reason why a single type of stem cell would be needed to treat all types of diseases. After all, people suffering from Parkinson's disease and diabetes do not care whether cures are derived from two different types of hASC lines or a single, pluripotent hESC line. It might be aesthetically elegant to cure all diseases by beginning with a single cell, but this is hardly a practical requirement.

There are, however, several better reasons that explain why the vast majority of scientists in the field believe that hESC research should be pursued in addition to hASC research. First, as discussed above, there might be some types of cells for which there are no adult stem cells and that thus could be treated only with hESCs. We know that hematopoietic stem cells produce blood cells, but research suggests that there are no adult stem cells that produce the pancreatic beta cells necessary for insulin production.[44] Thus, current research on treating Type 1 diabetes stem cells has focused on coaxing hESCs into differentiating into the required cell type.[45]

Second, although some types of hASCs are found in large numbers in vivo (in the body) and are relatively easy to extract from live donors, others lack one or both of these features. It is likely, for example, that it will be much easier for scientists to differentiate hESCs into neural stem cells for research purposes than to extract substantial enough quantities of neural stem cells from donors. A related problem is that in tissues small numbers of hASCs are found intermingled with large numbers of other cells, making it extremely difficult to produce purified preparations of hASCs.

Third, hASCs usually do not live as long or proliferate as extensively in vitro while retaining their original properties as do hESCs.[46] With careful tending, the hESCs from a single blastocyst can produce a stem cell line of millions of cells in months. Scientists have not achieved this level of success with hASCs, which makes them less available even for basic research. More important, the limited proliferation potential of hASCs raises obstacles to the success of stem cell treatments because a major step in moving from basic science to clinical application is the ability to mass-produce a sufficient number of stem cells to treat patients. Put slightly differently, even when hASCs can do the job in theory, they are liable to present manufacturing problems that will be difficult and costly to overcome, if it is even possible to overcome them. Moreover, the progeny of hESCs appear to live longer and differentiate more rapidly and reliably than do the progeny of hASCs,[47] so some treatments produced with the former might be more successful and/or long-lasting.

There are several reasons to hope that it one day might be possible to obtain all of the benefits of hESCs from the less controversial hASCs. Some research has suggested that under certain circumstances it might be possible to coax adult stem cells into transdifferentiating—that is, to create different types of mature cells than they are normally programmed to create.[48] Although most scientists doubt that this is biologically achievable, there is a possibility that transdifferentiation could allow hASCs to mimic at least some of the potential of hESCs and hEGCs.[49]

Even more provocative are two very recent findings. In early 2007, researchers reported that they had isolated stem cells found in amniotic fluid that could remain stable in vitro and be made to differentiate into different lineages of specialized cells.[50] Other scientists immediately cautioned that these stem cells, which seem to be more developed than hESCs but less developed than previously identified hASCs, were unlikely to match the full potential of hESCs,[51] but only time and further research will tell.

Several months later, other scientists reported success in making skin cells in adult mice behave like ESCs by inserting four genes into the cells.[52] This feat has not yet been accomplished using human cells, and in mice the procedure caused high rates of tumor formation, so, again, caution is warranted. Still, it is possible that this technique might one day reduce the need to use embryos to produce pluripotent stem cells.

In short, scientific advances one day might prove that hASCs, when appropriately manipulated, can fulfill all of the aspirations that scientists have for hESCs, but that day has not arrived yet. It is simply too early in the development of stem cell technology to know for sure what benefits will be achievable with the range of stem cells that scientists have been able to identify. There is only one way the world will ever know for sure what medical advances are possible, and that is by conducting research using the full range of available tools.

With this background established, we are ready to leap into the swirl of complex and fervently contested policy issues that stand before us in the stem cell century.

# 2

# The Embryo Wars

In the summer of 2001, before the terrorist attacks of 9/11, before Hurricane Katrina, and before the U.S. invasion of Iraq, the biggest political story was the Bush administration's looming announcement of its policy concerning stem cell research. More specifically, attention focused on whether President Bush would or would not allow federal research grants to be awarded to scientists conducting hESC research. During that summer, polls indicated that 40–60 percent of Americans were following the issue at least "fairly closely." According to one Gallup Poll, 78 percent of those surveyed said the issue of stem cell research was "very important" or "somewhat important" to them.[1]

Lobbied hard since his election the preceding fall by scientists, bioethicists, clergy, and policy wonks of all persuasions, the president hunkered down at his Crawford, Texas, ranch, working on the first speech that he would deliver to the nation in prime time since assuming the presidency. Would he side with members of his pro-life constituency (as his pronouncements in the 2000 presidential campaign suggested that he would), who argued that research on embryonic stem cells approaches or even constitutes murder because it requires the destruction of embryos?[2] Or would he yield to the arguments of the scientific community and patient advocacy groups that early-stage embryos are suitable for research? Predictions ran both ways.

The president was not writing on an entirely blank slate. In 1995, Congress had attached a provision to a spending appropriation bill that came to be known as the Dickey Amendment, after Republican congressman Jay Dickey. The amendment prohibited the federal government from funding any research that destroyed or endangered human embryos.[3] Congress has renewed the Dickey Amendment every year since.[4]

When James Thomson and his colleagues at the University of Wisconsin created the first hESC lines in 1998, they had to do so without federal grant money because the process required embryo destruction. In the wake of that innovation, the Clinton administration determined that the Dickey Amendment did not prohibit federal funding of research on hESCs after the cells are extracted from embryos because research conducted at this later stage does not in fact destroy any embryos.[5] (This reading was an accurate literal interpretation of the Dickey Amendment, although critics claimed that it was inconsistent with the law's purpose of avoiding government complicity in embryo destruction.) The Department of Health and Human Services issued guidelines to this effect shortly before President Clinton left office, setting the deadline for an initial round of hESC research grant applications two months after the new president would take office.[6] When the Bush administration arrived in Washington, it postponed review of the applications pending further review of the policy.

According to accounts, in the summer of 2001, President Bush was thoroughly engaged with the issue of hESC research, often interrupting meetings on other subjects to ask aides or visitors their opinions.[7] When Bush reached his decision, his advisers gave the national news media only fourteen hours advanced notice that the president would address the nation. To the consternation of some Bush supporters and Republican activists, secrecy was maintained: before the address, no one outside of the president's top aides knew what he would say.[8]

On August 9, President Bush took to the podium in Crawford to announce his stem cell research policy. On one hand, the president explained, embryonic stem cell research had great promise for the treatment of disease. On the other hand, it was his belief that the embryos, even at the blastocyst stage, constitute human life and that it is morally wrong to destroy life, even as part of a research effort intended to save other lives. Consequently, he proclaimed that his administration would not fund any research on stem cell lines created after the date of his speech but that it would fund research on stem cell lines derived prior to that date.[9]

Superficially, the president's policy appeared Solomonic. Predictably, it angered both his supporters on the religious right, who opposed any kind of complicity in acts they equate with murder, and members of the scientific research establishment, who feared that limiting funding to existing cell lines would seriously hinder the development of any medical therapies and put American scientists at an enormous competitive disadvantage. At the same time, the president's decision played well with the public, winning the support of 50–60 percent of Americans and the disapproval of less than one-third.[10] Any controversial decision that angers partisans on either side but manages to satisfy the public at large might well be viewed as a political masterstroke, and perhaps it was. But for a host of reasons, there is substantially less to the president's logic than first meets the eye. At the same time, there is plenty not to like about the congressional alternative.

## The Moral Value of Blastocysts

The critical premise of the Bush policy is that five-day-old blastocysts are the moral equivalent of persons. This premise can be supported by two different types of claims: first, blastocysts and persons are identical in the qualities that give rise to moral worth; second, although different from persons in important ways, blastocysts have the potential to become persons and, as a result, enjoy the same moral worth as persons.

If the moral equivalence premise is valid on the basis of either argument, then it logically follows that it is improper to use embryos for research in ways that we would not use people.[11] If blastocysts lack the moral value of persons, however, then scientific research restrictions are inappropriate— even if blastocysts are assumed to have some "intermediate" amount of moral value rather than none at all. Assigning some lesser moral value to blastocysts might imply a moral obligation not to destroy them wantonly or haphazardly and perhaps to treat them with respect more generally, but it does not call into question the propriety of hESC research, where the importance of the goal—finding cures for acute and chronic human diseases—is unquestionable.

### PERSONHOOD

The first argument for the moral equivalence of blastocyst and person stresses the core biological similarity: each contains a functioning human genome that is (with the exception of identical twins) unique.[12] On the journey from zygote to fetus to infant to adult, a human animal transitions through a series of important developmental stages, but a blastocyst is just as human as a person—in the same way that a child is just as human as an adult even though children lack some competencies developed by adults.

The problem with this argument is that it assumes as true the contested claim that it is a person's genetic material alone that establishes his or her moral value. There is in fact a great deal of room for reasonable people to disagree about what specific features provide moral worth and thus whether a blastocyst falls into the same category as a person. The establishment of a unique genetic code is one potential point where the line might be drawn, but it is far from the most logical point. The blastocyst stage of development is obviously long before birth (approximately thirty-six weeks after fertilization) and long before viability outside of a womb (approximately twenty-six weeks). It is also long before organs begin to form (approximately four weeks) and substantially before the development of the primitive streak, signaling the beginning of neural development (approximately fourteen days). Other nations that are leaders in biomedical research, such as the United Kingdom and Singapore, permit the destruction of embryos for research purposes up until the fourteenth day of development,[13] and the National Research Council in the United States recommends the same cutoff date,[14] reflecting the implicit belief that some neuronal structure is at least a minimal requirement for acquiring the moral value of a person.

At five days post-fertilization, the blastocyst lacks consciousness, the ability to experience its surroundings, and the potential to feel pain. It has no emotions, no memory, no ability to reason, and no ability to imagine the future. It lacks any physical resemblance to a person. In short, it lacks every trait that could plausibly be considered a characteristic of human moral value except one: it has human DNA. Even were fertilization to have taken place in a fallopian tube rather than a Petri dish, a blastocyst would not yet even have implanted in the uterus at this point in its development. The implantation process begins around the sixth or seventh day after fertilization and takes three to four days to complete. The blastocyst cannot even properly be labeled a single individual at this point because twinning remains possible.

The intuition that a blastocyst lacks the moral value of a person is vividly demonstrated with the following hypothetical: Imagine that a fire starts in a fertility clinic and you must choose between saving a Petri dish containing two blastocysts and a five-year-old child.[15] Is there any question that you should (and would) save the child? The appropriate answer to the question is just as obvious if the blastocysts would be destroyed by the fire and the child only injured. The reason is that the child possesses not only human DNA but also such qualities as sentience, consciousness, emotions, the ability to interact with the environment, and the capacity to experience pain.

Contrast this with a different hypothetical: Imagine that you must choose between saving a five-year-old child and a twenty-five-year-old adult in a fire. Here it is far from obvious that you either should or would choose the twenty-five-year-old. If you did choose to save the adult, it almost certainly would not be because she is at a more advanced stage in human development. Beyond some point, a human's developmental stage is irrelevant to her moral worth. But prior to some point, the developmental stage does matter. The precise location of that point is difficult to determine, but it is less difficult to recognize that blastocysts have not reached it.

The well-accepted belief that the complete loss of brain function meets the definition of "death" further demonstrates the difficulty in attributing the moral worth of personhood to a blastocyst. Throughout most of history, "death" was understood to mean the cessation of all vital bodily functions, including circulation and respiration. This definition began to be reconsidered in the mid-twentieth century, when medical science became able to maintain these functions artificially. In the latter half of the century, most American jurisdictions rewrote their legal definitions of death to include the complete and irreversible cessation of all brain function, even if other bodily systems continue to function. Since 1980, most U.S. states have adopted the Uniform Determination of Death Act, which explicitly codifies this principle.[16]

The shift in our understanding of death makes it legally possible to cease heroic medical interventions on individuals who have suffered brain death and to harvest their organs for transplant, and—unlike abortion, for example—the practice engenders scant opposition. But if individuals with functioning circulatory and respiratory systems are considered to lack the moral worth of persons if they lack brain function, it is difficult to construct a logical explanation for why blastocysts, which also lack brain function, should be considered the moral equivalent of persons. A distinction might be made between a blastocyst and a brain-dead individual on the grounds that the former has potential that the latter lacks, but this is a form of the argument based on potential (addressed separately below) rather than on the blastocyst's existing traits.

For many who believe blastocysts share the moral value of persons, the conviction is rooted in religious belief that by its very nature cannot be contradicted with analytical reasoning. But it is even unclear whether a blastocyst constitutes "human life" according to the theological tradition of the Roman Catholic Church, which is usually identified as among the most conservative institutions on such matters. The current position of the Church is quite clear: in a 1995 encyclical, Pope John Paul II wrote explicitly that a fertilized egg constitutes human life, and he condemned scientific research that resulted in embryo destruction.[17] But the Church has historically defined human life as requiring a "soul," and some leading Catholic theologians believe that this criterion cannot be met until some time after fertilization—be it when an embryo can no longer twin, when embryonic cells begin to differentiate, or when the primitive streak appears.[18]

## POTENTIAL

The second argument against embryo research on the grounds that blastocysts enjoy the same moral value as persons is that a blastocyst has the potential to become a person. While this assertion is true if "potential" is understood very broadly, the argument gives more moral force to the concept of potentiality than the concept can sustain. As supporters of hESC research are fond of observing, an acorn's potential to become an oak tree hardly makes it one.[19] A person who crushes an acorn is unlikely to be viewed as committing a harm equivalent to a person who chops down an enormous oak.

In order to equate the moral value of one item with the moral value of another on the grounds that the first has the "potential" to become the second, and to do so without conflating the value of a great many things that have little relationship to one another, the concept of potentiality needs to be bounded in some meaningful way. Two possible approaches are to require that an item be able to become something else on its own without external assistance (self-actualizability) or to require that an item have a high degree of likelihood of becoming something else (likelihood).

If the definition of potential is bounded by the self-actualizability or likelihood qualification, a blastocyst cannot be said to have the moral value of a person based on its potential. An embryo fertilized ex utero has no potential to become a human being on its own; it must be transplanted into a womb to have any potential whatsoever.[20] Thus in vitro blastocysts fail the test of self-actualization. Even if created in what might politely be called the "traditional" way, any given blastocyst is relatively unlikely to ever become a person; most estimates put the chance of a blastocyst successfully implanting in the uterus at only 20–40 percent, and the chances of its being carried to term are significantly lower than this because of the high rate of spontaneous miscarriage early in pregnancy.[21] Thus blastocysts also fail the likelihood test of potentiality.

If a five-day-old in vitro blastocyst is inviolate because of its potential (understood without any bounds) to develop into a human life, it is hard to say why each individual egg or sperm cell does not have the same potential and therefore deserve the same consideration. Under appropriate conditions, with help from humans, and with a fair bit of luck, these cells (which also possess human DNA) also have the potential to develop into a person. If SCNT one day makes the cloning of humans possible, then it might also become literally true that every human cell of any type will have the potential to develop into a person, but it seems quite a stretch to think that this potential would render the destruction of any individual cell a moral transgression or that the value of a single skin cell should be considered comparable to the value of a person.

## Internal Inconsistencies

If the central premise of the Bush policy is the moral equivalence of blastocysts and persons, the finer distinctions incorporated in that policy are based on the philosophical principle that benefiting from a moral transgression is acceptable as long as causal complicity in the transgression is absent.[22] According to this principle, the government should do nothing to cause the alleged moral wrong—in this case, embryo destruction—but neither need it refuse to benefit from the fruits of bad acts perpetrated by others.

In practice, this principle led President Bush to authorize the NIH to fund research on the hESC lines that had already been created. For these lines, the damage had already been done; the embryos that had been destroyed to create the lines could not be saved. Funding for research using any new hESC lines would be prohibited, however, because such funding would encourage scientists to commit new moral transgressions—that is, destroy more embryos—in hopes of obtaining grant money to study their cells, and the government would be causally complicit.

On close examination, however, the path that the Bush policy attempts to steer between encouraging "bad" acts and merely profiting from them fails to satisfy the policy's basic implicit distinction. In fact, the policy fails in two ways, and it is thus subject to attack from diametrically opposing positions. The policy allows too little research, in that it refuses to support science that would neither directly cause nor even encourage further embryo destruction. At the same time, it allows too much research, in the sense that it makes the government causally complicit in other acts of embryo destruction. Legal scholars would describe the policy as both underinclusive and overinclusive relative to its implicit goal.

If one supports research on hESC lines developed prior to August 2001, it makes little logical sense to oppose research on hESC lines developed after that date using embryos that as of that date were already slated for destruction. The president's funding policy does exactly this, however.

The most readily available source of embryos for stem cell research is IVF clinics, storehouses of embryos created using gametes provided by couples who wished to conceive a child. A cycle of fertility hormones enables a woman to produce 10–20 (or more) eggs at one time.[23] Clinic physicians then employ a surgical procedure to harvest these eggs, and they typically attempt to create embryos from all of them.[24] Fertilization fails in some cases, but quite often the process produces 8–12 embryos.[25] From these, the physicians then select the "best" embryos for implantation—that is, those judged most likely to implant successfully based on factors like number of cells and symmetry.[26] An average of just over three embryos is implanted per cycle, with variations depending on the age of the woman and clinic proclivities.[27] In a recent study, fully 97 percent of American IVF clinics reported that they create more embryos than they intend to implant in a given treatment cycle.[28] Most couples cryopreserve the remaining embryos.[29] After the couple has successfully conceived its desired number of offspring or given up trying, the remaining embryos are excess. If they are not used for research, nearly all will be destroyed, and most will be destroyed sooner rather than later.

Defenders of the Bush policy might well point out that permitting the funding of research using hESC lines derived from excess IVF embryos could encourage more people to take advantage of IVF technology and IVF practitioners to create a larger "cushion" of excess embryos for the IVF process. Thus, funding research on cell lines derived from such embryos might encourage the production of more embryos in the future and thereby make the government causally complicit in future embryo deaths.[30]

The problem with this reasoning is that it does not argue against the funding of research on cell lines derived from embryos that were *already* in frozen storage in IVF clinics as of the date of Bush's policy announcement. That is, if the policy permits the funding of research using hESC lines created before August 2001 because, as the president put the point, "the life and death decision has already been made,"[31] it also should permit research on hESC lines derived from embryos already slated for destruction as of that date for precisely the same reason. The key to this point is recognizing that the alleged moral wrong that forms the basis of the Bush policy is not the development of hESC lines per se but the destruction of embryos necessary to create those lines. Permitting scientists to harvest stem cells from existing excess embryos would not encourage any additional embryo destruction. In fact, if we assume for the sake of argument that blastocysts have equivalent moral value to persons, destroying embryos in pursuit of scientific advancement is far more ethical than allowing the embryos to be destroyed with no offsetting benefits.[32]

For excess embryos already in cold storage, there is, in theory, the possibility of so-called "embryo adoption." In reality, however, only an infinitesimally small fraction of excess embryos become human beings through donation and implantation into unrelated women: as of 2005, there were only eighty-one children known to have been born this way.[33] Studies have found that while many couples entering IVF treatment indicate a desire to donate excess embryos to other infertile couples, they rarely do so when the time comes.[34] And few couples are interested in adopting embryos, preferring either to employ the IVF process using their own gametes (or at least gametes of one member of the couple) or to adopt a child. It therefore seems quite unlikely that permitting the NIH to fund research on hESC cell lines created from embryos that already existed as of August 2001 would have resulted in the destruction of even a single embryo that would not otherwise have been destroyed.

Had Bush decided to permit the funding of research on cell lines derived from these embryos, not only would his policy have been more logically coherent, but the consequence would not have been trivial. According to an oft-cited study, as of 2002 nearly four hundred thousand embryos sat frozen in IVF clinics in the United States alone.[35] As discussed below, this number does not suggest that four hundred thousand, or even tens of thousands, of hESC lines could be created from these embryos. But the cryopreserved embryos as of August 2001 could have been transformed into a significant number of cell lines if used for that purpose.

If, given its guiding principle, the president's policy is too narrowly drawn in one respect, it is too broadly drawn in another. Permitting the funding of some hESC research—even though the permission is limited to cell lines derived before August 2001—is certain to contribute, albeit indirectly, to the future destruction of embryos, making the government causally complicit in that destruction. The reasoning is quite simple: the NIH will fund research only if it believes that the research is likely to advance scientific knowledge. As the scientific community's understanding of stem cells improves, the incentives of nonfederal funding sources (that is, private industry, philanthropic organizations, state governments, and foreign governments) to create and conduct research on new hESC lines will increase.

## Lack of Fit between Means and Ends

Perhaps what is most noticeable about President Bush's Crawford address and his later comments on the subject of embryo research is what has not been said. The president has not called for the enactment of a federal law that would prohibit research on hESC lines that were ineligible for federal funding under his policy. Neither has he proposed a law that would outlaw research that directly destroys embryos.

These facts do not indicate that the Bush policy has not had a significant negative impact on the development of stem cell technology. The federal government provides most of the nation's funding for basic medical research—at more than $28 billion per year, as much as 90 percent or more of the total national funding by some estimates[36]—so limiting federal grant support has serious ramifications. But if it is immoral for the government to have any complicity in the destruction of embryos, consistency demands that the government outlaw the practice and attempt to prevent it from occurring in addition to cutting off funding. A knowing failure to take any action to stop the practice certainly demonstrates complicity in it.

More generally, the Bush policy is fundamentally inconsistent because of the mismatch between its basic premise (blastocysts have the same moral value as persons) and the policy tool used to support it (restrictions on federal spending). Even the most ardent libertarians believe that the government is justified in acting to protect human life. But the obvious tool to achieve this end is the government's power to regulate behavior, not its ability to spend (or not spend) public funds. Governments prohibit murder. It would be odd indeed for the government to announce that it will not subsidize murder but that private citizens are free to engage in the activity as long as they foot the bill.

A principled rejoinder to this argument could be made on federalism grounds. That is, supporters of expansive state power and a limited federal government might contend that hESC research should be criminalized locally rather than by Washington. This position is not advocated by Bush or his allies either, however, perhaps because it would be squarely inconsistent with the administration's positions on related issues. The Bush administration supports a congressional prohibition on therapeutic cloning for stem cell research. (The legislation is analyzed in detail in Chapter 3.) The administration also has sought, unsuccessfully, to prevent Oregon doctors from participating in that state's physician-assisted suicide program, despite the policy's approval by local voters on two separate occasions.[37]

An alternative argument that might logically suggest a ban on federal funding but not legal prohibition is that the government should not fund activities that a significant number of citizens find abhorrent, out of respect for that subset of the population, even if the majority of citizens do not share those beliefs. Government funding for stem cell research would come from tax dollars provided by all citizens. Forcing opponents of such research essentially to spend their money on something they find repugnant, so this argument implies, would be worse than forcing them merely to live with the activity.

There is some political precedent for this viewpoint, most notably in the passage of the Hyde Amendment, which prohibits federal funding of abortions.[38] But the principle is honored mostly in the breach, and its logic breaks down under any scrutiny at all. We have a political process for allocating government resources because no government spending could ever win unanimous consent among all citizens. Every taxpayer indirectly funds some government programs with which he or she disagrees, sometimes vehemently, and conflicting views of morality are often at stake in such policy battles. This is why liberals have been known to sport bumper stickers that say things like, "Wouldn't it be great if the schools had all the money they need and the Air Force had to hold a bake sale to buy a bomber?"

## The Congressional Alternative

Under the Constitution's separation of powers, the president does not have the final word on stem cell funding. Congress alone appropriates money, and Congress can decide where that money is spent. With a federal budget that runs into the trillions of dollars, it would be quite impractical for Congress to earmark every dollar it appropriates, so in most cases it allocates funds to broad areas and relies on executive branch agencies to make specific spending decisions. Such is the case with grant money for scientific research. Congress appropriates funds to the NIH (and to some extent other agencies), and it relies on the NIH administrators to parcel out the money in the form of grants. The head of the NIH reports to the secretary of health and human services (in whose department the NIH resides), who reports to the president. It is because of this chain of authority that the president can issue policy declarations about who will and will not be granted federal research funds, even though he himself lacks the power of the purse.

### THE STEM CELL RESEARCH
### ENHANCEMENT ACT

Congress can overturn the president's ill-conceived policy, if it is motivated to do so, simply by enacting legislation directing the NIH not to discriminate against grant applications that propose to work with hESC lines, whenever created. And although it took more than four years after President Bush's 2001 speech, Congress eventually attempted to do precisely this.

The House of Representatives took the first step in May 2005, when, by a vote of 238–194, it passed the Stem Cell Research Enhancement Act (SCREA), designed to overturn the Bush policy by instructing the secretary of health and human services to "conduct and support research that utilizes human embryonic stem cells . . . (regardless of the date on which the stem cells were derived from a human embryo)."[39]

The House's passage of the act created political problems for the leadership in the Republican-controlled Senate. A number of Republican senators enthusiastically support hESC research and oppose the president's spending restrictions. A particularly outspoken and emotional advocate in the majority party has been Senator Arlen Specter. Appearing tired, ill, and noticeably without hair, Specter launched an offensive against the president's stem cell policy in the summer of 2005 while undergoing chemotherapy treatment for Hodgkin's disease, a form of cancer that scientists hope to be able to cure one day using stem cell technology. In a June 2005 interview, Specter told CBS News that he was "very angry" about the failure of the government to support stem cell research and called it "scandalous when we have the potential to save lives and we're not doing so."[40] The president's policy was also opposed by some steadfast pro-life senators, such as Utah's Orrin Hatch and then Senate majority leader Bill Frist, the latter having initially supported the president but then quite publicly switched sides in the debate. With the breadth of Republican support, there was never much doubt that the SCREA would pass the Senate; thus, bringing the bill to a vote would force a showdown between the Republican-controlled Congress and the Republican president, who had threatened a veto.[41]

More than a year after the House vote, the Senate leadership finally brought the SCREA to the Senate floor in July 2006.

It passed by a vote of 63–37, with nineteen Republicans voting in favor and one Democrat voting against.[42] The following day, President Bush wielded his veto pen, for the first time in five and a half years in office, to block the bill, as threatened.[43] An immediate vote to override the veto in the House failed, falling more than fifty votes short of the required two-thirds majority.[44] The shortfall was sufficient to ensure that even the large gains in the House by the Democrats in the November 2006 congressional elections would leave supporters of the SCREA about three dozen votes short of mustering a veto-proof majority, making Congress's second enactment of the bill in 2007 (followed by a second veto) mainly for show.

## LIMITATIONS OF THE SCREA

Although the SCREA would greatly expand federal funding if it were to become law, it would not fully open the doors to federal support for hESC research on an equal basis with other medical research for two reasons. First, the SCREA apparently would not reverse the Dickey Amendment's prohibition on the funding of research that destroys embryos. Although it calls for research that "utilizes" hESCs, the bill is silent on the subject of research in which hESCs are *derived* from embryos, which suggests that it would not supersede the Dickey Amendment.[45]

Second, the SCREA specifies that the federal government may fund only research conducted on stem cells derived from excess IVF embryos, to the exclusion of embryos specifically created for research purposes.[46] To some bioethicists who believe that embryos lack the moral value of persons but are entitled to special respect based on their potential, the difference between using embryos slated for destruction in any event and creating embryos specifically for the purpose of scientific research is morally quite significant. According to this "discarded-created" distinction,[47] the former is ethically acceptable because it does not cause an increase in the number of embryos destroyed, whereas the latter is unacceptable because it results in a net increase in embryo destruction.

These limitations built into the SCREA obviously represent a political compromise struck so as to attract the votes of members of Congress who want to see hESC research progress but are at the same time deeply troubled by the destruction of embryos. But anyone who thinks that embryo destruction is even somewhat immoral or troubling should not be fooled into thinking that the limitations on funding in the SCREA provide anything more than an empty gesture toward their concerns.

By permitting the funding of research on new hESC lines, the SCREA would encourage the creation of countless new lines and thus encourage embryo destruction, making the government causatively complicit. Maintaining the Dickey Amendment's prohibition on funding of the destructive acts themselves but not acts that will directly encourage the destructive acts should provide little solace to anyone who believes that blastocysts have the same moral worth as persons. In practical terms, however, if the SCREA were enacted, the continued obstacle of the Dickey Amendment probably would have a minimal effect on scientific progress. American scientists have created a large number of hESC lines since August 2001 using private funds, most notably at Harvard, where Douglas Melton alone had created twenty-eight lines as of 2005.[48] And even if most hESC lines had to be imported, the American biotechnology industry would not be at a substantial competitive disadvantage.

The more troubling falsehood perpetrated by the SCREA is the implicit suggestion that by refusing to fund embryos specifically created for research, the law would ensure that the government would support research only on embryos created for the purpose of reproduction. The reality is that most of the more than four hundred thousand embryos frozen in American IVF clinics were created not to make babies but for the convenience of the patients and the gamete donors (often but not always the same people).

As described above, most IVF physicians create as many embryos as possible from an egg-retrieval cycle, implant perhaps three of the ones perceived as most likely to succeed, and freeze the rest. If the initial implantation attempt does not produce a live birth, or if it does but the patient wishes to have another child, some of the frozen embryos may be thawed and implanted in a subsequent treatment cycle. But even if a patient wishes to initiate another cycle, she will not necessarily use any of the frozen embryos. IVF statistics indicate that the live birthrate is much higher for "fresh" than for frozen-then-thawed embryos,[49] so most women who undergo successive IVF treatment cycles choose to go through another round of hormone treatment, egg harvest, and embryo creation to maximize the likelihood of success.[50]

The common practice of creating as many embryos as possible per egg-retrieval effort gives physicians the largest possible number of embryos from which to select the "best" for implantation, and it affords women the option of undergoing multiple attempts at implantation without having to undergo the egg-retrieval process more than once. It is thus a quite sensible practice from the point of view of IVF patients who wish to minimize the pain and medical risks of repeated hormonal injections and egg-retrieval procedures and maximize the likelihood of pregnancy in any one cycle of treatment. Cost concerns also counsel for this practice: a single treatment cycle can cost patients as much as $10,000 or more.[51] For all these reasons, it is an appropriate medical practice for IVF clinicians, who owe professional duties to their patients. But this should not obscure the fact that the practice results in hundreds of thousands of embryos created with the full knowledge that only a limited number will ever be implanted and that the rest will be destroyed.

To suggest that all of these embryos are produced for the purpose of "creating life," however, is to use rhetoric to promulgate a blatant falsehood. If the nation's governing moral principle were to be that embryos should be created only for the purpose of creating life, IVF clinics would be permitted to create at any one time only the number of embryos that they were planning to implant immediately, and they would be required to wait to create more embryos until another treatment cycle became necessary.

Legislation to curtail the production of embryos by IVF clinics is rarely proposed; such regulation would constitute a gross interference in the personal choice of IVF patients and the professional autonomy of IVF clinicians. But as long as the nation is willing to permit the creation and ultimate destruction of hundreds of thousands of excess embryos for the convenience of people trying to conceive, it is pure hypocrisy to oppose the creation by scientists of a far smaller number of embryos on the grounds that it is morally wrong to create embryos for any purpose other than procreation. Maintaining the discarded-created distinction for stem cell research purposes while ignoring the embryo creation practices of the IVF industry is like holding a finger in a hole in a dyke while a tsunami propels hundred-foot waves over its top.

Limiting funding to research on excess IVF embryos, as
the SCREA would do, would be less problematic from a practical perspective if all embryos were equally valuable for research. But this is not the case. For several reasons, stem cell
lines derived from excess IVF embryos are likely to be less
useful over time to researchers than those from embryos
created specifically for research purposes. Because an IVF embryo's gamete donors are not selected for their genetic
makeup, such embryos can only by happenstance have disease
characteristics—or disease-fighting characteristics—of particular interest to researchers. Further, IVF gamete donors do
not make up a broad cross section of the population.[52] Because
of the high cost of IVF treatment, IVF gamete donors come
from disproportionately wealthy and disproportionately Caucasian backgrounds, and the excess embryos might lack the
heterogeneity necessary for study.[53] IVF embryos also disproportionately come from women who are older and who had
difficulty conceiving. Scientists believe that stem cell lines resulting from such embryos would be of generally lower quality and more prone to genetic defects.[54] Additionally, excess
IVF embryos are not a randomly selected subset even of embryos created for IVF. They are disproportionately embryos
that are the least likely to implant and develop into persons. It
is likely that stem cells derived from this subset of embryos will
not prove to be the best candidates for stable reproduction in
culture over a long period of time or use as regenerative agents.[55]

The enactment of the SCREA would be a step toward re-
alizing the medical potential of stem cells, but its limitations
would create meaningful obstacles to research without truly
addressing the concerns of opponents of hESC research. Blastocysts do not have the moral value of persons. If they have any
more moral value than any other tissues, it is outweighed by

the value of persons with crippling illnesses that regenerative medicine might alleviate or cure. The federal government ought to fund research proposals involving hESCs on the same basis—scientific merit—that it funds all other medical research. The only other internally coherent policy is to criminalize all hESC research as murder and prohibit IVF clinics from creating any embryos that are not immediately implanted.

## Practical Consequences
### hESC LINES

Not long after President Bush's August 2001 speech, it became clear that the stem cell lines eligible for federal funding would be far less valuable than the president's description suggested. Of the hESC lines cleared by the NIH as eligible for federal funding under the Bush policy, only twenty-one are currently available for use in research, about one-third of the number Bush estimated in his national address.[56] In testimony before the Senate two years ago, John Gearhart, the innovator of human embryonic germ cell lines, explained that the federally eligible hESC lines offered little help in studying the development of specific diseases because they were not derived from embryos selected for their disease-specific attributes.[57]

To make matters worse, it is likely that none of the eligible lines could ever be used to create cells that could be safely transplanted into human patients. In order for hESCs to live and reproduce outside the body, scientists must mix them in a solution that contains nutrients. Early attempts to create stem cell lines—including all of the existing federally "eligible" lines—relied on mouse cells for this purpose.[58] Although mouse cells worked well to keep the stem cells alive and allow them to propagate, they have the potential to infect the stem cells with mouse viruses, and it is possible that the viruses (which are now confined to the mouse population) would not be apparent for some time. Most scientists believe that it is unacceptably risky to inject humans with stem cells grown with mouse feeder cells.[59] Finally, although embryonic stem cells could conceivably be coaxed into proliferating indefinitely, the quality of the existing crop of hESC lines appears to degrade over time.

For all of these reasons, two conclusions are clear: first, if scientists are ever successful in developing treatments for diseases using hESCs, this promise will not be accomplished with the federally eligible lines; second, the federal funding restrictions have slowed progress in hESC research to some degree, although to what degree is certainly debatable.

## RESEARCH PROGRESS AND INTERNATIONAL COMPETITIVENESS

When President Bush announced his hESC funding policy in 2001, a near tidal wave of predictions of a brain drain followed, with visions of vast numbers of American scientists decamping for nations with more supportive government policies. These fears perhaps were fueled by the well-publicized move of U.C. San Francisco biologist Roger Pederson to Cambridge University in the summer of 2001, even before the Bush policy was put in place.[60] Since Pederson's departure, a handful of high-profile American stem cell scientists have been wooed overseas by offers of state-of-the-art laboratory facilities and government research funding. Judith Swain and Edward Holmes moved their labs from U.C. San Diego to Singapore, Neal Copeland and Nancy Jenkins turned down offers to join Stanford University's stem cell research program in favor of moving to the Asian city-state, and Lawrence Stanton left his research post at Geron for Singapore as well.[61] These well-publicized cases demonstrate that the political climate in the United Kingdom and Singapore offers certain advantages at present, but there is little hard evidence of a brain drain of serious proportions, although claims of it continue to appear in print from time to time.[62] It is also difficult to find evidence substantiating predictions that junior scientists who might otherwise become stem cell researchers would avoid the field for fear of funding difficulties, although this possibility is more plausible.

One recent study documented that the U.S. share of published scientific papers on hESC research declined precipitously between 2002 and 2004, and one of its authors raised an alarm that U.S. scientists are being eclipsed by those in countries with governments more supportive of stem cell research.[63] But as that study itself indicates, the absolute number of papers increased substantially for American as well as non-American scientists.[64] Although the United States today is not the world's behemoth in stem cell research that it might have been with higher levels of federal funding, it is still the world's leader. The simple reason is that notwithstanding the federal funding limitations, stem cell research receives far more financial support in the United States than in any other country.

*Federal Funding*

Often lost in the political battles over stem cell research is the fact that even with funding restrictions in place, federal support in the United States exceeds government funding for stem cell research in the rest of the world combined. A British report on the U.K. Stem Cell Initiative estimated that 2005 public support for stem cell research was about $40 million in the United Kingdom, $16–$19 million in Singapore, $17.7 million in South Korea, $18 million in Sweden, $4–$10 million in China, and $5–$7 million in Israel.[65] (Other sources suggest that U.K. funding might be as high as $85–$90 million in 2007.)[66] These are the nations most often named as challengers to the United States for scientific supremacy in the field. In comparison, in 2005 the NIH spent $239 million to support human stem cell research—$40 million for research involving the federally eligible hESC lines and $199 million for hASCs—and an additional $370 million on nonhuman stem cell research.[67]

### Philanthropy

In the years since 2001, a large amount of private funding has enabled scientists to create and study hESC lines not eligible for federal funding. With a few exceptions—most notably the Geron Corporation, which funded pioneering work at the University of Wisconsin and Johns Hopkins that led to the creation of the first hESC and hEGC lines—biotechnology companies have been reluctant to invest in stem cell research: the distance between understanding how stem cells work and the manufacture of marketable products is still considered too large and the risks too great. But the willingness of philanthropists, both nonprofit foundations and private donors, to put their money where the government will not put its own has been impressive.

Much of this private funding has surfaced in the form of gifts to research universities. In 2006 alone, Ray Dolby donated $16 million to the University of California at San Francisco for a stem cell center, Eli Broad gave $25 million to build an institute for integrative biology and stem cell research at the University of Southern California, New York mayor Michael Bloomberg donated $100 million to Johns Hopkins University to support stem cell research, and Harvard announced it had raised more than $30 million in private funds for its stem cell institute.[68] These amounts are small compared to the $28+ billion annual budget of the NIH, but they are significant, and they are even significant in comparison to the amounts that governments of other countries spend to fund stem cell research.

### State-Level Activity

Although the most attention has been paid to federal policy concerning hESC research, there has been far more legal action at the state level. At least nine states ban research on in vitro embryos altogether, going further than the Dickey Amendment or the Bush funding policy.[69] These statutes appear on their face to prohibit the development of hESC lines from embryos but not subsequent hESC research that makes use of the stem cells themselves. A handful of state laws that prohibit research on aborted fetuses, embryos, or organs or tissues derived therefrom might also ban hESC research, depending on how terms such as "abort," "embryo," and "tissue" are interpreted.[70]

At least five states have enacted statutes that prohibit the use of state funds for hESC research, more or less paralleling the Bush policy. Arizona, Nebraska, and Virginia explicitly prohibit the use of state funds for such research.[71] Missouri law defines an embryo, even if in vitro, as a "child," and it prohibits the use of state funds for research on a "living child" if the purpose or likely result of such research is to kill, harm, or target the child for destruction, as well as research on any "deceased child" if the parents consented to another person causing the child's death.[72] The former prohibition precludes the use of state funds to harvest embryonic stem cells. The latter prohibition would seem to preclude the use of state funds for any research involving embryonic stem cells. At least three states—Indiana, Michigan, and Virginia—provide tax breaks, loans, or other financial incentives to the biotechnology industry but specifically exclude hESC research from these benefits.[73] Other states, however, have lined up against the president's policy, enacting statutes that officially permit and/or promote hESC research. In 2002, the California legislature became the first to proclaim its support for hESC research,[74] and at least a half-dozen others have followed suit.[75]

In 2004, California used its initiative process to amend its constitution to establish a right to conduct hESC research.[76] That initiative, Proposition 71, also established the California Institute of Regenerative Medicine (CIRM) and provided it with the authority to issue $3 billion in bonds over a ten-year period. The bond revenue is earmarked to support stem cell research, with preferential treatment accorded to research that is ineligible for NIH funding under the Bush policy. Issuance of the bonds was stalled until the summer of 2007 by litigation alleging that Proposition 71 violates the California constitution. The plaintiffs' primary argument was a frivolous claim that the authority the initiative grants to CIRM makes that agency too distant from the control of the state's elected officials.[77] A state trial court ruled firmly for CIRM in April 2006, but it took an additional thirteeen months before the appeals process was finally exhausted. In the meantime, the day after President Bush's first veto of the SCREA, California governor Arnold Schwarzenegger asked the California state treasurer to loan CIRM $150 million from the state's general fund, to be paid back with bond revenue received after the litigation ends, thus allowing CIRM to award its first series of grants in 2006.[78]

One remarkable side effect of the legal wrangling in California demonstrates the power of private philanthropy in the arena of stem cell research. In order to provide some initial funding for research while the litigation ensued, CIRM was able to obtain commitments from philanthropic organizations to buy $45 million in bond anticipation notes.[79] These notes will now become bonds, but they would have been converted to donations if the agency lost and the courts ruled that the bonds could not be issued.[80]

While California is the eight-hundred-pound gorilla of states providing financial support for hESC research, it is not alone, and the field appears to be getting more crowded each year. New Jersey created a stem cell institute, and the Garden State was the first to actually award grant money to researchers.[81] Connecticut's legislature has committed $100 million over ten years to stem cell research, with preference given to hESC research.[82] The governor of Illinois has provided a total of $15 million in funding to support stem cell research by executive order,[83] and Maryland's legislature has authorized annual stem cell research grants based on the availability of state funds ($15 million was provided in the law's first year).[84] Lawmakers in yet other states have proposed additional financial commitments to stem cell research—most notably New York, where Governor Eliot Spitzer has called for a research and development bond initiative that would provide more than $1 billion for stem cell science over the span of a decade.[85]

State and private research funding has its disadvantages when compared to federal funding, and the scope of the resources available is not the only one. Another is the fact that multiple funding sources are less efficient than a single funding source: many overhead expenses have to be duplicated. It is nice for scientists if each state decides to build its own gleaming stem cell institute, but it is not very cost effective.

Still another disadvantage is the problem of segregating research on ineligible hESC lines from federally funded projects. Major research universities rely heavily on federal grant support for scientific research. The Bush funding policy requires these universities to adopt careful procedures to prevent any intermingling of federal grant dollars that support other projects with support for research on ineligible hESC lines. This means, for example, that a microscope purchased with a federal grant awarded for research on adult stem cells—or for an entirely unrelated line of research—cannot be used, even briefly, by a scientist conducting ineligible research. If the construction of a university laboratory building was funded in part with federal grant money, ineligible research may be conducted in that building, but the university must ensure that private funds contributed to that building in proportion to the amount of space used by the ineligible projects.[86]

The complicated bookkeeping required by the federal policy, along with fear of political repercussions should errors be made, has caused some universities to take even more extreme precautions to prevent the intermingling of funds than the government requires. These precautions often increase the cost of conducting even privately funded research. At Harvard, a portion of one building used for research on ineligible lines has been sealed off, and special keycards are needed for access. The purchase of all supplies for this portion of the building, right down to the light bulbs, is handled separately.[87] Stanford, still recalling a 1980s scandal over the improper use of federal grant funds, is constructing an entirely new building for stem cell research that is ineligible for federal funding.

*Expectations of Regime Change*

The final explanation for the continued U.S. leadership in stem cell research is the belief that the federal funding prohibition will be relatively short-lived. The failure of the Congress to muster a veto-proof majority for the SCREA makes it likely that the funding restrictions will remain in place until Bush leaves office in January 2009. When a new occupant enters the White House, however, the odds are extremely high that he (or she) will lift the ban. If the Democratic nominee prevails in the 2008 presidential election, this is a foregone conclusion. But it is also a likely, albeit far from certain, consequence of a Republican victory. As of this writing, the three leading candidates for the Republican nomination—Senator John McCain, former New York City mayor Rudy Giuliani, and former Massachusetts governor Mitt Romney—favor increased federal funding of hESC research. (McCain voted in favor of the SCREA.)

The support of both Republican and Democratic candidates is not surprising given that hESC research is popular with the American public. A 2005 *Wall Street Journal* poll found that 65 percent agreed (17 percent disagreed) that if most scientists believe stem cell research will improve our ability to prevent diseases, we should allow it, and 72 percent agreed (15 percent disagreed) that stem cell research should be allowed if conducted on embryos that would otherwise be destroyed.[88] A Harris Poll taken the same year found 70 percent favored hESC research, with 19 percent opposed.[89] As people become more aware of hESC research, the likelihood of their supporting it increases substantially, suggesting that the trend of increasing public support is likely to continue.[90] A 2006 Gallup Poll found that 61 percent of respondents believed medical research using stem cells obtained from human embryos was morally acceptable, up nine points from the 51 percent of respondents who said the practice was morally acceptable in 2002.[91] A Pew Research Center poll found that in 2002 only 43 percent of respondents said it was more important to conduct stem cell research than to protect embryos and 38 percent thought it was more important to protect embryos, but in

2004 the former had risen to 56 percent while the latter had declined to 32 percent.[92]

When the question is whether the government should fund stem cell research, support remains strong according to most polls. A 2005 CNN/USA Today/Gallup Poll found that 56 percent thought the federal government should fund embryonic stem cell research, compared to 40 percent who thought it should not, while 53 percent favored eliminating or easing current federal funding restrictions. In early 2007, a Harris Poll reported that 65 percent of respondents support expanding federal funding for hESC research.[93]

## Is Common Ground Possible?

In the case of hESC research, revolutions in technology have created possibilities that raise divisive moral questions. It is conceivable that further technological advancement might avoid those questions altogether, as well as the societal divisions that they create. As time wears on, however, the possibility of such technology eliminating the deep social conflict seems less and less likely.

As an example of how intractable the fundamental disagreement is, consider the August 2006 publication of a study that claimed to have taken a major step to bridge the gap.[94] Modifying the procedure they had demonstrated with mouse embryos two years earlier,[95] scientist Robert Lanza and colleagues were able to create two hESC lines using individual cells taken from three-day-old embryos, each of which was made up of only 8–10 cells. This was significant because we know that eight-cell human embryos can lose one cell and still develop into a person. When parents are known carriers of certain genetic diseases, IVF clinics often conduct preimplantation genetic diagnosis (PGD) of in vitro embryos in exactly this way, by removing and testing one of the cells. If that cell is free of genetic impairment, the embryo, now with seven cells, can be implanted in the womb and result in a live birth.[96]

Some opponents pointed out that attempting to remove a single cell from an eight-cell embryo can potentially destroy the embryo, and others pointed out that we do not know for sure whether a person who develops from a seven-cell embryo bears differential health risks.[97] Babies born after the PGD process have shown no signs of suffering ill effects to date. But since PGD has existed for little more than a decade, researchers do not know for sure whether people born after PGD carry with them a propensity toward unknown problems later in life.[98]

These criticisms, however, misunderstand the full implications of Lanza's discovery. It is true that opponents of research that destroys embryos logically might also object to removing one of the embryo's cells solely for research because of the risk that the procedure could harm the embryo. But Lanza's technique shows that if an IVF clinic were to extract a cell for PGD purposes, that cell could be permitted to divide once, and one of the resulting two cells could be used for research while the other was used for PGD.[99] In theory, hESC lines could be created with no additional harm or additional risk to the embryo.

Lanza's technique is, at this point, relatively inefficient in the sense that it would take many embryos to make just one cell line if only one cell per embryo were used. In their experiment, in fact, Lanza and his group used multiple cells from each embryo and destroyed the embryos, thus provoking a small uproar among people who failed to understand that their point was to demonstrate that hESC lines *could be* created without harming embryos rather than to actually create them without harming embryos.[100] In addition, creating hESC lines in this way would limit the pool of eligible embryos to those developed for IVF purposes (and a small subset of those if only embryos that would undergo PGD anyway were chosen), meaning that the technique would not be useful for creating specialized embryos with particular disease profiles. Notwithstanding these shortcomings, however, Lanza's approach would seem to be immune from criticism on the grounds that it puts embryos at risk. In triumph, Lanza proclaimed that "there is no rational reason left to oppose this research."[101]

As it turned out, Lanza underestimated the opponents of hESC research. Critics quickly pointed out that although it has never been accomplished with any mammal, it is possible that a single cell removed from an eight-cell embryo could develop into a person.[102] This point generated opposition to Lanza's technique on the grounds that even if it is practiced in a way that does not harm embryos, the cells that are used for research could themselves be potential persons. After Lanza's findings were announced, Senator Sam Brownback, one of the leading congressional supporters of the Bush stem cell policy, seized on this line of reasoning, issuing a statement equating Lanza's approach to "creating a twin and then killing that twin."[103] Other critics hypothesized that a cell extracted for PGD purposes could die while scientists wait for it to divide, which would constitute harm attributable solely to the attempt to make it useful for research.[104] If PGD could not be conducted on the cell as a result, the embryo presumably would not be implanted, with the result being that the embryo's ultimate destruction could be attributed to the attempt to use it for research.

President Bush quickly indicated that he had not been won over by Lanza either. Immediately after Lanza's results were announced, the White House issued a statement saying that "any use of human embryos for research purposes raises serious ethical concerns. This technique does not resolve all those concerns."[105] Although admittedly opaque, this statement might suggest a shift in the president's position from "it is wrong to *take* a life to save a life" to "it is wrong to *use* a life to save a life." If so, it is difficult to imagine how any scientific advance could ever soften the opposition to hESC research of President Bush and his allies.

# 3

# Cloning, Congress, and the Constitution

In the 1976 novel *The Boys from Brazil*, the infamous Nazi concentration camp doctor, Josef Mengele, who disappeared after World War II, never to be found, has created ninety-four clones of Adolf Hitler. The children, sent to live with German families around the globe, are being raised in circumstances that Mengele has chosen to mimic Hitler's upbringing. Now that the clones have reached the age at which Hitler's father died, Mengele sets out to have each of the ninety-four stepfathers murdered. The stoic Mengele thinks nothing of the bloodshed, of course. It is just one more necessary step in his plan to breed a new "Fuehrer" who will lead a reconstructed "Fourth Reich." In the movie version, Gregory Peck portrays Mengele, while Laurence Olivier plays the Nazi hunter, a character based loosely on Simon Wiesenthal, who successfully foils the plot.

The depiction of a man called "the angel of death" attempting to create nearly one hundred replicas of arguably the most evil man ever to walk the planet for the purpose of world domination does not portray cloning in a favorable light—to put it mildly. Most depictions of cloning in popular culture, while not this extreme, are similarly negative.

In 1996, Ian Wilmut and his research team at the Roslin Institute in Scotland—with the assistance, of course, of a mature female sheep who supplied the necessary womb—gave birth to the first cloned mammal. The lamb was created by inserting the nucleus of a cell from an adult sheep into an enucleated sheep ovum and using electrical impulses to stimulate the resulting cell to divide as if it were a newly fertilized zygote. Notwithstanding Wilmut's attempt to bring some levity to the circumstances—he named the soon-to-be famous lamb "Dolly," after Dolly Parton, because the somatic cell used in her creation came from mammary tissue—the sheep's birth was taken quite seriously across the globe when it was announced six months later.[1] Dolly's scientific value was often viewed as secondary to her implications for human reproduction.

By suggesting that the technology might one day be available to create a cloned human being, the announcement of Dolly's birth gave rise to an immediate and virtually unanimous chorus of opposition to human cloning, in the United States as well as abroad. Although they were not enacted, bills were introduced in the House and Senate in the following two weeks that would prohibit human cloning.[2] President Clinton issued a presidential directive prohibiting the use of federal funds for the cloning of humans, and he instructed his National Bioethics Advisory Commission to produce a report on the ethical implications of human cloning.[3] Several months later, that commission called for a prohibition on the creation of human clones.[4]

Ten years later, little has changed. A few iconoclasts and provocateurs write essays extolling the virtues of human cloning, but virtually all bioethicists, scientists, and elected officials who speak on the issue of reproductive cloning oppose the practice, and most favor a strict legal prohibition on any attempts. This includes the entire membership of the President's Council on Bioethics, which unanimously recommended in a 2002 report that reproductive cloning be banned.[5]

Against this background, it is hardly surprising that scientists who wish to use an adult cell and an ovum to create a blastocyst with the same genotype as the adult cell and then use the blastocyst's stem cells for medical research often wince when the term "cloning" is used to describe their endeavor, even when modified by the word "therapeutic." In fact, largely as a public relations matter, many informally boycott the term "therapeutic cloning," preferring the less loaded, if somewhat impenetrable, "somatic cell nuclear transfer" or "nuclear transplantation."[6] Unfortunately for those researchers, however, biology does provide a valid reason for comparing the creation of Dolly the sheep to the use of SCNT for stem cell research: both reproductive and therapeutic cloning begin with the same process of inserting an adult cell's nucleus into an enucleated ovum and stimulating it to begin the process of cell division. It is therefore unlikely that SCNT can be fully divorced from the broader cloning wars.

## Cloning Legislation

Given the vivid fears that the specter of reproductive cloning raises, it is unsurprising that a number of states have enacted comprehensive cloning bans that are insensitive to the purpose for which a cloned embryo is created. To date, at least five states—Arkansas, Indiana, Michigan, North Dakota, and South Dakota—have enacted statutes that prohibit all human cloning, for therapeutic as well as reproductive purposes, within their borders.[7] Some of these statutes make engaging in the prohibited activities a felony, while others punish transgressions only with civil fines.[8] Most of these laws prohibit not only creating a cloned human embryo but also receiving one. These statutes might preclude any research on hESCs derived from a cloned embryo, although they might be interpreted to permit scientists to import and conduct research on stem cell lines derived elsewhere from cloned embryos. Other states, most notably those that actively support hESC research, explicitly support the practice of SCNT for therapeutic purposes.[9] The statutes of these states clearly distinguish (and prohibit) reproductive cloning.[10]

At the federal level, in contrast to the case of hESC research generally, there is a congressional ban on federal funding of cloning, even if done for therapeutic rather than reproductive purposes. The annual renewal of the Dickey Amendment, which prohibits funding of research that destroys human embryos, also prohibits the use of federal funds for the creation of human embryos.[11] In so doing, it implicitly bars federal financial support for cloning, whatever its purpose.

Also in contrast to hESC research generally, there is significant support in Congress for imposing a regulatory prohibition on cloning, rather than merely refusing to fund the technology. The House of Representatives has twice passed a bill, the Human Cloning Prohibition Act, [12] which would outlaw the production of cloned embryos whether their intended use is reproduction or therapeutic research, and it has done so by a comfortable margin of just over one hundred votes in 2001 and just under one hundred votes in 2003.[13] Significantly, the bill would also prohibit the import of "any product derived" from a cloned embryo.[14] This provision suggests that American scientists would not be able to conduct research on hESCs harvested (overseas) from cloned embryos and that

American consumers would not be able to receive treatments created from such hESCs, at least in the United States. Whether an American who traveled internationally to receive a stem-cell-based treatment created from a cloned embryo would violate the importation ban by returning home with the biological product inside his or her body would violate the statute is uncertain, as the term "import" is not defined. If enacted, the bill would subject violators to a criminal penalty of up to ten years of imprisonment and, if the violator profited from the act, not less than $1 million in civil penalties.[15] The bill has faltered in the Senate so far, but sponsors continue to reintroduce it in both houses in each Congress, and President Bush called for its enactment in his 2006 State of the Union Address.[16]

Congressional opponents of a complete ban, without any visible exceptions, support bills that would prohibit cloning for reproductive purposes but allow the use of SCNT technology for stem cell research. While overwhelming opposition to reproductive cloning would seem to suggest that a reproductive cloning ban would pass easily, these bills have been stymied by proponents of a comprehensive prohibition who hold the reproductive cloning ban hostage to their insistence that therapeutic cloning also be outlawed.[17] Somewhat surprisingly, then, other than the Dickey Amendment, which concerns only federal funding, there is no federal law of any kind on the subject of cloning.

## Opposition to Therapeutic Cloning

The medical argument for pursuing therapeutic cloning technology is compelling. SCNT would enable scientists to study the progression of any disease by taking a single cell from a diseased adult, creating an hESC line from it, and following the differentiation process of the resulting cells. Even more important, SCNT offers the unique potential for future recipients of stem-cell-based treatments to receive cells genetically identical to their own. This would eliminate the significant problem of tissue rejection, which could prove to be the most substantial impediment to the clinical success of regenerative medicine.

To be sure, there are some serious obstacles to overcome, both technical and industrial, before cloning-based stem cell treatments become a reality. The inability to date of scientists to perfect the cloning technique with a human somatic cell is only one of the problems. A second is that SCNT does not produce a pure clone because cells in the new embryo retain small bits of mitochondrial DNA from the egg donor. Thus it is possible that problems of immune system rejection will not be wholly solved by SCNT.[18] Still another problem is that the cost of truly individualized treatments, which would require technicians to create a cloned embryo from a patient's cell, extract the hESCs, and create a new cell line, might be prohibitive, at least in the short run. Notwithstanding these obstacles, however, the potential for therapeutic benefits is so substantial that the endeavor is worth pursuing.

Against the potential of therapeutic cloning, opponents advance at least three types of arguments as to why the law should ban the research effort: the creation and destruction of embryos that would be required, the unnaturalness of the procedure, and the fine line between therapeutic and reproductive cloning.

EMBRYO CREATION AND DESTRUCTION

Some arguments against therapeutic cloning reiterate those proffered by opponents of hESC research generally or against hESC research under certain conditions. First, at least given currently available technology, therapeutic cloning requires the destruction of blastocysts. For most people who oppose all hESC research for this reason, it logically follows that therapeutic cloning is also improper. Second, therapeutic cloning by definition entails the creation of embryos for research purposes, in addition to their destruction. Most people who believe it is improper to create embryos for purposes other than reproduction—whether or not they find embryo destruction for research problematic—also oppose therapeutic cloning, although some bioethicists believe that the creation of a cloned embryo for research is less troubling than the creation of one through fertilization because the former would lack a unique genome.[19]

Chapter 2 argued that it is inconsistent to oppose the creation of embryos for stem cell research while not opposing the widespread IVF clinic practice of creating hundreds of thousands of excess embryos with the knowledge that they will never be implanted into a womb. It seems difficult to contend that stem cell research that might cure terrible diseases is not a sufficiently good reason to create embryos that are destined to be destroyed but that reducing the likelihood that an IVF patient will have to go through more than one cycle of treatment before becoming pregnant is. It is more consistent to oppose therapeutic cloning and common IVF practice, but the sensibility of this position necessarily must rely on the premise, also contested in Chapter 2, that embryos have the same moral value as the human beings who could be helped by stem cell research.

There is one important way in which this set of arguments, when made against therapeutic cloning, takes a different approach than when the arguments are raised in the context of hESC research that does not involve cloning. Opponents of hESC research generally have focused, at least at the federal level, on the issue of government funding. Some individual Americans undoubtedly would support either a prohibition against any research that destroys embryos or a prohibition against creating embryos for research purposes, but there is relatively little popular support for either, at least as far as popular support can be judged by the position of members of the legislative or executive branches of the federal government. In the context of therapeutic cloning, however, the battle-ground issue is prohibition, not merely federal financial support. Because of this difference, the debate over cloning raises a series of constitutional issues that are usually not present in the hESC research debate. These issues will be considered below.

## UNNATURALNESS

Distinct from arguments against hESC research using fertilized embryos, other arguments against cloning emphasize the "unnaturalness" of creating an embryo with the genes of a single parent. Such claims more routinely surface as criticisms of reproductive cloning, but they are sometimes used to criticize therapeutic cloning as well: creating embryos through SCNT is either morally unacceptable in principle or problematic as an indication of mankind's willingness to engineer human life, which shows moral hubris.[20]

What are essentially intuitions about morality based on what repulses us or makes us feel uncomfortable can be a signal of deeper wisdom, as Leon Kass, the former chair of the President's Council on Bioethics, has written.[21] But the problem with relying on such intuitions without a reasoned justification is that they are just as often indications of unfamiliarity and prejudice. It was only a half century ago that most

Americans thought interracial marriage was unnatural and immoral.[22] When the Supreme Court struck down a Virginia anti-miscegenation statute as unconstitutional in 1967, sixteen states still had such laws on their books, and fourteen others had repealed their laws only within the previous fifteen years. Today it is the fact that people once believed such laws were appropriate that seems immoral. Closer to the subject of SCNT, artificial insemination and IVF technologies were criticized as immoral interference with the natural process of procreation when they debuted; today they cause little controversy at all.[23]

## THE SLIPPERY SLOPE

A third type of argument against therapeutic cloning relies on the claim of a "slippery slope" between therapeutic and reproductive cloning: permitting SCNT for therapeutic purposes either increases the likelihood of or will inevitably lead to reproductive cloning.[24] Assuming that reproductive cloning would be undesirable—an issue that goes beyond the scope of this book—a slippery slope that leads from therapeutic to reproductive cloning could potentially justify a prohibition on the former even if therapeutic cloning itself is not ethically problematic.

Slippery slope arguments take the following form: "A is unobjectionable in itself, but allowing A is ill advised because it will increase the likelihood of B, which is objectionable." The implied causal mechanisms embedded in slippery slope claims are varied, however, and when fleshed out, they often undermine either the premise that A is itself unobjectionable or the premise that B is itself objectionable. For example, a common slippery slope argument is that if society permits A, which appears similar to B, people will become accustomed to A, and this familiarity, in turn, will reduce their revulsion toward B. The problem with this line of argumentation is that, on one hand, if exposure to A reduces revulsion to B, perhaps B is not so bad after all, and we need not fear it. On the other hand, if B genuinely is as terrible as we think it is and A is not terrible at all, there is scant reason to think that exposure to A will cause people to decide that B is acceptable.

The slippery slope argument against therapeutic cloning is significantly more powerful, however, because it rests not only on the fear that A's acceptance will change public morality (and thus that the population will come to accept reproductive cloning) but also on the fact that A's acceptance will tangibly interfere with the practical ability of society to police against B.[25] If SCNT were illegal, it would be difficult, although probably not impossible, for a renegade scientist to create a cloned embryo without being discovered by colleagues and reported. If SCNT is legal for therapeutic purposes but not for reproductive purposes and becomes widespread, however, the act of creating a cloned embryo would not raise any eyebrows. With the widespread use of IVF, implanting an embryo in a woman's uterus is already commonplace, and this part of the procedure is relatively low tech and simple. A rogue scientist bent on reproductive cloning could relatively easily take a cloned embryo created as a routine part of one process (SCNT) and use it for another routine process (IVF).[26]

This slippery slope claim appears quite powerful and would seem, at a minimum, to force a careful balancing of the potential benefits of therapeutic cloning against the potential costs of reproductive cloning. For two reasons, however, this argument is much less powerful that it first appears. First, there is a substantial obstacle to the slide down the slippery slope; second, prohibiting therapeutic cloning will not keep us off that slope in the first place.

The biological facts are more complicated than the slippery slope claim implicitly assumes, and the risk of rogue scientists creating illicit babies with legally cloned embryos is considerably less likely than one might fear. As it turns out, creating a cloned baby is considerably more complicated than inserting a cloned embryo into a female's uterus. The nucleus of the somatic cell used to create the cloned embryo must be reprogrammed in a way that returns it to its embryonic state before it can successfully develop into a fetus and lead to a live birth. This reprogramming is extremely difficult because during the process by which a sperm cell fertilizes an egg cell, a chemical process important for proper embryonic development occurs to which the sperm and egg genomes react differently. In the SCNT process, however, there is no separate sperm and egg genome—just the single genome of the donor cell. In order to program the nucleus of that cell correctly, scientists would have to first divide its genome into its two original donor genomes, an ability beyond scientists' current capabilities.[27] According to an important article by MIT biologist Rudolph Jaenisch, however, one of the field's leaders, this step is not required in order for a cloned embryo to create usable embryonic stem cells.[28] The upshot is that the slippery slope concern, while it could become significant in the future, is based more on science fiction than scientific fact at present.

If and when technology advances to the point at which it becomes trivial to program cloned embryos to develop into babies, a less restrictive alternative to prohibiting SCNT for research purposes because of slippery slope fears would be to regulate SCNT research by requiring that it include a step that would make the reproductive use of cloned embryos impossible. Such technology appears to be on the horizon. Jaenisch's laboratory recently created cloned mouse embryos that were unable to implant into a mouse uterus because the scientists deactivated a gene in the donor cell that facilitates implantation.[29] After harvesting stem cells from the embryos and creating cell lines, the scientists reactivated the gene and demonstrated that the resulting cells could differentiate appropriately.[30] This technique, dubbed altered nuclear transfer (ANT), was created in an attempt to moot some moral concerns about SCNT. Because an ANT embryo cannot implant, so the argument goes, creating one does not create a potential life, and destroying one to extract embryonic stem cells does not destroy a potential life.

That ANT or a process like it will win over opponents of hESC research who object to the creation or destruction of blastocysts seems quite doubtful. Surely it is mere semantics to say that an embryo that is altered so that it cannot implant in a womb is not actually an embryo. This point was not lost on the U.S. Conference of Catholic Bishops, a representative of which said that ANT is just as morally objectionable as SCNT.[31] On the other hand, pragmatists who support SCNT for research purposes but fear it could make it easier for rogue scientists to create human clones should find the concept behind ANT useful in suggesting that therapeutic cloning need not make reproductive cloning unavoidable.

Whatever the likelihood that widespread therapeutic cloning will lead to reproductive cloning, prohibiting the former in this country alone would do little to forestall the latter, even if the goal is only to prevent reproductive cloning in the United States. When the technological obstacles to therapeutic cloning in humans are overcome, other nations on the cutting edge of stem cell research will embrace it. When that happens, a rogue scientist will be able to steal a cloned embryo from a laboratory in one of those nations and hop an international flight to the United States almost as easily as one might take a cloned embryo from a stem cell research laboratory in this country and drive it across town to an IVF clinic.

Staying off the slippery slope would require that all the leading nations in scientific research band together to prevent SCNT. The prospects for such a coordinated action are virtually nil. A recent U.S.-supported attempt in the U.N. General Assembly to pass a resolution prohibiting cloning for any purpose, including research, failed miserably.[32] Substantial support for therapeutic cloning in that body led it to enact instead a generally worded resolution that prohibits human cloning and other research contrary to "human dignity," leaving to each nation the decision of how broadly the ban ought to extend.[33]

## Constitutional Concerns

As noted above, the debate over the rules that should govern hESC research, at least at the national level, generally concerns public funding. The political process alone will determine how these issues are eventually resolved. Because the issue of prohibition is central to the public controversy over cloning, however, constitutional concerns are also implicated here. Before cloning can be prohibited, its opponents must not only succeed in the political crucible of the Congress but also navigate the choppy waters of judicial review. For the reasons explained below, none of the constitutional issues is likely to prove significant enough to trump the political process under the relevant jurisprudential views of the current Supreme Court. However, a congressional cloning ban would undermine the constitutional principles of limited federal power and individual liberty rights. These features of the ban provide an independent justification for opposing its enactment.

## FEDERALISM AND THE COMMERCE CLAUSE

Under our federal system, the national government lacks general regulatory authority: Congress's ability to enact legislation is limited to the powers granted it by the Constitution. Between 1937 and 1995, this fact was little more than vaguely interesting trivia for policy wonks. The Supreme Court interpreted the Constitution's commerce clause—the grant of power "to regulate Commerce with foreign Nations, and among the several States"[34]—so expansively that the Court found no act of Congress exceeded that body's authority. The landmark 1995 decision of *United States v. Lopez,* however, reinvigorated the commerce clause and placed some limits on federal power.[35]

Alfonso Lopez, Jr., a high school senior in San Antonio, brought a concealed handgun to school. Although this act constituted a crime under Texas law, Lopez was charged with and convicted of violating a federal statute that prohibited the possession of a firearm in a school zone. The federal court of appeals reversed his conviction, and the Supreme Court upheld the reversal on the grounds that the federal law exceeded Congress's power under the commerce clause. The Court concluded that the statute regulated a purely local activity, the effect of which on interstate commerce was too attenuated to justify federal regulation. Five years later, the Court reaffirmed *Lopez* in *United States v. Morrison,* in which a rape victim sued her assailants under the federal Violence Against Women Act.[36] Asserting that the commerce clause draws a line "between what is truly national and truly local," the High Court held that

Morrison's "remedy must be provided by the Commonwealth of Virginia, and not by the United States."[37]

In 2005, however, the Supreme Court's decision in *Gonzales v. Raich* called into doubt whether *Lopez* and *Morrison* heralded a significant contraction of congressional power.[38] *Raich* concerned the federal Controlled Substances Act (CSA), which, among other things, makes the production and possession of marijuana a federal crime. Under the authority of the CSA, which the government claimed was permissible under the commerce clause, federal drug agents seized and destroyed six of plaintiff Diane Monson's marijuana plants following a three-hour standoff. The *Raich* plaintiffs, including Monson, were Californians permitted by that state's Compassionate Use Act to use marijuana for medicinal purposes with a doctor's prescription. They contended that their marijuana use existed within the boundaries of a traditional state concern (the practice of medicine), had no substantial effect on interstate commerce, and was therefore beyond the realm of federal regulation. Justices Anthony Kennedy and Antonin Scalia, part of five-justice majorities in *Lopez* and *Morrison*, joined the four dissenters in those cases—Justices John Paul Stevens, Stephen Breyer, David Souter, and Ruth Bader Ginsburg—to uphold Congress's power.

The *Raich* opinion relies heavily on an analogy between intrastate production and use of marijuana and the intrastate production and use of wheat in the New Deal–era case of *Wickard v. Filburn*.[39] *Wickard* concerned a federal regulation designed to boost wheat prices during the Great Depression that limited the number of acres Filburn was permitted to cultivate with that crop. Filburn argued that the federal government had no authority to regulate his production of wheat for his private use because such production was a purely intrastate activity that had no effect on interstate commerce. Ruling for the government, the Supreme Court found federal regulation was proper because Filburn's production of wheat for personal use, when aggregated with similar production of other farmers, would affect interstate commerce.

In *Raich*, the High Court applied the *Wickard* aggregation principle to Diane Monson's marijuana, holding that in the aggregate, intrastate marijuana production and possession could substantially affect interstate commerce by seeping into a market that the government was legitimately attempting to prevent altogether. In finding *Wickard* a more appropriate precedent than *Lopez* or *Morrison*, the Court also drew a line between "noneconomic" activity, at issue in the latter cases, which Congress cannot regulate under the commerce clause, and "economic" activity, at issue in the former case, that subjects even intrastate activity to the aggregation principle.[40] By defining the class of economic activities extremely broadly to include any production, distribution, or consumption of commodities[41]—a definition strongly criticized by the dissent[42]—the Court determined that the intrastate production and consumption of marijuana was economic in nature and subject to the same analysis that governed *Wickard*.

As a predictive matter, the reasoning in *Raich* strongly suggests that the Supreme Court would uphold a cloning ban against a federalism challenge. Congress clearly possesses the authority to prohibit the interstate transmission of cloned embryos. The question is whether it also has the power to prohibit the intrastate creation of cloned embryos. Under *Raich*, creating an embryo would presumably be considered an "economic" activity because it entails the production of a commodity, even if the production is for a noncommercial purpose such as basic scientific research. Employing the aggregation principle, the

*Raich* reasoning suggests the conclusion that cloned embryos produced within states could seep into the interstate market and thus, in the aggregate, substantially affect interstate commerce, even though—as is the case for marijuana—there is no legal interstate market. Therefore, the government's power to prohibit interstate commerce in cloned embryos gives it the power to prohibit the intrastate production of cloned embryos by way of the "substantial effects" test and the aggregation principle.

There are paths of reasoning that the Supreme Court justices could take that would lead them to strike down a cloning prohibition on commerce clause grounds, but it is unlikely that they will choose to follow them. The Court could determine that cloned embryos are not "commodities" and therefore not subject to analysis under *Raich* because, unlike the case with marijuana, there is no market—legal or illegal—for cloned embryos. The problem with this analysis is that the lack of a market results from technological limitations—specifically the fact that no one has yet created a cloned human embryo—rather than the character of cloned embryos. One can easily foresee a day in which there will be either a legal or black market for cloned embryos.

Alternatively, the Court could narrow its conclusion that the production of any commodity is within the realm of "economic" activity that the commerce clause permits Congress to regulate under the substantial effects test. Arguably, therapeutic cloning conducted by academic scientists seeking to improve our understanding of the body's regenerative potential, as opposed to the same activity conducted by corporate scientists with the aim of developing a commercial product, is noncommercial in nature, much like the operation of schools at issue in *Lopez*. This analysis seems improbable, however, because it would require the Court to directly overrule a significant part of its *Raich* analysis.

Notwithstanding the likelihood that a cloning prohibition would survive commerce clause review by the courts, a cloning ban undermines important federalism values. This fact constitutes an independent argument against congressional action, above and beyond beliefs about the potential benefits of therapeutic cloning specifically and the value of scientific research generally. The jurisprudential principle central to the *Lopez* and *Morrison* decisions was that federal legislation should not encroach on areas of "traditional state concern."[43] Proposals to prohibit cloning are motivated primarily by the perceived moral impropriety of the technology. Although there is no readily agreed upon definition of what precisely comprises the category of traditional state concerns, the regulation of morals ought to fall within it.

In some instances, laws driven by moral or ethical concerns bear directly on interstate commerce. In such cases, federal regulation is appropriate under the commerce clause, whatever Congress's primary motivation. This point is exemplified by the facts of one of the Supreme Court's most famous commerce clause opinions: *Heart of Atlanta Motel, Inc. v. United States.* In that decision, the Court properly found that the commerce clause provides Congress with the power to ban racial discrimination in motels because such discrimination impedes interstate travel, even if the regulation was motivated primarily by Congress's desire to redress a moral wrong.[44]

In contrast, the Human Cloning Prohibition Act lacks any significant commercial justification at all. The bill's clear goal is not to regulate interstate commerce in cloned embryos by preventing it, nor is the bill even useful for that purpose. The bill's proponents wish to prevent the intrastate conduct of an activity that they perceive to be ethically improper and that has only the most tangential relationship to interstate commerce concerns. That relationship might be sufficient to satisfy the expansive view of the commerce clause to which the Supreme Court adhered for most of the twentieth century and to which it returned in *Raich*. But a principled division between federal and state regulatory power ought to place judgments about the ethics of human cloning in the states' bailiwick, along with the regulation of schools, at issue in *Lopez*, and the regulation of violence, at issue in *Morrison*.

## THE RIGHT TO PURSUE MEDICAL TREATMENT

A legitimate challenge to federal cloning prohibitions also could be raised under the Fifth Amendment's due process clause by persons suffering from maladies that might be cured one day as the result of therapeutic cloning technology.[45] More than twenty years ago, the Supreme Court recognized that individuals have a "liberty interest" under the due process clause to refuse medical treatment.[46] A "liberty interest" is generally understood to enjoy constitutional protection but not as much as a "fundamental right"—another term used when the courts analyze the due process clause—although the Supreme Court has never articulated the precise difference between the two terms.

In the wake of the publicity over the Terri Schiavo case, in which the husband and parents of a woman in a persistent vegetative state battled over whether she should be kept alive by artificial methods, a good deal of popular attention has been paid recently to this constitutional principle. Rarely, however, does the government, at any level, attempt to interfere with the ability of individuals to obtain medical treatment for their maladies, and when it does, the usual reason is to protect them from harm that could be caused by unsafe or ineffective remedies. Consequently, the constitutional principle of protecting individual liberty from unwarranted government interference is rarely discussed in the context of access to medical treatments. The liberty principle is implicated in this context too, however, and therefore in government attempts to prohibit medical research, such as therapeutic cloning, that could lead to the development of new treatments.

The landmark decision of *Roe v. Wade* is known for the Supreme Court's pronouncement that the right to privacy prevents states from proscribing abortion during the first two trimesters of pregnancy and that countervailing interests permit state prohibitions during the final trimester. In explaining that states may regulate abortion in the third trimester, however, the Court noted, almost in passing, that prohibitions— even at this point—are not permissible when abortion "is necessary to preserve the life or health of the mother."[47] Although *Roe* is perhaps the most controversial Supreme Court decision of our time, the majority found common ground with Justice William Rehnquist's dissent on this point.[48] The implication of this reasoning is that a pregnant woman has a constitutionally cognizable right to pursue medical treatment (in this case, an abortion) when her health is in jeopardy. If this were not the case, it would make little sense that the Court precluded state interference with abortion when a woman's health is at stake, even at the point of the pregnancy at which the Court explicitly recognized that the state had a countervailing interest in protecting fetal life.[49]

Nineteen years after *Roe*, a plurality of the Supreme Court, writing in *Planned Parenthood v. Casey*, replaced *Roe*'s trimester framework with the less rigid "undue burden" test for determining the constitutionality of state laws that interfered with the exercise of abortion rights.[50] Yet the *Casey* Court maintained that abortion prohibitions are flatly unconstitutional, even after fetal viability, if abortion is necessary to protect either the life or health of the mother.[51] In 2000, the Court applied this rule explicitly in *Stenberg v. Carhart*, finding Nebraska's "partial-birth abortion" ban unconstitutional because it did not contain an exception to the prohibition when necessary to preserve the health of the mother.[52]

Thus the law is clear that the government may not interfere, under any circumstances, with a woman's attempt to obtain an abortion when doing so is necessary to protect her health. It arguably follows that the government may interfere with medical research, including therapeutic cloning, designed to lead to treatments and cures for disease, only when doing so serves a compelling government interest, the standard that the government must meet to be permitted to interfere with a fundamental right.

To be sure, the analogy between abortion jurisprudence and therapeutic cloning requires inferential reasoning on several points. The most obvious difference between the circumstances is that the abortion cases preclude the government from interfering with a woman's ability to preserve her health by removing something (a fetus) from her body, whereas a government ban on medical research would only impede an individual from seeking an external treatment to introduce into the body. On close analysis, however, this internal/external distinction collapses. In both cases, a condition internal to the body—be it pregnancy or a malady such as Parkinson's disease or diabetes—threatens an individual's health. The issue is whether the government may prohibit the individual from using the assistance of others to intervene in that internal condition to restore health. In both cases, the individual requires the assistance of one or more third parties to preserve health, be it a physician or scientific researchers. And in both cases, the right claimed is not an affirmative right to have the government provide an abortion or fund medical research but merely the negative right to be free of government interference in the pursuit of treatment.

Another potential difference between the two contexts is that when pregnancy threatens a woman's health, abortion is a known "cure" that offers immediate results, at least in many cases, whereas therapeutic cloning and stem cell research more generally offer only the uncertain potential of cures in the future. But whether patients have a fundamental right not to have the government impede their search for a cure should not depend upon the likelihood of a cure's being available. Indeed the Supreme Court made this point in *Stenberg*, determining that the constitutionality of Nebraska's partial-birth abortion ban did not depend on how likely it was that the banned procedure would be more conducive to preserving a patient's health than alternative procedures. In that case, despite substantial disagreement in the record over whether the banned procedure had any positive health benefit, the Court found it sufficient that a "significant body of medical opinion believes a procedure may bring with it greater safety for some patients."[53] Analogously, there is widespread belief within the scientific and medical communities that patients suffering from a range of diseases might one day be cured or their suffering alleviated by innovations arising from stem cell research, although such an outcome is far from certain and there are many doubters.

A recent decision of a panel of the D.C. Circuit Court of Appeals in *Abigail Alliance for Better Access to Developmental*

*Drugs v. Von Eschenbach* provides legal support for this argument. The panel held that terminally ill patients have a fundamental right not to be prevented by the FDA from using potentially life-saving drugs that have passed that agency's Phase I trials—which means that the drugs have been judged safe enough in small-scale clinical trials to proceed to larger-scale trials—but have not been approved by the agency for general use.[54] The decision did not require the FDA to approve the drugs at issue for use by the terminally ill because the agency might identify a compelling interest sufficient to override the fundamental right. But it did articulate a presumption against government interference in patients' attempts to seek medical treatment, at least under certain conditions.

As a practical matter, it seems unlikely that the Supreme Court would either uphold the D.C. Circuit ruling in *Abigail Alliance* or determine that the due process clause provides patients with a right to seek therapeutic cloning.[55] The majority of justices currently serving on the Supreme Court have, in previous opinions, articulated a relatively narrow view of the substantive due process doctrine. Under this prevailing perspective, the only rights protected by the due process clause that are not explicitly enumerated in the Constitution are those specific rights that traditionally have been recognized as such in Anglo-American law.

In *Washington v. Glucksberg,* for example, the Court refused to recognize physician-assisted suicide as a right guaranteed by the due process clause, thus leaving legislatures free to prohibit the practice if they see fit.[56] The Court majority relied mainly on the observation that the practice of assisted suicide—and, indeed, suicide in general—enjoyed no historical tradition of support in the United States or in Great Britain prior to the American Revolution.[57] More generally, the Court pronounced that substantive rights under the due process clause must be "deeply rooted in this Nation's history and tradition" and stated that constitutional rights cannot be "simply deduced from abstract concepts of personal autonomy."[58]

The *Abigail Alliance* court attempted to inoculate itself against the current Supreme Court's negative view of unenumerated rights by claiming that there is a "long-standing tradition in our Nation that would protect individual access to life-saving medication."[59] The factual support to which the *Abigail Alliance* opinion refers for this claim, however, is the lack of regulation of pharmaceuticals prior to the twentieth century, rather than any evidence of governmental recognition of an affirmative right. This approach turns the reasoning of *Glucksberg* on its head, shifting the burden of proof on the question of historical tradition from individuals claiming a right to government actors denying the existence of any such right, and it is not likely to be accepted by the Supreme Court's current majority. In any case, the justices would be unlikely to agree to consider a challenge to therapeutic cloning legislation at the level of generality of a "right to medical treatment." Proponents of a history-based due process jurisprudence attempt to define rights claims as specifically as possible and as such would likely frame a constitutional challenge as a claim for a right to pursue "therapeutic cloning" specifically. This analytical technique bodes ill for therapeutic cloning, a technology with no history and thus no history of support in Anglo-American law.

The *Abigail Alliance* decision highlights, however, that congressional interference with the ability to seek medical treatment outside the politically charged context of abortion does raise constitutional concerns. The principle of constitutional liberty would be compromised more, in fact, by a cloning ban than by the FDA's refusal to permit the terminally ill access to unapproved drugs. The reason is that under the Food, Drug, and Cosmetics Act, the FDA balances the benefits to patients of access to medications against the costs of access to those patients, including the possibility that the drugs will be unsafe or ineffective. A line of federal court cases dealing with challenges to FDA authority observes, quite reasonably, that any individual liberty interests to use particular pharmaceuticals are counterbalanced by the government's interest in protecting the public health.[60] In the case of a cloning ban, by contrast, Congress would not be seeking to impede the search for health-enhancing technologies because of the risks that therapeutic cloning would entail for its potential beneficiaries but because of concerns totally unrelated to the health of the potential beneficiaries. Congress should erect an impediment in such circumstances only when the interests it seeks to protect are particularly compelling.

## REPRODUCTIVE RIGHTS

A broad congressional ban on cloning would prohibit reproductive cloning, in addition to therapeutic cloning, and in so doing implicate constitutional concerns that arise from clearly established constitutional rights related to reproduction and child rearing.

In *Skinner v. Oklahoma*, the Supreme Court recognized marriage and procreation as "basic civil rights of man."[61] In *Griswold v. Connecticut*, the Court held that the Constitution protects the fundamental right of married couples to use contraceptives.[62] It extended this protected zone of privacy to the use of contraceptives by unmarried couples in *Eisenstadt v. Baird*, observing that "if the right of privacy means anything, it is the right of the individual, married or single, to be free from unwarranted governmental intrusion into matters so fundamentally affecting a person as the decision whether to bear or beget a child."[63] In *Roe,* the Court found a fundamental right of women to terminate a pregnancy in the first two trimesters,[64] and it essentially reaffirmed this ruling nearly two decades later in *Casey.*[65] In related cases, the Court has invalidated legal bans on interracial marriage,[66] found a general fundamental right to marry,[67] and struck down various governmental attempts to interfere with parents' decisions concerning child rearing.[68] Recently, in *Lawrence v. Texas,* the Supreme Court articulated a fundamental right of privacy in the realm of sexual behavior.[69]

Given the general reluctance of the current Supreme Court to recognize any substantive rights under the due process clause that lack a clear pedigree in Anglo-American legal history, it is unlikely that a majority of justices would even consider whether its holdings in these cases ought to be expanded by analogy to laws prohibiting cloning. But even assuming that a Supreme Court majority overcame its general hostility to unenumerated rights (that is, those not explicitly listed in the Bill of Rights) and adopted the jurisprudential view that constitutional interpretations should evolve alongside technological and social change,[70] there would remain a question as to how broadly the holdings in the Court's due process cases could be fairly interpreted.

The Supreme Court's plurality opinion in *Casey,* jointly authored by Justices Sandra Day O'Connor, Kennedy, and Souter, refers to the Court's tradition of protecting individual freedom to make "intimate" decisions.[71] If *Casey* and the prior decisions on which it relies stand for a proposition this broad, protection of the right to use cloning technology seems appropriate as well. The selection of a method of producing a baby seems just as "intimate" as the choices at issue in the Court's related landmark cases.[72] If the precedents are read somewhat more narrowly as protecting freedom of choice in matters relating to sexuality, freedom from interference with one's body's reproductive capabilities, or even liberty necessary to ensure gender equality, it is less clear that the Court's holdings are applicable to the issue of cloning. By definition, cloning is unrelated to sexual behavior because sexual intercourse cannot create a clone, and a ban on cloning would seem to burden men and women roughly equally.[73]

If the Supreme Court were to determine that its previous decisions supporting individual freedom of choice in the area of reproduction and familial relationships imply a constitutional right to make use of reproductive cloning technology, due process doctrine still would allow the government to prohibit cloning if it could demonstrate a significant countervailing justification for doing so.[74] Here the argument for cloning protection seems stronger. That is, if the pursuit of cloning technology were recognized as a fundamental right, or even a liberty interest, the government would fail to establish an interest in interfering with that right sufficiently compelling to satisfy the requirements of constitutional doctrine.

The two strongest arguments in support of the importance of the governmental interest in prohibition are conceptually quite different. One rests on the need to protect potential clones and the other on the need to protect everyone else in society. As to the first, the reproductive cloning of nonhuman mammals has, to date, not been particularly healthy for the clones. Put simply, science has not yet been able to reproduce mammals through SCNT that are as healthy, on average, as those reproduced through more traditional methods.[75]

At least given present technology, human clones would likely suffer the same disadvantages.[76] If so, a plausible argument that the fundamental rights of a would-be parent to reproduce asexually, even if recognized, might be outweighed by the government's interest in protecting the competing claims of the potential offspring to be created by methods that offer the best chance of good health and longevity.[77]

If this argument is understood to be that the government has a compelling interest in ensuring that children are born with the *maximum likelihood* of living a long and healthy life, it could have the perverse consequence of indicting reproduction through sexual intercourse. With current technology, a potential child arguably has the best possible chance of being born in good health with maximum expected longevity if he or she is conceived through an IVF process in which embryos are screened for genetic diseases and only healthy embryos are implanted in the mother's uterus. If the government has a compelling interest in maximizing the expected health and lifespan of children that justifies its interference with reproductive choice, it would seem to follow that it would have the power to ban sexual reproduction, a "technology" that does not screen either gametes or embryos. It is scarcely imaginable that the Supreme Court would adopt a position that would suggest Congress may ban sexual reproduction.

A more moderate version of the anti-cloning position would be that the government has a compelling interest in protecting potential children from *substantial risks* of being born with serious health problems. This argument faces both a conceptual and a practical problem. The fact that a child produced through cloning is more likely to suffer ill health than a child produced through sexual reproduction seems to be relevant only on the assumption that a potential parent who wishes to create a cloned offspring would in fact resort to sexual reproduction if cloning were prohibited. Some would-be parents might do just this, but others likely would not. Potential parents interested in cloning who cannot sexually reproduce—single people, homosexual couples, or heterosexual couples in which one member is infertile—might choose to forego reproduction altogether if the only legal option is to engage a sperm or egg donor and create a child with one-half of its DNA contributed by an outside party.

Even assuming for the sake of argument that a substantial risk of a child being born with a significant health impairment is worse than a child not being born at all—a contestable and contested position—as a practical matter, this risk is likely to decline over time. The government might have a significant interest in protecting clones from being born today on this ground, but if cloning efforts in other countries reduce these risks substantially in time, that interest could evaporate.

The second, and very different, argument for a constitutionally cognizable government interest in prohibiting cloning focuses on the potential harm to society that too much cloning could conceivably create. Presumably, humans reproduce sexually because sexual reproduction arose in our ancestors. Through the evolutionary process, by shuffling DNA, each generation creates constant changes in the genetic makeup of the human species; such changes help to keep us one step ahead of bacterial and viral agents that seek to invade and destroy us by learning how to evade or overcome our antibodies.[78] No individual clone creates a risk to the continued viability of the human species, but a world in which cloning becomes a common method of reproduction could conceivably create such risks. Prohibiting cloning entirely, it might be argued, is the only nondiscriminatory method of protecting against such future risks. This argument has a compelling logic to it, but cloning would have to be so widespread for the species to be endangered that it is unlikely this would ever become a practical concern.[79]

Other arguments in favor of a ban on reproductive cloning are relevant from a policy perspective but seem far from sufficiently critical to outweigh a constitutionally protected fundamental right or a liberty interest in cloning, if such a right were ever recognized. Many people feel an intuitive negative reaction to the idea of cloning.[80] But one person's disgust, even with government support, should not override another's constitutionally protected right. A large number of people are morally opposed to abortion, and many are offended by various specimens of constitutionally protected speech. Yet in neither case have the courts held that supporting such popular sentiments provides a sufficient legal basis to override individual rights.

Others fear that parents would attempt to engineer their children by selecting a DNA donor (whether it be one of the parents or a third party) in order to maximize a child's physical or intellectual capabilities.[81] Although perhaps different in degree from what is possible using sexual reproduction, it is hard to argue that such behavior would be different in kind from what some parents already do. Nothing prevents people from choosing their spouses on the basis of their genetic endowments; many people quite explicitly select gamete donors on such a basis. With sexual reproduction, of course, it is no sure thing that any offspring will inherit his or her parents' desirable endowments. It is similarly less than a sure thing with clones, for genes interact with the environment, and the environmental influences on a donor and a clone will always be different.

Still other cloning opponents argue that clones would be psychologically harmed by being denied a unique identity.[82] This claim is not only quite speculative, but it is also likely to be false. There is little reason to believe that identical twins suffer undue psychological harm from the fact that they share their DNA. The generational difference between clone and donor could cause a clone to experience sharing a genome differently than would twins, with a clone perhaps viewing the course of his life as preordained by that of the donor.[83] But this fear suggests an unjustified degree of genetic determinism. Genes alone are not destiny; environment and choice are just as important.

Given the Supreme Court's reluctance to recognize new substantive due process rights, it seems unlikely that it would read its jurisprudence on reproduction to require the recognition of a right to pursue cloning technology. But this prediction about the outcome of hypothetical litigation does not undermine the fact that a cloning ban clearly would raise serious constitutional concerns because of its effect on reproductive and child-rearing decisions, just as it would raise constitutional concerns because of its implications for the pursuit of medical treatment and its implications for federalism. This set of constitutional concerns, like the others discussed in the previous two sections, provides a powerful argument against a congressional ban on the use of cloning technology.

# 4

# Stem Cell Patents

The cover of *Time* magazine for August 20, 2001, has a large photograph of a scientist, then age 42, with blue eyes. At once mild and confident in appearance, he is wearing a blue shirt and a white lab coat. The subject is Dr. James A. Thomson, veterinarian and molecular biologist of the University of Wisconsin, whom the article describes as conscientious, altruistic, and extremely hard working—but also given to hang gliding and flying model airplanes. In his on-duty hours, Thomson operates out of an off-campus laboratory under a nonprofit arrangement with the Wisconsin Alumni Research Foundation (WARF). His work has received funding in part by the biotechnology firm Geron.[1]

As Chapter 1 describes, Thomson was the first scientist to create cell lines from primate ESCs, and then, in 1998, he became the first to successfully sustain cell lines for a long period of time using hESCs—accomplishments for which the U.S. Patent and Trademark Office awarded WARF three patents.

This chapter is coauthored by Stephen R. Munzer.

For his path-breaking work, Thomson has obtained rock-star status in the scientific research community. WARF has earned a reputation for interpreting the patents broadly and asserting its rights aggressively.

Amazingly to most people (even lawyers) not schooled in patent law, WARF does not merely claim a right to charge for the particular hESC lines that Thomson actually created, the use of which presumably would require the shipment of cells from Wisconsin. WARF claims the legal right to prevent anyone from using any and all hESCs, cultured in any laboratory and by any method, if it so desires.

For many years, individual scientists have complained about the cost and restrictiveness of the contracts WARF demands they sign before the organization will provide them licenses to use the claimed technology. In 2006, WARF created a slightly noisier storm of protest when it publicly demanded a cut of any income the state of California might earn from sponsoring hESC research. Although it backed away from this demand, WARF continues to assert its right to royalties on any commercialized process developed with the use of hESCs.

The boldness of WARF's expansive intellectual property claims has generated more than just gripes. A public interest group filed a formal petition asking the U.S. Patent and Trademark Office (PTO) to reexamine the WARF patents, and in March 2007, the PTO issued a preliminary ruling that, if it becomes final, will revoke all three patents in their entirety. With both sides now having tasted victory—WARF with the initial grant of the patents, its opponents with the preliminary revocation—the battle is likely to continue until at least the end of this decade in the patent office and then in the federal courts.

At stake in the legal battle are fundamental issues concerning ownership of intellectual property in the stem cell century: Should patent protection extend to substances found in the human body? If so, how broadly should it extend? To what extent should the pioneers of basic innovations be able to interfere with the creation of various applications of those innovations? This chapter explores and analyzes these controversies from a broad public policy perspective and the narrower perspective of patent law.

## The WARF Patents
### WHAT HAVING A PATENT MEANS

The U.S. Constitution grants Congress the power "to promote the Progress of Science and useful Arts, by securing for limited Times to Authors and Inventors the exclusive Right to their respective Writings and Discoveries."[2] Congress exercises this power through the Patent Act, the most recent full version of which was enacted in 1952,[3] along with statutes relating to copyright and trademark. Chief among the benefits of patent protection is the legal power to exclude others from using the invention or discovery without first securing a license at a price satisfactory to the patent holder. Until recently, the patent period was seventeen years from the issuance of a patent; to accommodate U.S. international legal obligations, it is now twenty years from the date the patent application is filed.[4]

As a form of intellectual property, a patent differs from a copyright, a trademark, and a trade secret. A copyright is a property right, not in ideas themselves, but in the original expression, fixed in a tangible medium, of ideas broadly understood. You may use the ideas expressed in this book in your own book (please give proper attribution!), but you may not copy the expression. A trademark is a name or symbol used to market goods or services. The name "Nike" and the familiar swoosh are trademarks used to sell athletic shoes and apparel. You may manufacture and sell sports shoes, but you may not adorn them with the Nike name or swoosh. A trade secret is information that can be used in a commercial enterprise and that is sufficiently valuable and confidential to provide an economic advantage to that enterprise over others. The formula for Coca-Cola is a trade secret. In the United States, trade secrets are protected under state law for an indefinite duration, but the law does not prevent competitors from mimicking a product if they independently create it or reverse engineer the original. Patents, although limited in time, provide the holder a right under federal law against any other producer of an identical innovation, even if independently discovered. In return for this right, the patentee must make information about the invention available to the public. In biotechnology, where reverse engineering and independent invention pose considerable risks, most inventors attempt to obtain patents.

To obtain a patent, the inventor must file an application with the PTO that states what the invention is and why it is new and useful. The PTO then appoints an examiner to decide whether a patent should be issued. During the examination process, which may take months or even years, the examiner often asks the inventor to clarify the nature of the invention, or to narrow exactly what the inventor claims is new or useful about it, or both. If a patent application meets a series of legal requirements, the PTO issues a patent.

An issued patent is presumptively, but not definitively, valid.[5] Its validity can be challenged in the PTO in the form of a petition for reexamination, it can be directly challenged in federal court, and it can be challenged as a defense in a lawsuit claiming patent infringement.[6] In addition to reviewing the propriety of the PTO's grant of a patent, a reviewing court also may reevaluate a patent's scope.[7] Thus, the fact that WARF obtained patents never definitively meant that it possessed the full extent of the rights that it claimed.

A patent does not itself authorize the inventor to practice, manufacture, or sell a physical embodiment of the invention or discovery to the general public. Regulation has never been the province of the PTO but rather the domain of various federal or state agencies and statutes. For instance, a gun manufacturer may be able to patent a novel type of semi-automatic rifle but will be barred from selling it if the sale is prohibited by federal or state law. Similarly, a pharmaceutical company may be entitled to patent a new drug for the treatment of Alzheimer's disease, but it must satisfy the exacting requirements of the FDA before physicians may prescribe it for patients.

## LICENSING THE TECHNOLOGY

Between 1998 and 2006 the PTO issued WARF a series of three patents based on Thomson's work. All three share the same title, "Primate Embryonic Stem Cells," although the second and third claim rights to the more specific category of hESCs. The patents claim rights to a product (in patent jargon, a "composition of matter") defined as hESC lines that can remain stable, undifferentiated, and pluripotent for at least one year. Secondarily, the patents claim rights to a particular method of producing this product, but these "process" claims are redundant if the product claims are upheld because the product claims would allow WARF to block others from producing the product using any process.[8]

Because of the Dickey Amendment's ban on federal funding of research that destroys embryos, Thomson received funding for his attempt to create hESCs from Geron. In return, Geron demanded certain rights to any successes that might arise from the work. Post-1998, the relationship between Geron and WARF has been rocky, with several renegotiations of licensing rights and threats of litigation. The current agreement between the parties gives Geron worldwide exclusive rights to develop diagnostic and therapeutic products from three types of specialized cells derived from the use of hESC technology.[9] It also gives Geron nonexclusive rights to develop diagnostic and therapeutic products from a range of other types of cells that can be derived from hESCs.[10]

The agreement between WARF and Geron provides that academic, nonprofit, and governmental researchers may obtain a license to use patented hESC lines without any fees or royalty payments. As of mid-2006, WARF claimed to have signed agreements with 324 U.S. academic institutions.[11] WARF (through a subsidiary called WiCell) also reached an agreement to provide hESC lines created by Thomson's group directly to the U.S. Public Health Service (PHS) without charging a licensing fee.[12] The no-cost licenses, however, are restricted to noncommercial uses of the hESC lines, and WARF claims that users who develop commercially useful inventions must negotiate a new licensing arrangement with it, just as WARF demands of commercial research organizations.[13] Reports claim that WARF has sought a $100,000 up-front fee and a $25,000 annual maintenance fee from companies wishing to buy commercial licenses.[14] As of January 2005, WARF had entered into only seven commercial licensing agreements.[15]

On March 30, 2006, the *Los Angeles Times* reported that WARF was seeking compensation for hESC research funded by the California Institute for Regenerative Medicine (CIRM). One of the inducements for voters to support Proposition 71,

California's $3 billion stem cell initiative, was its promoters' claims that the state would earn royalties on resulting scientific discoveries. An analysis commissioned by supporters of Proposition 71 estimated that the state might receive as much as $1.1 billion in revenue, though the nonpartisan legislative analyst opined that the amount of revenue was not predictable.[16] When CIRM announced that its grant recipients would be required to share up to 25 percent of revenue earned if state funding leads to marketable innovations, WARF claimed a right to demand licensing fees. Said WARF spokesman Andrew Cohn, "We feel there should be a discussion about how the University of Wisconsin gets a benefit."[17] In a separately reported interview, WARF General Counsel Elizabeth Donley was more blunt: "We feel we should get a share of [the action]."[18]

In January 2007, WARF, battered by criticism from the research community, adopted a somewhat less aggressive posture. It dropped its demand that CIRM purchase a license, and it announced that it would allow private companies to sponsor hESC basic research at nonprofit institutions without first obtaining a license.[19] These moves did not, however, indicate that WARF had changed its view of the scope of its rights. It reiterated its position that companies that wish to develop marketable products with any hESCs must negotiate a license from WARF.[20]

Should research using hEGCs ever become as widespread as research using hESCs, a parallel conflict is likely to result. Johns Hopkins University holds three patents on hEGCs resulting from the work of John Gearhart's laboratory.[21] Gearhart, like Thomson, received most of his initial funding from Geron. Under the conditions of Geron's grant to Gearhart, any researchers who wish to use germ cells patented by Gearhart must sign a restrictive agreement.[22] As Gearhart described the situation, "Our stuff is solely licensed through this company, so they control all the levers." He continued: "People come to us and we work up [material transfer agreements that] state that if you get anything good that is patentable, we have the right to negotiate a license. This is not something many investigators want to do. . . . It can be a barrier to investigators working in the area."[23]

## How Broad Should Stem Cell Patents Be?
### THE NEED FOR STEM CELL PATENTS

One justification for awarding patents is simple. A useful invention can be tremendously valuable to society, and awarding patents encourages the production of such inventions. Without a patent system, we would enjoy much less innovation: people would spend the time and effort necessary to produce an invention only when the invention is very easy and very cheap to create or extremely difficult to copy. Few people would spend much time or money to perfect an invention if the value could be easily appropriated by copycats.

In the case of hESCs, if no patent protection were available, a very valuable innovation might have been delayed for many years. Perhaps some academic researchers, such as Thomson himself, would have pursued the goal of creating hESC lines even if patent protection were unavailable, provided that they enjoyed salaries from their universities and were able to obtain research funding for their labs from the government or private foundations. Many academic scientists are motivated to innovate by some combination of their love of science and their pursuit of tenure and academic prestige, rather than the lure of patents. Even when scientists themselves are not motivated by the desire to obtain a patent, however, corporate funding sources—such as Geron, which funded Thomson's research—would have little incentive to invest in research. Without patent potential, Geron almost certainly would have demanded, at a minimum, that Thomson refrain from publishing his results or sharing his cell lines. Such demands might have enabled Geron to use the innovation for several years before any other researchers could figure out how to duplicate it. This result would have been terrible for society because a tremendous amount of effort would have been wasted by scientists reinventing Thomson's method rather than producing new hESC lines or investigating the properties of hESCs. By requiring innovators like Thomson to disseminate a description of their inventions as a quid pro quo for obtaining a patent, society gains a valuable benefit in return for its grant of monopoly rights.

## PATENT BREADTH: A HAPPY MEDIUM

Although the need for patent protection is clear, the difficult question is how broad patent protection should be. This question is difficult because it pits the interests of early innovators ("pioneers") against the interests of later ("secondary") innovators who would like to improve the pioneer's invention or apply it to other or more specific uses. Encouraging innovation at one level discourages it at the other, but both types of innovation are good for society.

We can think of the possible scope of an hESC patent as spanning a continuum between "very narrow" and "very broad." A very narrow patent would give WARF property rights only in the particular stem cell lines Thomson created in his laboratory. It could prohibit others from using those cells themselves or identical ones, but other scientists would be free to copy Thomson's methods to produce different hESC lines. In the center of the continuum would be a patent on the specific process that Thomson used to create stable hESC lines and on the nutrient mix in the culture medium that he used or, alternatively, on a composition of matter including both hESCs and any unique chemical mix developed by Thomson to keep the hESCs stable and undifferentiated. This level of patent protection would enable WARF and Geron to prevent other researchers from using any uniquely functional or efficient methods Thomson's group developed, even though the other scientists would be creating hESC lines with unique genotypes. A very broad patent would confer a monopoly on the production of all hESC lines. Other researchers would need a license from WARF to produce any hESC lines at all, regardless of the methods used or the genetic makeup of the cells involved. This very broad scope is reflected in the language of the WARF patents, as well as the position that WARF has taken publicly concerning the extent of its property rights.

If WARF could patent only the specific cell lines Thomson created, companies like Geron would be less likely to fund pioneering research in the future or, at a minimum, would demand that researchers keep their methods secret from other scientists rather than disclose them publicly. Such a rule would risk slowing future scientific progress and thus probably would provide too little patent protection.

Awarding WARF very broad patent protection for all future hESC lines would encourage future investment in pioneering research, but it might cause two other types of problems. First, ironically, it could encourage too much investment in pioneering research. Imagine, for example, that it would cost approximately $100 million to create a pioneering invention but that the creator would earn broad patent rights that could be converted into tens of billions of dollars of profits in the future. Rather than two or three biotechnology companies investing in research geared toward creating the invention, perhaps dozens or even hundreds of companies would join the race, which could divert resources and effort—most of which would end up being wasted—from other valuable endeavors without increasing the social value of the pioneering invention at all. To understand the problem better, imagine how many people would have quit their jobs and rushed to California in 1849 to prospect for gold if the first person to locate a nugget of the precious metal could have obtained a right to preclude anyone else from mining gold anywhere in the country without purchasing a license from the pioneer.

The second problem with granting very broad patents is that it could discourage other inventors from improving upon Thomson's method of creating hESC lines or, more important, from using hESC lines to develop scientifically and commercially useful products, such as clinical therapies. WARF could require other potential inventors to pay for a license before building on Thomson's patents.

In theory, broad patent rights need not inhibit valuable innovation. According to the Coase Theorem—familiar to lawyers and economists as the proposition that private transactions will ensure that resources are ultimately assigned to those who can make efficient use of them[24]—WARF and the would-be innovator should simply divide the profit potential of future innovations. For example, imagine that a scientist has an idea for an innovation using hESCs that would create $10 million in profits and WARF demanded $100,000 for a license to use hESCs. The scientist should happily pay the WARF fee and create his invention because he would still expect to earn $9,900,000 in profits. In this example, broad patent protection could even be socially useful because WARF could use its position as a gatekeeper for research efforts to ensure that multiple scientists do not compete to create the exact same invention, thus wasting resources.[25]

Unfortunately, the Coase Theorem relies on a number of heroic assumptions, including zero transaction costs, no holdout problems, and certainty about the cost and feasibility of creating follow-on inventions. In the real world, negotiating licenses can be expensive, bargaining can break down, and the parties can have wildly different assessments of the profit potential of secondary research. In such a world, broad patents are quite likely to inhibit the development of at least some valuable secondary inventions.[26] For example, the corporate sponsors of the scientist with the $10 million idea might believe that there is only a one in two hundred chance of the innovation ever making it to market and thus refuse to pay $100,000 to WARF for the necessary license. WARF, in turn, might refuse to lower the price it demands, either because it believes the scientist is severely downplaying the profit potential of her idea in order to improve her bargaining position or because it does not want to create a precedent of discounting. As a result, the potentially valuable research might not proceed, to society's detriment.

For these reasons, the level of patent protection that WARF claims is too broad and, if validated by the PTO and the courts, is likely to inhibit scientific progress to some degree. Anecdotal claims already have surfaced that WARF's demands for licensing fees have driven some scientists out of the field of commercial research on hESCs.[27]

The happy medium consists of providing patent protection for the process and nutrient mix developed by Thomson to create the first sustainable hESC lines. On one hand, WARF should be able to require scientists who wish to use the process or medium described in Thomson's patent applications—assuming that these represent a significant advance over previously known methods and media—to pay a license fee for the rights to do so. On the other hand, scientists who are able to create hESC lines that are genetically different from Thomson's using a functionally different process (for example, one that better spurs cell proliferation or better reduces the number of genetic mutations during proliferation) should be permitted to do so without negotiating a license from WARF. Such an approach would assure a substantial enough financial return for the pioneer to justify future pioneering efforts. At the same time, it would avoid making the reward for pioneering inventions so large relative to secondary inventions that too many future scientists would attempt to become pioneers and too few would devote their efforts to improvement and application.

This approach has two other virtues to recommend it as well. First, it would respond to noneconomic concerns about issuing patents on biological materials. WARF's broad claims to patent protection, if upheld, would enable it to prohibit individuals from developing tailored stem cell treatments from their own, individual cells. Imagine, for example, that SCNT technology one day makes it possible to extract an egg cell and an adult cell from a woman to create an hESC line with her genome that can then be used to regenerate damaged or diseased cells in her body. Upholding WARF's broad patent claims would mean that WARF could prohibit the woman from undergoing the treatment without first purchasing a license. This possibility would extend patent protection farther than is defensible, even if WARF were to charge such a small licensing fee that no individual would forego the treatment rather than pay or even if it were to agree in a fit of benevolence to waive the fee altogether. Nevertheless, if the patient's individualized stem cell therapy were created by maintaining the hESC line in the culture medium invented by Thomson, WARF should be entitled to a fee for the use of that recipe.

Second, this approach, by limiting what WARF could patent, would respond to international competitiveness issues facing American scientists that could well prove more significant than the Bush administration's limitations on the federal funding of hESC research (considered in Chapter 2). Neither WARF nor Geron has been able to obtain patent protection for hESCs in Europe.[28] The reason is that the European Patent Convention (EPC) prohibits the issuance of patents that violate "*ordre public*," or morality,[29] and an ethics panel, created by the EPC,[30] decided in 2002 that patenting unmodified hESCs ought to be prohibited on this basis (it judged that patenting modified hESCs was acceptable).[31] The Patent Office of the United Kingdom later explicitly adopted a similar approach.[32]

In a world in which science is international and capital moves freely across borders, significant differences in the patent protection offered by nations can affect the business of scientific research. If WARF is able to prevent American scientists from using hESCs for commercial purposes if they refuse to pay a substantial licensing fee but no such restrictions exist in Europe or elsewhere, private enterprise will fund scientific research overseas. Some anecdotes suggest that a flight of capital to avoid WARF's licensing demands has already become reality, at least to some extent. Eventually, corporations might have to negotiate a license from WARF before they are able to market their stem cell products in the United States, but this is a problem that most commercial funding sources would prefer to grapple with in the future, after they have created products with demonstrable commercial value.

## Legal Analysis of the WARF Patents

The best public policy would be to allow WARF to have patents on original aspects of Thomson's specific process for creating hESC lines and any uniquely useful aspects of his culture medium, but not for hESCs themselves. Although patent law is self-consciously utilitarian, however, it does not operate by loosely balancing the costs and benefits of various degrees of patentability. Rather, patent law specifies a number of statutory requirements necessary for a valid patent. It is to these requirements that the PTO looks when it evaluates patent applications and requests for reevaluation and to which the courts look when PTO decisions are challenged through litigation.

The Patent Act grants twenty years of monopoly power to a person who meets the act's subject matter requirement—specifically, to one who "invents or discovers" a "process, machine, manufacture, or composition of matter"—and whose invention is novel, useful, and nonobvious and who discloses the invention as part of the patent application in a way that enables others to replicate it.[33] To qualify as novel, the invention or discovery must not have been disclosed to the general public earlier than one year prior to the date of the patent application.[34] To satisfy the utility requirement, the invention must have a "specific, substantial, and credible" real-world application.[35] To be nonobvious, the invention must not be so trivial as to have been anticipated by a person having ordinary skill in the art.[36] Finally, to satisfy the written description and enablement requirements, the invention must be spelled out in sufficient detail to allow a person of ordinary skill in the art to reproduce it.[37] The inventor may not receive a patent on overly broad claims by "extrapolating" potential inventions and discoveries from experimental data.[38]

To challenge WARF's broad patent claims, a convincing case must be made that the hESC innovations fail to satisfy one or more of these complex requirements. Four plausible arguments can be made against the validity of or the expansive scope of the composition of matter claims in the WARF patents, and at least three (all but the "moral utility" claim) have a nontrivial chance of ultimate success. It will probably take several more years before patent office and judicial appeals are exhausted and the stem cell community knows precisely what intellectual property rights, if any, belong to WARF.

## PRODUCTS OF NATURE

The first issue raised by the breadth of the WARF patent claims is whether the underlying innovations, important as they are, satisfy the basic subject matter requirement of the Patent Act. Although the Constitution allows Congress to give intellectual property protection to "*discoveries*" and the Patent Act claims to provide intellectual property protection for "inventions and *discoveries*," U.S. patent law does not, in fact, allow the award of a patent for a mere discovery of something that occurs in nature, whether it is a single substance or a relationship between substances, such as $E = mc^2$. The U.S. Supreme Court made this point in an early biotechnology case more than fifty years ago. In invalidating a patent for a combination of bacteria, the Court held that "he who discovers a hitherto unknown phenomenon of nature has no claim to a monopoly of it."[39] The policy reason for this exclusion is that patents on natural phenomena would be so broad as to often impede scienti-

fic progress[40]—precisely the concern with the WARF patents
generally—but courts have disagreed on the statutory basis for
the doctrine. The usual basis is that products of nature are not
"processes," "machines," or "compositions of matter" within
the meaning of the Patent Act,[41] although courts have also held
that they fail the novelty requirement because they are not
"new,"[42] and others have argued that they do not demonstrate
the necessary inventiveness.[43]

Prior to 1980, U.S. patent law had long assumed that living organisms were unpatentable under the "products of nature" rule. In that year, the Supreme Court decided *Diamond
v. Chakrabarty.*[44] This case refocused the legal inquiry from
the characteristics of the subject matter for which patent protection was claimed to the effect of the claimant on the subject matter. Chakrabarty, a microbiologist, genetically altered
*Pseudomonas* bacteria so that they had the capacity to break
down hydrocarbons, a property that made them useful for
cleaning up oil spills. Over a dissent that argued that Congress
intended to exclude living organisms from patent protection,[45]
the Court in a 5–4 decision held that Chakrabarty was entitled
to a composition of matter patent on the altered bacteria
themselves.[46] Quoting from the legislative history of the Patent
Act of 1952, the *Chakrabarty* Court concluded that Congress
intended the Patent Act to cover "anything under the sun that
is made by man."[47] Thus whether something is "natural" in the
sense that it is living is irrelevant as far as patentability is concerned. The critical inquiry is whether the product is found in
the world without human engineering or modification.

The *Chakrabarty* holding alone does not resolve the
question of whether hESCs are patentable. Chakrabarty's bacteria were altered by human ingenuity and are nowhere found
in nature. In contrast, hESCs are themselves found inside em-

bryos just as they are found when scientists take them out of embryos. Isolating embryonic stem cells and coaxing them to reproduce outside the womb requires a substantial investment of capital and scientific ingenuity. But this fact alone does not make stem cells patentable subject matter, any more than a naturalist who relies on hard work and scientific expertise to discover a previously unknown species of bird could patent that bird.

The legal question is whether embryonic stem cells isolated from blastocysts are "made by man" or are "naturally occurring" ("natural phenomena").[48] The answer depends on precisely how one characterizes Thomson's innovation. One argument is that the important contribution to science made by Thomson and his research team was the invention of a *method* that makes stem cells usable for scientific research. On this view, Thomson might deserve a patent on his process of creating hESC lines or on the mix of nutrients in the medium that he created, assuming that these are original and inventive. But Thomson and his team did not invent hESCs themselves, which are a product of nature, so WARF should not be able to claim a right to exclude other scientists from using stem cells that are isolated, purified, or maintained using a different method from that of Thomson's team.

That a naturally occurring substance cannot practically be used for research without manipulation of the matter around it, this view continues, should not mean that creating a process that makes the object useful entitles its inventors to a patent on the object itself. An inventor of a cage that allows an otherwise wild species of bird to be caught and studied by scientists would be entitled to a patent on the method of capturing the bird with the cage. But he or she should not be entitled to a patent on the species of bird, which he or she clearly did not invent, or even to a patent on "birds in a cage," even though "birds in a cage" do not exist in nature. By the same logic, taking steps that make stem cells useful for study does not qualify researchers to a patent on the stem cells.[49]

The contrary view emphasizes that the Thomson team created a phenotypically and functionally new type of matter that is different from stem cells as they exist inside of blastocysts and thus in nature. On close analysis, the WARF patents do not claim property rights in "embryonic stem cells" without qualification. Rather, they claim "preparations" and "purified preparations" that have specific characteristics such as enabling the cells to proliferate in vitro without differentiating.[50] Embryonic stem cells are, of course, found in nature (inside embryos). Purified preparations with these characteristics are compositions of matter that just as obviously do not occur in nature: inside embryos, for example, the cells do differentiate quickly. According to this view, the process and the nutrient mix do more than constructively "cage" the embryonic stem cells. They change the functional characteristics of the cells. Thus the end product has been manipulated by man and should pass muster under the *Chakrabarty* test.

No court has yet passed judgment on whether hESCs are unpatentable under the product of nature doctrine, but rulings in analogous cases concerning biological patents suggest that the courts are likely to view in vitro hESCs as a composition of matter sufficiently "touched by man" to be patented. As far back as 1977, the Court of Customs and Patent Appeals (the predecessor of the U.S. Court of Appeals for the Federal Circuit, which hears all patent appeals) held that a purified culture of the microorganism *Streptomyces vellosus* was patentable despite the "product of nature" doctrine because it was never found in nature in its pure form and could be made only under specified laboratory conditions.[51] Several court decisions also have upheld the validity of patents issued on purified fetal and neonatal[52] and adult hematopoietic stem cells.[53] Perhaps more important, similar analysis has led courts to uphold patents on isolated and purified genes, even though the genes themselves occur in nature.[54] Recent studies have identified more than 4,200 issued patents on human genes and more than 39,000 issued patents that include a claim to some sequence of DNA.[55] The validity of all of these patents would be put in doubt by a judicial ruling that hESCs are unpatentable products of nature.

The international legal community seems in accord with the principle that a purified substance can be patented even if the same substance is found in nature in an unpurified state. A 1998 directive of the European Community, also concerned with the patentability of biotechnological inventions, concludes that "biological material which is isolated from its natural environment or produced by means of a technical process may be the subject of an invention even if it previously occurred in nature."[56]

The prediction that the courts would not find the WARF patents invalid under the product of nature doctrine, based on analogous recent cases, suffers from one glaring weakness: none of the key cases was decided by the U.S. Supreme Court. A recent High Court opinion on a related topic gives some hint, albeit a very modest one, that the Court *might* be inclined to interpret the product of nature exclusion somewhat more expansively than lower courts have done in recent years. If so, this could place the WARF patents in some peril.

The issue in *LabCorp v. Metabolite* was whether patent protection could extend to the process of "correlating" an elevated level of an amino acid in a patient's blood with a specific vitamin deficiency.[57] Justice Breyer, writing for himself and Justices Stevens and Souter, answered the question in the negative, finding that the relationship between the amino acid's presence and a vitamin deficiency is an unpatentable law of nature. The case dealt with a "law of nature" rather than a "product of nature," but Breyer's analysis rested on the reasoning that patent protection should not be awarded to discoveries so basic to future research that the patent system would impede further scientific progress. The same reasoning would seem to support disallowing WARF's broad hESC patents.

Unfortunately, the record provides no hint of whether the other six justices agree with Breyer's analysis, much less whether they would find it applicable to hESCs. Chief Justice John Roberts recused himself in *LabCorp,* and the other five justices voted to dismiss the writ of certiorari as improvidently granted; that is, the Court's majority decided not to consider the merits of the case after all, and it did so without explaining why. Whether the Supreme Court will use the case of the WARF patents to reinvigorate the "product of nature" doctrine that has been interpreted very narrowly in the lower courts since *Chakrabarty* was decided remains uncertain.

## MORAL UTILITY

A different question—but one obviously related to the product of nature inquiry—is whether hESCs should be unpatentable on moral or public policy grounds because such patents effectively create private property rights in human material. In stark contrast to the European Patent Convention, which includes the *ordre public* provision that incorporates moral considerations into patent law, no provision in the U.S. Patent Act explicitly conditions patentability on the morality of an invention or its consistency with public policy.[58] However, there is a judicial doctrine of "moral utility" (sometimes called "beneficial utility"), which dates to an early-nineteenth-century case called *Lowell v. Lewis.*[59] The doctrine holds that an otherwise patentable invention that lacks a morally permissible use may not receive a patent.

Originally used to deny patents on gambling machines and early medical frauds, the moral utility doctrine fell into disuse in the twentieth century, as courts adopted the view that patent law is intended to be morally neutral.[60] (Recall that a patent gives its holder the right to exclude others from using the invention, but the government may still exercise its regulatory power to prohibit all production.) In April 1987, however, the commissioner of the PTO issued a statement that his office would not consider claims pertaining to human beings to be patentable subject matter under the Patent Act.[61] Among several justifications, the PTO seemed to rely on the dormant moral utility doctrine, for it interpreted the Patent Act's utility requirement to exclude certain types of inventions that are "injurious to the well-being, good policy, or good morals of society."[62] In addition, some scholars have argued that courts should revive the doctrine and use it to create a public policy limitation on patentability similar to the European Union's *ordre public* clause.[63] The WARF patents could be a place to start.

In the 1999 case of *Juicy Whip v. Orange Bang,* however, the Federal Circuit ruled that the moral utility doctrine is unsupported by and inconsistent with the Patent Act.[64] Subsequently, the PTO later backed away from, without explicitly repudiating, its policy statement that seemed to rely on the doctrine.[65] And, of course, the PTO did issue broad patents to WARF. With no statutory language in the Patent Act that suggests patentability should be determined by reference to any nonutilitarian principles, it seems quite unlikely that the federal courts will reverse course and move U.S. patent law in the direction of European patent law.

One provocative side note is in order: As part of annual appropriations bills beginning in 2004, Congress has enacted the Weldon Amendment, which bans the use of federal funds "to issue patents on claims directly related to or encompassing a human organism."[66] The amendment has no effect on previously issued patents, like those held by WARF, but it could affect the ability of the patent office to issue certain patents related to stem cells in the future.

So far no court has rendered a published decision concerning the Weldon Amendment, and it is difficult to predict how the courts will interpret its language. The amendment might be interpreted to prohibit the issuance of composition of matter patents on human clones, and possibly SCNT process patents, because clones either are or can become (depending on one's philosophical position) human organisms. The Weldon Amendment probably does not affect the ability to patent stem cells because even pluripotent hESCs lack the ability to grow into a human organism. This interpretation is far from certain, however. The European Union has taken the position that unmodified stem cells are not patentable because "such isolated cells are so close to the human body . . . that their patenting may be considered a form of commercialization of the human body."[67] The PTO or the federal courts could conclude that the significant potential of stem cells makes them closely enough "related to . . . a human organism" to fall within the Weldon Amendment.

## "WRITTEN DESCRIPTION" AND "ENABLEMENT"

The Patent Act's "written description" element requires that, to qualify for patent protection, the specifications of an invention must be fully disclosed in the patent application. Courts have explained that this requirement is necessary to enable a skilled practitioner to reproduce the patented substance.[68] This is the means by which the patentee teaches others how to produce the invention in return for his or her time-limited monopoly. It ensures, too, that the claimant "was, as of the filing date sought, in possession of the invention."[69]

Determining whether a patent application's written description is sufficient to support its scope can be quite difficult. Some protection beyond the text of its claims almost always must be given to the inventor in order for patents to have value. Leeway is necessary to prevent copycats from avoiding infringement liability by making only a slight, inconsequential change to the invention specified in the application. A patent on a washing machine, for example, would be of little value if an imitator could legally copy the patent holder's design merely by adding a single bolt. This example illustrates the "doctrine of equivalents," which the courts evolved to make sure that insubstantial differences would not allow copycats to escape an action for infringement.[70]

Courts have sometimes invalidated or limited the scope of patents when the patent holder claimed ownership of a broad category of innovations but described only one or a small number of examples in that category. The most famous illustration is Samuel Morse's nineteenth-century telegraphy patent. It claimed ownership of "the use of motive power of electric or galvanic current . . . however developed for marking or printing intelligible characters."[71] In *O'Reilly v. Morse,* the U.S. Supreme Court found the patent invalid because Morse had disclosed only a single method of doing what he claimed.[72]

In the context of gene and gene-related patents, courts have applied the written description requirement quite aggressively, resulting in the narrowing of patent protection. Genes contain sequences of nucleotides that create amino acids, which in turn comprise proteins. A particular nucleotide sequence produces a single amino acid sequence. Altering a nucleotide in the sequence sometimes results in a change in the resulting protein's functionality, and sometimes it does not. Gene patents frequently specify a nucleotide sequence that scientists have identified as creating a protein and then claim rights not only in that specific sequence but also in all other sequences that create a protein with an identical function. The Federal Circuit has held these types of claims to be overbroad and has limited patentees' monopolies to the sequences described in the patent.[73]

The gene patent cases suggest that a court could narrow the scope of the WARF patents without invalidating them altogether, by focusing on either the specific nutrient mix described in the patents or the specific genomes of the hESC lines created by Thomson and his colleagues. Recall the argument that in order to avoid being considered attempts to patent products of nature, the compositions of matter over which WARF claims ownership should be viewed as combinations of hESCs and nutrient mix, or culture medium. It follows from this premise and the gene patent decisions that WARF is entitled to patent protection only for the combination of hESCs and culture media that it specifically describes, not all possible combinations that exhibit the same functional characteristics. This means that although the doctrine of equivalents perhaps should protect WARF's rights against copycats who make minor, inconsequential changes to the nutrient mix (switching an inactive ingredient for an equivalent one, for example), other scientists should be able to work around WARF's patents by developing substantially different nutrient mixes that are also capable of enabling hESCs to proliferate without differentiating in vitro for long periods of time, especially if the alternative approach increases the functionality of the hESCs (that is, increases proliferation rate, reduces copying errors, etc.).

Courts could plausibly interpret the scope of the WARF patents even more narrowly by emphasizing the fact that every blastocyst, and thus every hESC line, has a different genetic makeup. This fact suggests that the patents' scope should be limited to lines of hESCs with the genotypes of Thomson's. The doctrine of equivalents arguably should expand the coverage of WARF's patents to hESC lines with genotypes functionally equivalent to those actually created in Wisconsin, but it is quite likely that genotypic differences among hESC lines will be functionally relevant for stem cell research and potential therapies. For example, hESC lines with certain genetic mutations certainly will be more useful for studying the disease effects of those mutations, and some genotypes might make hESC lines more stable, longer lived, easier to differentiate into certain types of specialized cells, etc. Scientists are currently in the process of comparing the differentiation efficiency of different hESC lines, hypothesizing that differences in genetic endowments might make some cell lines more suitable than others for particular uses.

It is difficult to predict with confidence how a court would assess such challenges. As one patent law treatise notes, "no precise equation allows us to determine whether a particular patent claim suffers from 'undue breadth' in view of the disclosure of the patent's specifications."[74] But this avenue of challenge would stand a good chance of success both because it is consistent with the way courts have treated gene patents and because it would result in the narrowing of but not the elimination of WARF's patent protection—the happy medium that is justified on broader policy grounds. Narrowing WARF's claims via the written description and enablement doctrines would also be more cautious, and thus more likely to appeal to the courts, than expanding the products of nature doctrine or reviving the moral utility doctrine. The former approach would not threaten to upset the long-standing and settled expectations of companies that own the thousands of gene-related patents issued by the PTO since 1982.[75]

## NONOBVIOUSNESS

The PTO itself may reconsider whether a patent was properly issued in the narrow circumstance in which an objecting party alleges that the patented invention lacked originality at the time it was issued. In 2006, the Foundation for Taxpayer and Consumer Rights (FTCR) sought such a reevaluation of the WARF patents by the PTO, alleging that the applications failed to satisfy the Patent Act's novelty and nonobviousness requirements.[76]

To show that an invention fails the novelty requirement, there must be a *single* item of so-called "prior art," such as a patent issued or article published prior to the inventor's patent application, that discloses all of the claims in the supposed invention. In contrast, to demonstrate that an invention fails the nonobviousness requirement, a challenge can appeal to *multiple* prior art references and the assumption that a "person having ordinary skill in the art" would be able to make logical, incremental improvements to the published technology.[77]

Hence, technically, obviousness is an easier argument on which to prevail than lack of novelty. For practical purposes, however, the issues merge into the following question: Given information available prior to the filing of the Thomson patents, could an ordinarily skilled practitioner of ESC research have accomplished what Thomson's group did? If the answer is yes, the grant of a patent is inappropriate, for the sensible reason that the innovation is quite likely to have been made without the incentive of monopoly rights.

The very breadth of WARF's patent claims increases their vulnerability to assertions of obviousness: because WARF claims ownership of all hESCs maintained in a stable and undifferentiated state for at least one year, preexisting instructions that would have enabled a skilled practitioner to create such a cell line using any method undermine the patents' validity. At issue specifically in the FTCR's challenge are the teachings of two patents and four articles that were published prior to the filing of Thomson's first patent application in 1996 that describe methods of creating ESC lines.[78]

In a series of preliminary, nonfinal opinions (one for each of the three WARF patents) issued in March 2007, the PTO indicated that it found the arguments of the FTCR compelling and that it would shift the burden of persuasion back to WARF to demonstrate the nonobviousness of its claimed inventions.[79] If the PTO ultimately maintains this position and determines that the patents were improperly issued, WARF may appeal the decision to the Board of Patent Appeals and Interferences.[80] If that body upholds the PTO's decision entirely or in part, WARF may appeal that decision to the Federal Circuit.[81] The dust is not likely to settle for some time.

The most immediately apparent differences between the published prior art and the WARF patents are the species from which ESC lines are derived. Most of the prior art describes methods of creating mouse ESCs rather than primate or human ESCs. Arguably, an ordinarily skilled stem cell researcher would have been motivated by descriptions of mouse ESC lines alone to use the same steps to create an hESC line. The two prior art patents, however, provide even more specific direction by explicitly asserting that the same process that they show can produce mouse ESC lines could also be used to produce hESC lines.[82] In addition, an article by a Singaporean research group describes how it actually created an hESC line in culture and maintained it for a short period of time.[83] Taken together, the prior art seems quite clearly to encourage the creation of hESC lines using the same approach demonstrated with mouse blastocysts.

But would this course of action have produced the composition of matter of which WARF claims ownership in its patents: an hESC line capable of being maintained undifferentiated for a year or more? If so, the WARF patents should be revoked as having failed to satisfy the nonobviousness requirement. This question cannot be definitively resolved without a laboratory, but there is reason to be skeptical. Although the FTCR claims that the only difference between the processes described in the WARF patents and at least three of the prior art references is the species of blastocyst used,[84] a close reading of the materials indicates some subtle differences in methodology, including the precise composition of chemicals used at various steps of the process. Given that none of the prior art publications describes a successful attempt to create a sustainable hESC line, it seems quite likely that following the precise recipes provided in the prior art while using a human blastocyst would not have yielded a sustainable cell line.

Assuming that none of the precise methods described in the prior art would produce viable hESC lines, the final issue is whether an ordinarily skilled practitioner would have made the subtle adjustments to the prior art necessary to produce the result that Thomson actually achieved. In resolving this type of question, the courts have tended to assume that ordinarily skilled practitioners are relatively dim automatons, able to follow instructions but not to exhibit much creativity.[85] Specifically, the Federal Circuit has held that obviousness is not shown if the prior art invites experimentation or if the inventor could have tried different possibilities until achieving the desired result.[86] At the same time, the Federal Circuit has found that the commercial success of an invention, the demonstrated ability to sell licenses, and the prior failure of others to demonstrate the achievement—all of which are present in the case of the WARF patents—all weigh heavily in favor of a finding of nonobviousness.[87] If these precedents are faithfully applied, the WARF patents are likely to be reaffirmed in final analysis.

In the rarified world of highly knowledgeable ESC researchers with Ph.D. degrees and laboratory experience, however, an ordinarily skilled practitioner would, at a minimum, be bright enough to mix and match culture ingredients and methods described in the prior art, and nonobviousness analysis should take this into account. In other words, because stem cell scientists are a pretty smart bunch, it should take a greater quantum of inventiveness to qualify for a patent than might be required in more "low-tech" fields. This might seem a bit unfair to researchers like Thomson, but it is appropriate given that the purpose of the nonobviousness requirement is to try to limit patent monopolies to innovations that would be made only if that incentive is offered.

Regardless of which side ultimately prevails in this extremely technical dispute, the nature of the disagreement reinforces the notion that any hESC patents should be issued for a particular method or elements thereof or for a particular culture medium that renders a cell line uniquely useful for research. It is these items that are potentially inventive and thus deserving of patent protection, not the hESCs themselves.

## A "Safe Harbor" from Infringement Claims

Even if WARF's composition of matter claims are ultimately upheld by the PTO and the courts and interpreted broadly, a separate provision of federal law should provide scientists who wish to use hESCs considerable latitude to do so. The latitude would probably not be sufficient, however, to enable most researchers to avoid negotiating a license from WARF.

In general, selling or using a patented invention during the patent term without a license from the patentee constitutes infringement and subjects the infringer to legal liability. In 1984, however, Congress enacted as part of the Hatch-Waxman Act an exception to this rule. It provides that "it shall not be an act of infringement to make, use or sell a patented invention . . . solely for uses reasonably related to the development and submission of information under a Federal law which regulates the manufacture, sale, or use of drugs," including those under which the FDA exercises its authority.[88]

Congress created this "safe harbor" provision to allow manufacturers of generic drugs to begin the process of winning FDA approval for their copycat products before the originals go off patent.[89] Generic drug makers may obtain FDA approval by demonstrating the bioequivalence of their product and the brand-name version of the drug.[90] Creating data for this purpose necessarily requires using the original, patented compound. If makers of generics are prohibited from even beginning this process until the patent on the original compound expires, the effective term of that patent would be much longer than the actual term. A patent that is supposed to provide a twenty-year monopoly would in fact keep competing products off the market for twenty years plus the additional years needed to navigate the FDA process.[91]

In the 2005 case of *Merck KGaA v. Integra Lifesciences I, Ltd.*, the U.S. Supreme Court interpreted this safe harbor provision liberally. The defendants produced several amino acid sequences referred to as "RGD peptides" and used them in a series of tests designed to identify compounds that would inhibit a process called angiogenesis, which plays a part in some diseases. The plaintiff, which held patents on the RGD peptides, sued, claiming infringement.[92] A unanimous Court ruled for the defendants on the ground that their research was "reasonably related" to the development and submission of data that the FDA would require to approve a new drug.[93] The Court explained that the safe harbor is so broad that it is not necessary for the defendants to have planned to submit experimental results obtained by using patented materials to the FDA if the experiments were successful. Because of uncertainties as to what information the FDA might demand before approving a drug, the safe harbor can be invoked under the "reasonably related" test, even when data collected are left out of subsequent FDA submissions.[94]

*Merck's* broad interpretation of the "reasonably related" test implies that many uses to which researchers would put hESCs are protected from infringement lawsuits. Scientists who wish to differentiate hESCs into specialized cells and use them to test the toxicity or efficacy of new pharmaceuticals would create a scenario extremely similar to the facts of *Merck* itself. The FDA has taken the position that clinical treatments derived from hESCs would require FDA premarket approval.[95] This position suggests that research aimed at developing therapeutic uses of hESCs might also be protected from infringement claims since such research could result in data that would later be submitted to the FDA. It also suggests that creating hESC lines from SCNT-created blastocysts to provide personalized stem cell treatments could be protected from infringement actions.[96]

Whether *Merck* will be interpreted broadly enough to protect *all* research using hESCs is a more difficult question. Researchers could contend that the ultimate goal of all hESC research is to create therapies that will require FDA premarket approval. This demonstrates that all hESC research is "related" to the "development and submission" of data to the FDA in some sense, but is the relationship of basic research on hESCs that is not designed to create a particular treatment for a specific disease too attenuated from the development of a therapy to qualify as "reasonably related" under the statute?

The underlying problem with extending the safe harbor this far is that unlike prescription drugs, on which Congress focused when it enacted Hatch-Waxman, hESC lines are not themselves products marketed to the public that require FDA approval. Rather they are "research tools," in the sense that their market is other scientists who will use them to conduct further research. By permitting generic drug makers to use name-brand drugs that are still under patent, Hatch-Waxman does not deprive the drug patents of their entire value. The patentees still enjoy a twenty-year monopoly (from the date of the patent application) on the right to sell the compound. But if Hatch-Waxman is interpreted to cover all uses of biomedical research tools, like hESCs, the patents on such tools would decline substantially in value—a patentee could hope to earn licensing revenue only if its tool led to commercial products that received regulatory approval prior to the patent's expiration. This could significantly reduce the incentive to produce such research tools in the future.

Such an outcome quite certainly was not intended by Congress when it enacted Hatch-Waxman. This point was probably not lost on the Supreme Court, which explicitly stated that Merck was not using the RGD peptides as a research tool and that its decision in that case is not intended to address the status of research tools generally.[97] The Hatch-Waxman safe harbor should protect from infringement the use of hESCs to test the effects of potential pharmaceuticals on them and to test their efficacy as direct treatments of disease, as these uses fall clearly within the text of the statute, even if the enacting Congress did not specifically intend even this breadth of protection. But the courts should decline to extend the safe harbor to the use of hESCs for basic scientific research not directly related to the development of drugs or therapies. Patent protection for hESCs should be limited but not completely eviscerated.

# 5

# The Taxpayers' Stake
# in Stem Cell Profits

When the promoters of California's Proposition 71 placed that initiative on the state's ballot in 2004, they promised the public technological innovation: stem cell research, the initiative's initial declarations claimed, could potentially lead to treatments and cures for many serious medical conditions, including "cancer, diabetes, heart disease, Alzheimer's, Parkinson's, spinal cord injuries, blindness, Lou Gehrig's disease, HIV/AIDS, mental health disorders, multiple sclerosis, Huntington's disease, and more than 70 other diseases and injuries." But they combined the description of such lofty humanitarian aspirations with a business proposition of sorts: if taxpayers would agree to pony up $3 billion over ten years to fund the research, they would be rewarded with a share of the profits that the research would generate.[1]

The initiative instructs CIRM to balance the opportunity of the state to benefit from the intellectual property created with its funding with the need to avoid hindering medical research, but it leaves it to the agency to determine precisely how this should be done.[2] CIRM's solution was to make a revenue-sharing arrangement a condition of its grantees' profiting from their state-funded innovations. Nonprofit grant recipients (primarily universities and their faculty scientists) are free—even encouraged—to patent inventions made possible by state funding and to license them, but they have to share their licensing revenues with the state. The grantee can retain the first $500,000 earned, above and beyond any amounts shared with the individual inventor and the direct costs of patenting the invention. For any revenues that exceed that threshold, however, the grantee must return 25 percent to the state's general fund to pay off the bonds issued to fund stem cell research or to meet other public needs.[3]

For-profit companies are also eligible for CIRM stem cell funding. For-profit grantees are subject to the same rules as nonprofits if they license their state-funded inventions, except that they must share only 17 percent of revenues over $500,000. If for-profit grantees choose to bring their own inventions directly to market, they must pay royalties on sales to California after product revenues reach the $500,000 mark until three times their grant amount is returned. The state is due extra bonuses in the case of "blockbuster" inventions that produce more than $250 million per year in revenue for the grantee.[4]

What is most striking about the California revenue-sharing plan is the extent to which it diverges from the federal government's policy concerning who benefits from the fruits of government-funded scientific research. Under current law, the federal government demands very few benefits—and no cash return—from the recipients of the billions of dollars in research and development (R&D) funds it distributes every year, no matter how valuable the resulting innovations. If federal restrictions on funding of hESC research are lifted after the 2008 presidential election, as predicted in Chapter 2, California's financial commitment to stem cell research might wane in significance. But even if, in retrospect, Proposition 71 ends up being a footnote to the stem cell revolution rather than a headline, careful consideration is due the questions it raises about how intellectual property produced as a result of publicly funded stem cell research should be shared between the government agencies that supply the financial capital and the scientists who provide the human capital.

## The Bayh-Dole Act and the Fruits of Government Funding

Prior to 1980, the federal government lacked a single, coherent policy governing ownership of technological innovations produced by nonfederal employees with federal financial support. Since World War II, when federal support became a significant source of the nation's overall spending on technology R&D, government officials and academics had debated the merits of two alternative strategies.[5] One group believed that technological innovations produced with public funding ought to belong to the public. Most members of this group favored government patenting of inventions generated by publicly funded research, combined with a policy of making the technology available to anyone who wished to exploit it. Others favored a policy of placing such inventions directly into the public domain and not seeking patents at all.

Members of the competing camp believed that either of these policies would inhibit, rather than promote, the commercialization of inventions because private businesses would not be willing to invest the funds necessary to bring a good idea to market without proprietary rights in the invention. Because they saw exclusive dominion over an invention by a party with an incentive to bring it to market as critical, this group preferred allowing private and nonprofit entities that receive federal grant support to patent their resulting innovations. Armed with the patents, these nongovernmental entities could either invest the money necessary to move an innovation from the laboratory to the marketplace themselves or license the innovation to other private actors with the ability to do so.

For several decades, federal agencies followed a variety of different rules concerning ownership of government-funded inventions, with different combinations of these divergent theoretical views holding sway in different corners of the government. In most cases, the government held title to inventions and (usually) offered the use of them freely, but in other cases, agencies allowed grantees or contractors to take title. In the late 1970s, federal agencies followed as many as twenty-six different patent policies.

In 1980, Congress enacted legislation known as the Bayh-Dole Act.[6] Bayh-Dole created a uniform set of federal rules governing ownership of federally funded innovations, and in doing so, it sounded a victory for the proponents of vesting property rights in inventions in grant recipients. Under Bayh-Dole, small businesses and nonprofit entities—most notably universities—were given the right to patent inventions created with federal support, and they were encouraged to do so in return for their commitment to seek the commercialization of those inventions. With a profit incentive, these entities would presumably transfer control over their inventions, through the sale of licenses for flat fees or royalties on future product sales, to the commercial entities best suited to bring the inventions to market. Although large corporations were not originally included as beneficiaries of the Bayh-Dole Act, a statutory amendment and executive order effectively extended the scope of the legislation to include them as well.[7] Under the statute, government funding agencies can restrict grantee patenting only in "exceptional circumstances" and only if burdensome procedures are followed.[8]

Universities are required to share the licensing revenue with the faculty members personally responsible for the inventions, but no grant recipients are obligated to share any licensing revenues with the federal government. An early draft of Bayh-Dole included a revenue-sharing requirement of 15 percent of licensing revenue and 5 percent of revenues from product sales, but the provision failed to make it into the statute's final text.[9] Under Bayh-Dole, the provision of grant money entitles the federal government only to the right to nonexclusive licenses to use funded inventions.[10] According to the statute, the government also retains the right to take over a patent or force its holder to license it if the patentee fails to effectively commercialize an innovation. The possibility that it conceivably could exercise these so-called "march-in rights" occasionally improves the government's bargaining leverage when it seeks to pressure a patent holder into exploiting a technology more quickly than it otherwise might, but the government has never exercised these rights.[11]

The reasoning that led to Bayh-Dole's passage with little opposition is easy to understand, particularly in light of the time period in which it was enacted. In the late 1970s, economic stagnation had created widespread fears that the United States was losing is global leadership position in the development of technology. International economic competitiveness requires not only the production of innovative ideas but also their incorporation into marketable goods and services. Congress received data indicating that only a small fraction of inventions in the government's patent portfolio had ever been used to make commercial products, whereas the percentage was much higher when government grantees were permitted to patent the inventions.

This comparison was at least somewhat misleading because most of the data originated from Defense Department programs, which permitted contractors first choice over whether to patent innovations and left the government with title to the least commercially viable inventions.[12] Nonetheless, it is fair to say that the record demonstrated that the federal government had not been very successful at commercializing the inventions for which it had paid. With the political winds of the era blowing in the direction of deregulation and privatization, the available information seemed to reinforce the view that private inventors would be better than federal bureaucrats at satisfying Bayh-Dole's stated goal of "promot[ing] the utilization of inventions arising from federally funded research or development."[13]

The historical record demonstrates that after the enactment of Bayh-Dole, the number of university-held patents increased sharply,[14] as did the annual number of licenses issued by universities and the revenue generated by them.[15] In the legislation's wake, many universities that had had no formal method of sharing technology with private industry created technology transfer offices, where staffers work closely with faculty to patent inventions and then license them to private industry for commercial purposes, either in the form of exclusive licenses to exploit a particular technology or a particular application of a technology or in the form of nonexclusive licenses.[16] And although some universities clearly benefit much more than others from technology licensing, the trend toward the increased commercialization of inventions across academic institutions has been broad in addition to deep.[17]

Total license income in 2004 for 196 reporting universities totaled nearly $1.4 billion, a relatively small amount compared to the $27.7 billion those same universities received in research funding from the federal government, but still a substantial sum.[18] And licensing income is particularly valuable to universities because its use is unrestricted. Faculty scientists benefit as well from their share of the licensing revenues that Bayh-Dole mandates. Private industry benefits by being able (often) to procure exclusive licenses to exploit a technology, thus justifying the investment necessary in bringing it to market. Taxpayers benefit, although indirectly, from the creation of new and useful products, which themselves create jobs for workers and utility for consumers.

The conventional wisdom is that Bayh-Dole has been an enormous success. The *Economist,* for example, has called Bayh-Dole the "most inspired piece of legislation to be enacted in America over the past half-century" and has credited it with single-handedly "revers[ing] America's precipitous slide into industrial irrelevance."[19] Such fawning praise suggests not only that the federal government should leave well enough alone but also that states that aspire to become leading sources of funding for stem cell research, such as California, ought to emulate the Bayh-Dole model.

In the last decade, however, serious scholarly inquiries have questioned both the power of Bayh-Dole as the primary explanation for universities' becoming the nation's leading source of technological innovation and the net value of the act itself. What might be called revisionist critiques of Bayh-Dole point out that the increase in the rate of university patents observable after the enactment of the act actually began in the 1970s, mirroring the rise in biotechnology, a large expansion in federal funding of biomedical research, and a relative shift by the federal government away from defense related R&D funding and toward biomedical-related funding.[20] Relative to defense-related research, which dominated the federal R&D budget in the 1950s and '60s, biomedical research is more likely to be conducted in universities rather than in private industry and is more likely to lead to patentable inventions. In other words, the economy's changing innovation mix might explain more than does Bayh-Dole.[21]

Moreover, echoing the debates of the 1940s and '50s, the revisionists question whether the structure of Bayh-Dole provides the best possible innovation policy. On the positive side, as noted, universities have a greater incentive to patent innovations and exclusively license them to private firms who wish to bring the innovations to market. But there is a downside as well. By providing universities with incentives to claim property rights over their inventions, Bayh-Dole undermines the free exchange of ideas and information among researchers both within and outside of the academy. License agreements with industry often require faculty to delay the publication of inventions and sometimes permit the licensee to demand that useful information not be published at all. Faculty involved in potentially profitable research often decline to share their findings with colleagues. Such actions can inhibit creativity and increase transaction costs, and in so doing retard technological innovation. The revisionist critiques of the Bayh-Dole regime suggest, at a minimum, the need to carefully reassess government innovation policy in the context of stem cell research rather than simply assume that Bayh-Dole represents the optimal approach.

# Policy Choices for Public Funders of Stem Cell Research

Creating a policy for encouraging the creation and marketing of inventions requires attention to the following three questions concerning subsequent control over the technology:

> Who should determine whether a government-funded invention should be patented?

> Who should determine in what manner patents should be licensed?

> Who should profit from patent licenses and in what amounts?

By assigning all ownership rights in government-funded innovations to grant recipients, the Bayh-Dole Act effectively allocates all of the decision-making authority and all of the profits that follow from it to grantees. It is important to recognize, though, that there are many intermediate positions between providing grantees with all possible property rights in their inventions and none. In theory, decision-making authority and revenues could be decoupled, and each could be divided between public and private claimants in a number of ways. A careful evaluation of how the ownership of stem cell inventions should be allocated must consider the full range of possibilities.

## THE PATENTING DECISION

Whether the social benefits created by a patent exceed the social costs of granting an inventor a twenty-year monopoly depends in large part on two factors: the cost of producing the invention and the cost of commercializing it. As Chapter 4 discussed, patent rights are defensible in general on the grounds of encouraging innovation. Without the possibility of earning a patent, inventors would not invest large amounts of time and money in producing innovations for fear of having the profit potential eaten away by copiers who could take advantage of an invention's commercial potential without bearing the costs of creating it. If government grants pay the salaries and research costs of scientists, however, innovations that are costly to produce become nearly costless to the scientists and their employers, be they universities or private companies. Patent rights provide a less critical incentive in this context. Arguably, the incentive is completely unnecessary.

Even if the government pays the cost of invention, however, patents can still provide an important incentive to invest the capital necessary to commercialize the invention, assuming that the government does not wish to directly finance this part of the process, which it rarely does. But the necessity of patent rights for this purpose varies with the costs required to ready an invention for sale. Here, there is usually, although not always, a substantial difference between what are often called "basic" inventions, "upstream" inventions, or "research tools"—that is, inventions primarily useful as inputs to further inventions—and "downstream" or "applied" inventions— inventions of primary value to end users.[22]

James Thomson's method of creating hESC lines is an excellent example of an invention that falls into the former category. It has tremendous value to scientists who hope to create stem cell products but no direct value to patients or other consumers. A good example of an invention that falls into the latter category is a preparation of oligodendrocytes derived from differentiated hESCs of the type that Hans Keirstead has developed, as described in Chapter 1.

Keirstead's invention will require the investment of hundreds of millions of dollars before it can reach the marketplace, and there is substantial risk that it never will. First, treatment will require three phases of clinical trials to demonstrate the safety and efficacy required for approval by the FDA. In addition to the costly process of obtaining regulatory approval, an investment of untold millions of additional dollars probably will be needed to create an industrial process capable of mass-producing billions of oligodendrocytes. Such large quantities are not necessary for a laboratory scientist to demonstrate the usefulness of a stem cell preparation in principle, but they will be necessary for the mass production of a therapy.

Not only is attempting to bring such a product to market costly, but it is also quite risky. If the licensee is unable to either satisfy FDA requirements or create a technology able to reliably mass-produce the necessary raw materials, the investment will earn no return at all. It is unlikely that a private company would be willing to take such an expensive gamble without the compensating right to earn monopoly profits on the product, if successful, that a patent would provide.

Thomson's invention, in contrast, does not require substantial investment before it can be useful to its potential customers: other scientists. If WARF had not been able to obtain a patent on hESCs initially, the technology that Thomson's laboratory created would still be adopted widely, and if WARF eventually fails to win back its patent protection, there is no fear that the production of new hESC lines will cease. Armed with the instructions and relatively inexpensive equipment, other scientists could simply create new hESC lines in their own labs: many have done just this already. Researchers not wanting to devote the effort needed to master the technique would retain the option of purchasing samples of Thomson's hESC lines directly from WARF. Dissemination of the innovation in no way depends on patent protection. In fact, through the imposition of WARF's licensing fees and the transaction costs associated with negotiating and obtaining the licenses, patentability hinders—to a greater or lesser degree—the invention's dissemination.

Patents can burden the dissemination of inventions in other ways as well. In some instances, a patentee will not license a technology to a party that could successfully exploit it because the two will fail to agree on a price. This outcome is especially likely if the patentee is more optimistic about the future commercial potential of the invention than the potential licensee, and such differential optimism is itself exceptionally likely in new fields of technology with few market benchmarks.[23] In other instances, the costs associated with obtaining multiple upstream patents might be so great as to discourage potential downstream inventors, even if no individual patent presents a substantial obstacle.[24]

The freedom to patent inventions can also hinder the traditional sharing of research results by academic scientists. By statute, the PTO may not issue a patent on an invention that was "described in a printed publication" or "in public use" more than one year before the patent application is filed because prior publication prevents the application from fulfilling the "novelty" requirement.[25] Rather than rushing to publish their results as soon as possible in order to establish themselves as the first to an important discovery, scientists eyeing a patent have an incentive to delay publishing until a patent application is nearly ready.[26] Some empirical evidence suggests that the federal government's adoption of the pro-patent Bayh-Dole regime may have caused medical researchers to delay presenting research results at scientific conferences for fear that doing so would render their subsequent inventions unpatentable.[27] That patentability can slow the presentation and publication of important scientific innovations, and thus delay secondary innovation, must be counted as a significant social cost.

This analysis indicates that the overall social utility of patent protection varies, depending on the type of invention at issue. In some cases patent protection will be desirable, in other cases not. Grantees have a private incentive to patent all inventions with potential commercial applications, however, if they are permitted to do so. This is obviously the case for for-profit grantees, but it is also true for universities and other nonprofits. University technology transfer officers view their job as raising revenue, and revenue requires selling licenses.[28] Placing an invention in the public domain, even if doing so would redound to the benefit of the public, generates no revenue stream.

Government funding agencies lack this conflict of interest, and therefore it is sensible for them to determine whether the fruits of funded research should be patentable or must remain in the public domain. The decision should be based on whether the research project at issue is most likely to result in the creation of research tools or end-user applications that are more likely to require significant additional investment before being marketed.

There is, of course, the possibility that government agencies—even with institutional knowledge about a grantee's field of research—will mistakenly determine that inventions arising from such research should be nonpatentable when property rights would in fact be necessary to encourage commercialization or, in contrast, that the inventions may be patented by the grantee when in fact patenting would hinder dissemination without substantially increasing the likelihood of commercialization.[29] Scientific progress is not always linear or predictable; what starts out as basic research will sometimes yield an invention close to marketability, and research intended to be more applied often results in the creation of new research tools. In the former case, the problem can be remedied by allowing grantees to petition for reconsideration of a "no-patent" designation in light of new information. The settled expectations of grantees should preclude the government from revisiting the terms of a grant that originally permitted patenting, but mistakes in this direction would leave the government no worse off than it is under the Bayh-Dole regime.

There is also a risk that if patents are permitted on applied research but not on basic research, researchers might shift their emphasis from the latter to the former in an effort to take advantage of its profit potential. Put another way, even for a scientist with a university salary and government funding, engaging in basic research would entail opportunity costs—specifically, foregoing other types of research that might lead to licensing income—and might cause the scientist to choose more personally lucrative research projects over those with a greater expected social value.

Critics of Bayh-Dole at its time of enactment raised a similar concern: that the act would encourage scientists to shift from basic to applied research because the latter tends to present the greater opportunity to earn licensing revenue. Multiple researchers have concluded, however, that Bayh-Dole has caused little if any shift in research priorities among university scientists.[30] The explanation is probably that, although most university faculty scientists (like most other Americans) prefer more money to less, they receive other forms of compensation, such as tenure, academic prestige, and personal satisfaction with their research, which dilute their incentive to follow the money wherever it may lead. Even faculty scientists most concerned with maximizing income find that laboratory success that leads to important publications can generate significant remuneration through raises, promotions, lecture fees, and the like, mitigating the allure of patents to some degree.[31] This analysis suggests that prohibiting patents on government-funded upstream inventions is unlikely to skew the nature of university research to any significant extent.

CIRM delegates to grantees authority to decide whether or not to patent state-funded inventions, duplicating one of Bayh-Dole's greatest flaws. This decision might be justified, at least from a provincial perspective, by Proposition 71's goal of creating economic benefits for the state of California. Patents on CIRM-funded upstream inventions will hinder their widespread dissemination, but they will generate licensing revenue for California-based grantees that would be foregone if those inventions were placed in the public domain. But far from urging that its grantees patent all inventions for this reason, CIRM's intellectual property policy specifically states that it "does not encourage patent protection for 'upstream inventions' . . . and 'research tools'" because the "public interest is served primarily by ensuring [their wide availability]."[32] This statement drives a wedge between what CIRM says it favors and what its policy actually encourages: on one hand, the agency says it prefers broad dissemination of inventions over the private advantage of its grantees; on the other hand, rather than creating an institutional structure that ensures this trade-off is made, it mimics Bayh-Dole in giving grantees the ability to place their interests above the public interest.

To some extent, the negative effect of CIRM's policy on the dissemination of inventions is mitigated (at least within California) by a requirement that nonprofit grantees provide noncommercial licenses to other grantees.[33] It is important to recognize, however, that while such compulsory research licenses will speed the dissemination of research tools, this is only a half-measure compared to a requirement that upstream inventions be placed in the public domain. Researchers who improve on the patented invention may not sell the improved product to third parties without the third party's negotiating and purchasing a license from the original inventor. This means that scientists without public funding are less likely to invest in making improvements. It also means that if the secondary inventor patents an improvement, licensing the improved invention for commercialization might require the negotiation of multiple licenses.

## LICENSING DETERMINATIONS

The Bayh-Dole Act leaves to federal grant recipients whether and how to license patents, with the primary exception that the government retains "march-in" rights if the grantee does not take adequate steps to do so. As is the case with the decision of whether to seek patents, grantees need not necessarily be endowed with this discretion. The government could obtain patents and license them, or it could permit grantees to take title to patents but dictate the terms of subsequent licenses.

Assuming that patenting an invention (rather than placing it in the public domain) is socially desirable, the profit incentives of grantees usually will be well aligned with the public interest. The public interest is served if the patent is licensed to the company or companies best able to exploit the invention commercially. Since this company (or companies) will presumably also be the bidder (or bidders) willing to pay the most money for licenses, the grantee's profit incentive will usually lead to the socially optimal result.

Grantees also have a profit incentive to divide the licensed property rights in the most efficient way. One common decision is whether to exclusively license a patent for all possible uses to one purchaser or to grant multiple exclusive licenses to exploit particular aspects or uses of the technology to several purchasers. For example, an oligodendrocyte preparation, as described above, could be licensed to a single commercial entity, or it could be licensed to one entity for one application and to a second entity for a different application. Society benefits if the choice is made such that the innovation will be put to all of its uses in the most cost-effective way. The grantee has the same incentive because the most efficient division of licenses should yield the greatest licensing fees or royalties.

If a patent can be exploited most efficiently through nonexclusive licenses rather than one or more exclusive licenses, the public interest usually will be better served if the invention is not patented at all but instead placed in the public domain.[34] If producers will manufacture and market the innovation or its subsidiary products without the protection from copycats that exclusive rights provide, the primary reason for patenting publicly funded inventions is undermined. On the other side of the scale, nonexclusive license fees could discourage downstream inventors who might have commercially exploited the invention if it were in the public domain, and, at a minimum, they will add a cost to downstream inventions that can affect their ultimate market price, to the public's detriment. However, assuming the decision has already been made to permit patenting, the public is better served if the invention is non-exclusively licensed. The grantee's interests are consistent because the most efficient division of licenses should bring the greatest total revenues in the market.

The preceding analysis suggests that when it comes to determining how best to market licenses, grantees' private incentives are aligned with the public interest. This observation counsels for allocating authority of licensing decisions to grantees. In theory, the government funding agency could retain the right to negotiate licenses and attempt to do so in exactly the same way, but the profit motive makes private actors more likely than government agents to allocate licenses optimally and at the least possible cost. Even nonprofit entities, such as universities, will have an advantage over governments in this respect since revenues obtained can be used to fund the entity's mission and because such entities usually have a better ability than governments to create optimal incentives to motivate the individual employees charged with making licensing decisions.

Grantees might make errors, of course, granting exclusive licenses when nonexclusive licenses would allow for more effective exploitation of a particular technology, or vice versa. Critics of Bayh-Dole have argued that university technology transfer officials in particular are likely to sell exclusive licenses too frequently, not recognizing the broad potential market for nonexclusive licenses.[35] But this risk of error seems no greater than if the government were to decide whether to license an invention exclusively or nonexclusively. Data indicate that just over half of university technology licenses are nonexclusive, and just under half are exclusive.[36] Although these figures do not prove that university technology transfer officers always make the optimal licensing decisions, they do seem to suggest that the officers are not irredeemably biased in favor of exclusive licenses.

At the same time, granting too much discretion to individual government agents runs a risk of cronyism, and building too many layers of review or procedural steps into a government decision-making process to prevent this ill would increase the costs and delays imposed on potential licensees. Delegating licensing authority to grantees avoids both the disease and the cure. Another advantage of permitting grantees to make licensing decisions is that the geographical proximity to the scientists making the inventions and an ability to form personal relationships with them suggests that university technology transfer officers usually will be better able than funding agencies to work collaboratively with inventors in order to market licenses effectively and transfer technology to licensees efficiently. These advantages strongly suggest that grantees should control the licensing of patented technology, perhaps against a backdrop of "march-in" rights in case of unusual breakdowns in the process. This is just the balance reached by Bayh-Dole and by CIRM's new regulations.

## THE DISTRIBUTION OF LICENSING REVENUES

The prior analysis of whether grantees or government funding agencies are best positioned to make licensing determinations implicitly presumes that grantees will retain at least some of the revenues generated from licenses. In theory, the government could require grantees to license their patents and forward all revenue to the government, but such a policy would be as naïve as instituting a 100 percent personal income tax. Without some profit incentive, grantees would have no moti-

vation to patent their inventions, market their patents, or select licensees best able to exploit the inventions. Universities
would have no incentive to establish technology transfer offices,
and faculty inventors would have no incentive to spend their
time collaborating with the nonexistent technology transfer
personnel.

It does not follow from this observation, however, that
grantees should be permitted to keep all licensing revenue, as
Bayh-Dole permits, any more than it follows from the observation that a 100 percent tax rate is a bad idea that the rate
ought to be zero. It is true that the greater the percentage of licensing revenue that grantees can capture, the greater the incentive they will have to maximize the commercial potential of
their inventions, but this point proves too much. If the government not only permitted grantees to keep all licensing revenue but also matched that revenue dollar-for-dollar with unrestricted funds, grantees would capture 200 percent of their
licensing revenue and would have twice the incentive that
Bayh-Dole provides to disseminate their patented inventions
efficiently. If subsidies were provided on a five-to-one basis,
grantees would have five times the incentive that they enjoy
under Bayh-Dole. Obviously, the incentive created by permitting grantees to benefit from licensing their inventions must
be balanced against the cost to the public fisc of providing such
incentives. Other than administrative convenience, there is no
reason to think that allowing grantees to keep 100 percent of
the proceeds is any less arbitrary than setting the figure at 200
percent or 500 percent or 20 percent or 10 percent.

The problem of how much of the proceeds of government-funded innovation should be allocated to grantees is
similar to the problem that private sources of capital face when
they offer to fund technology research. Before funding a small

company with a promising idea, venture capital firms usually demand a percentage of future profits if the venture succeeds, either directly or in the form of an equity stake in the company. Sources of private capital also sometimes fund university research in exchange for licenses to use the resulting inventions or a share of licensing profits. In either case, private funders seek to offer their "grantees" enough of the fruits of success to convince them to (1) enter a joint venture with them, and (2) work hard at achieving success. The remainder of the proceeds they attempt to keep for themselves. Public entities willing to fund stem cell research should apply a similar analysis in structuring their intellectual property ownership policy.

Granted, public funding sources play a quite different role in the biotech innovation market than do private venture capital firms. The latter seek only to maximize their profits, whereas the former have an interest in creating socially valuable medical treatments and, perhaps, giving a boost to the polity's biotech economy. (California's Proposition 71 lists this as one of the goals of the initiative.) Indeed, if it were not for non-revenue-related goals, there would be no reason for government to fund R&D.[37] Private sources of capital are plentiful enough to fund research that is expected to earn market rates of return. Government funding is necessary for research that is either too risky or will require too many years before bearing fruit to offer an expected rate of return sufficient to interest the private capital markets.

Taxpayers must recognize that government-funded stem cell research will not earn a market rate of return on investment—not even close. In fact, a recent study of research expenditures and licensing revenues at U.S. universities, hospitals, and research institutes strongly suggests that each dollar spent on stem cell research is unlikely to produce more than eight cents in licensing revenue and less than five cents in real terms if the time lag between spending and return is taken into account.[38] But the fact that the amount of income generated by stem cell research is likely to be low relative to the total amount of funding does not mean that the government should simply give away what revenue there is. Public funders should aim to allow grantees to pocket just enough of the income so that a significant number of the best scientists are encouraged to engage in stem cell research and their organizations have an incentive to license the inventions with vigor. After satisfying this goal, public agencies ought to attempt to capture any remaining revenues for the public.

The appropriate question, then, is to how much of the future proceeds generated by successful government-sponsored stem cell inventions the government can lay claim without pushing the best stem cell scientists out of the field, discouraging the best future scientists from entering the field, and discouraging universities and technology companies from supporting those scientists. No one knows exactly, of course, what the right number is, but zero—the Bayh-Dole standard—is almost certainly too low. California has put the number at 25 percent of net revenues exceeding $500,000 for nonprofit organizations and 17 percent for for-profit companies. These numbers also seem too low. Fifty percent is probably more appropriate, especially in light of the high revenue threshold. Granted, there is no empirical support for the claim that 50 percent is closer to optimal than either 25 percent or 75 percent, but just as Bayh-Dole did not cause university scientists to switch from basic to applied research en masse, requiring grantees to split profits with the state would not cause many scientists or scientific institutions dedicated to the potential of stem cell research to move to other fields of study.

If scientists find that they are able to strike a better bargain with venture capitalists or other private funding sources, the state should be happy to allow private capital to provide the necessary funding; taxpayers will get the benefits of the research without having to foot the bill. From the perspective of California consumers, medical research funding presents what is often called a classic "public goods" problem. If other people wish to pay the cost of research, California's consumers will fare best by allowing the scientific work to go elsewhere, avoiding the costs while still benefiting from innovations in biomedical technology. If a different public funding source— perhaps another state government that follows California into the stem cell financing arena, the government of a foreign country, or even the U.S. government if it lifts its funding restrictions—offers grants to researchers on a more advantageous basis, the analysis becomes more complicated. Although losing a competition to give away money clearly would benefit California's consumers, this result would likely hurt California's biotechnology industry. If stem cell research is funded elsewhere, the jobs the state hopes will be created and the tax revenue that they will generate are likely to go elsewhere as well.

## REVENUE-SHARING ALTERNATIVES

A revenue-sharing arrangement between a public funding source and its grantees need not be a straight division of proceeds. There are an infinite number of creative ways of sharing revenues, some of which might be more mutually beneficial for all involved. In California, CIRM's intellectual property policies incorporate two creative amendments to its basic plan of a roughly three-to-one revenue split, and both are worthy of examination.

The first wrinkle of the California plan is, as mentioned above, that all grantees are permitted to keep the entire first $500,000 in licensing revenue. For nonprofit grantees, the amount of income not subject to revenue sharing is actually higher because the $500,000 exclusion amount is net of the direct costs of patenting and, more important, it is net of revenues that nonprofits must share with the individual inventor or inventors, as required by Bayh-Dole and by CIRM.[39] The implicit reasoning behind this exclusion is as follows: (1) even when direct research costs are paid for by public grants, some licensing revenues are needed before grantees recover other indirect costs, such as operating a technology transfer program, and (2) grantees should be made "whole" before taxpayers see a return on their investment.

Assuming that the state is better able than grantees to bear the high risk associated with funding cutting-edge scientific research—and, after all, this is the premise of public funding to begin with—permitting grantees to keep some amount of initial licensing proceeds in order to ensure that their costs are covered is entirely sensible. Two criticisms can be levied against CIRM's specific policy, however. First and most obviously, CIRM's policy sets a fixed amount of income per grant that is excluded from revenue sharing, with no consideration given to the size of the grant. Although it is impossible to pinpoint the optimal amount of revenue that grantees should be permitted to retain before revenue-sharing obligations set in, it is clear that the amount ought to vary somewhat with the size of the research project. The indirect costs associated with administering grants and licensing technology will be much larger for a $25 million grant than for a $25,000 grant, at least on average. Thus it would be more sensible to set the amount of licensing income excludable from revenue-sharing obligations as a percentage of the original grant.

Second, in return for the exclusion of initial income from revenue sharing, the state should demand higher returns as revenues increase. In other words, if the revenue-sharing plan minimizes risks to the grantees at the expense of taxpayers when revenues are low, the taxpayers should be compensated with a greater percentage of the "upside" potential. If the state is entitled to 25 percent of revenues above $500,000, it should lay claim to higher and higher percentages as revenues meet higher thresholds. CIRM's policy for nonprofits does not recognize this principle at all, and its for-profit plan recognizes it only to a very limited extent. The latter policy entitles the state to bonus payments on very successful inventions but only when the grantee chooses to produce and market the end product itself (rather than license it) and only when the product achieves true "blockbuster" status: $250 million in revenue in a single year.

## IN-KIND REVENUE SHARING

The goals of revenue sharing can be accomplished, in theory, through in-kind compensation as well as through cash compensation. The second wrinkle of the California plan is that it features in-kind benefit requirements in addition to the cash recoupment provision. CIRM grants obligate commercial third-party licensees to (a) sell resulting products at a discount to the state and/or low-income Californians and (b) create a plan to provide access to resulting therapies to uninsured Californians.[40] Both of these requirements make for good public relations copy, but neither is good policy.

CIRM's regulations for nonprofit grantees operationalize the first requirement by providing that licensees must sell therapies developed from CIRM-funded innovations to certain low-income Californians at a discount. The current version of the agency's proposed regulations for for-profit grantees calls for discounts to be given to the state itself. These provisions have a certain appealing equitable sensibility: the state funds the research, and the state and its needy residents receive the fruits of that research at a discounted price. The provisions are inefficient, however, compared to the sharing of cash revenues. By imposing limitations of any kind on the commercial licensor of technology, the value of the license will decline, resulting in lower licensing fees to the grantee and thus a smaller return to the state through the revenue-sharing requirement. The state and some residents will benefit, of course, when it comes to paying the medical bills, but they benefit only if they choose to purchase the stem cell product at issue. The implicit revenue in the form of drug discounts cannot be spent on non-stem-cell medical treatments, highway construction, education, prisons, or any of the hundreds of other state priorities that policy makers might find more pressing in any given year.

Ardent supporters of stem cell research might favor discount requirements over cash precisely because the former implicitly force the state to spend at least a portion of its return on stem cell investments on stem cell products, whereas the latter makes it possible for bureaucrats to "squander" the proceeds on programs that advocates believe are less important. But it is not properly the decision of CIRM to tie the hands of state officials when it comes to deciding how to spend any proceeds of the state's investment in stem cell research. The agency should invest the $3 billion of state funds dedicated to stem cell research in the most promising scientific projects, recoup as much of the profit that is earned from that investment as possible without discouraging the best scientists from seeking state grants or discouraging private companies from investing in the commercialization of state-funded innovations, and then let other officials decide how to allocate the proceeds. If the taxpayers think state officials are making poor decisions, the remedy is well known: throw the bums out at the next election.

The requirement that licensees provide a plan of access to the uninsured is an even worse idea than discounts to the state. That 45 million Americans lack private or public health insurance is a serious problem, but it is not one that producers of medical treatments are well positioned to address. At best, CIRM's vague demand will force licensing contracts to include equally nonspecific and meaningless pledges concerning access to treatments. At worst, the need to figure out a way to satisfy this requirement will cause private companies to hesitate commercializing CIRM-funded inventions or reduce the amount they will be willing to pay in licensing fees.

# 6

# Autonomy and Informed Consent

Once upon a time, the U.S. Public Health Service recruited 399 African American men from rural Alabama for a medical research study with the promise of free treatment, free food, free transportation, and, if they were to die, a burial stipend for their families. The men suffered from late-stage syphilis, but the doctors did not tell them this. They said that the men had "bad blood," a generic folk diagnosis for a range of possible ailments. The purpose was to study the progression of the disease over time, so the men were not given treatment appropriate for their condition.

At first, the doctors gave the men the best available medication for syphilis, but in small doses that the doctors knew would have no therapeutic effect. The doctors then persuaded their subjects to submit to painful lumbar punctures for the purpose of tracking the ongoing effects of the syphilis by falsely telling them that they were receiving a "special treatment" in the form of a spinal shot. When penicillin was invented and proven to be highly effective for syphilis, the men were neither offered the treatment nor told about its availability. Later in the study, the doctors responded to demands from the subjects for more treatment by providing aspirin, which they called the "pink medicine."[1]

What is most shocking about this now infamous Tuskegee Syphilis Study is that it did not take place in our country's distant history, before modern conceptions of morality or, more specifically, modern views of medical and scientific ethics. The forty-year experiment began prior to World War II but continued until after the *New York Times* reported it on July 26, 1972.[2] This was a full twenty-five years after American war crimes judges in postwar Germany had drafted the "Nuremberg Code" of ethics in response to the Nazi atrocities visited on concentration camp prisoners in the name of medical research. That statement of principles provides that experimental subjects must not only consent to research participation but that they should have "sufficient knowledge and comprehension" of the experiment to make "an understanding and enlightened decision" to participate.[3]

The Tuskegee scandal, along with evidence of other grossly unethical treatments of experimental subjects, led Congress to create a commission to study the treatment of human subjects of research and ultimately to the creation of federal regulations to protect these subjects. These regulations, known as the "common rule" because seventeen different federal agencies have adopted them, require that research that uses federal funds and involves human subjects be reviewed and approved by an institutional review board (IRB).[4] Among other responsibilities, the IRB must determine that risks of the research are reasonable in relationship to anticipated benefits and that they are minimized.[5] The IRB must also ensure that "appropriate informed consent" is obtained from each research subject.[6]

The common rule's informed consent requirement is designed to supply research subjects with all the information they need to perform an autonomous risk-benefit analysis.[7] It states that researchers *must* disclose the following information: the description, purpose, duration, and experimental nature of the study; reasonably foreseeable risks or discomforts to the subject; reasonably expected benefits to the subject or to others; appropriate alternative procedures or treatments that might be advantageous to the subject; extent of privacy and confidentiality of records that identify the subject; availability of compensation or treatment for possible injuries; contact information in case the subject has questions or concerns; and the subject's right of withdrawal from the study at any time without penalty.[8] In addition, an IRB *may* require that other information be given to the subjects when "the information would meaningfully add to the protection of the rights and welfare of subjects."[9]

Independently of the common rule, a requirement that physicians obtain the informed consent of their patients in therapeutic settings became firmly ensconced in American tort law over the course of the twentieth century. The idea that patients have a right to accept or decline medical intervention dates back at least to Judge Benjamin Cardozo's early twentieth-century pronouncement in *Schloendorff v. Society of New York Hospital* that "every human being . . . has a right to determine what shall be done with his own body."[10] The 1957 case of *Salgo v. Leland Stanford Jr. University Board of Trustees* introduced the term "informed consent" into the legal lexicon.[11] In that case, concerning an invasive radiological study of a patient's aorta that left him paralyzed, the court held that the physician was obligated to disclose the risks of the procedure "necessary to an informed consent."[12] Today, depending on the jurisdiction, physicians may face lawsuits for damages if they fail to provide a patient with the information that a reasonable physician would provide in recognition of the patient's right to make an autonomous treatment decision or if they fail to provide the information that a reasonable patient would have wanted in order to make an informed treatment decision.[13] Generally the subjects of mandatory disclosure include the nature of the treatment, the likelihood of success, reasonably foreseeable risks, alternative treatments, and clinical prognosis if the patient declines treatment.[14]

These two distinct but overlapping bodies of law, the common rule and informed consent, create rules designed to protect the autonomous decision making of participants in medical research. In the most common medical research setting, the clinical trial, researchers provide treatment to patients while simultaneously collecting clinical data. In such cases, both sets of rules concerning informed consent apply.[15] When stem cell research leads to the creation of new medical treatments, this regime will govern their testing, and the issues raised will not be unique because those treatments come from stem cells.

The advent of biotechnology and the rise of biomedical research, however, have challenged the doctrine of informed consent to adapt to the context in which medical treatment and scientific research are decoupled, such that subjects participate in research without receiving treatment. In the stem cell context, scientific progress will require the procurement of various bodily tissues and embryos from individuals who are not receiving any treatment as part of the research. How issues of research subject autonomy that arise in this context should be resolved under the principles of informed consent are, in some cases, far less clear. This chapter analyzes these unique issues.

# Nontherapeutic Research Outside
# of the Common Rule

The common rule does not apply to all scientific research that requires the participation of human subjects. It applies only if the research is funded with federal money or if the institution conducting the research has given "assurances" to the federal government that the research will comply with the common rule.[16] In many areas of scientific inquiry, the finite scope of the common rule is of little practical import because most research is supported by federal funds or conducted at research universities and institutions that receive federal funds and have agreed to comply with the common rule in all of their research endeavors.[17] A large amount of research that falls outside of this framework is sponsored by pharmaceutical companies and involves drugs for which FDA approval will be sought, subjecting it to very similar FDA requirements.

Current restrictions on federal funding of hESC research make stem cell science unusual in respect to the common rule. The interest of states, nonprofit foundations, and (to a lesser extent) private firms in funding basic research in the field means that a nontrivial amount of stem cell research in the United States might be conducted in laboratories not subject to the rule's requirements. Many of these funding sources are likely to require that its researchers follow the common rule itself or substantively equivalent requirements—in fact, California's CIRM has already issued proposed regulations that would do this—but there is no legal requirement that they do so.[18] If research not subject to the common rule is conducted by physician-researchers within the context of clinical treatment, the informed consent requirement imposed by tort law would apply. But a potentially important issue in stem cell research is whether scientists conducting research not covered by the common rule are under a legal obligation to obtain the informed consent of human tissue donors—a duty not imposed on most recipients of goods or services.[19]

As it turns out, authority that would support the proposition that stem cell researchers have a legal obligation to obtain informed consent from tissue donors is both sparse and weak. In *Whitlock v. Duke University*, a federal district court considered a claim brought by a diver who had participated in a Duke University study of the effect of deep underwater pressure on the human nervous system. The diver sustained an injury and then sued, claiming that he had not been fully informed of the study's risks.[20] The court concluded that it was "self-evident" that the North Carolina law required informed consent in the context of nontherapeutic research in which "the researcher does not have as an objective to benefit the subject," even in the absence of a statute to that effect, but it offered no explanation of why this was the case.[21] The court's assertion that this conclusion was in fact self-evident was undermined by the Maryland Supreme Court's decision in *Grimes v. Kennedy Krieger Institute, Inc.*, in which that court stated that Maryland law implied no such duty.[22] In any event, *Whitlock* concerned an experiment in which the subject was the object of experimentation, whereas tissue donors merely provide raw materials that are themselves studied or manipulated. This difference, at least arguably, could affect the obligations of experimenters.

In *Greenberg v. Miami Children's Hospital Research Institute, Inc.*, a federal district court in Florida faced the issue in a context more similar to that likely to be of concern in the context of stem cell research. The plaintiffs in *Greenberg* were the parents of children afflicted with Canavan disease (a rare and fatal genetic disorder that occurs mainly in Ashkenazi Jews) and a variety of organizations that work with Canavan sufferers.[23] The plaintiffs made initial contact with Dr. Reuben Matalon in 1987 and requested his help in searching for the gene or genes that cause Canavan disease.[24] To assist Dr. Matalon in his research, the Canavan families supplied him with epidemiological information from a confidential Canavan registry, as well as blood, urine, and autopsy samples from Canavan patients.[25] In 1993, Dr. Matalon successfully isolated the gene responsible for Canavan disease and proceeded to submit a patent application claiming the gene sequence and related therapeutic and diagnostic applications.[26] The patent was issued in 1997 and assigned to Miami Children's Hospital (MCH), Dr. Matalon's employer.[27] A year later, MCH informed the plaintiffs of its intention to enforce its patent rights and to limit Canavan disease testing through a campaign of restrictive licensing of the patent.[28]

The plaintiffs sued Dr. Matalon and MCH, alleging, among other charges, that they had failed to obtain the plaintiffs' informed consent.[29] Responding to a motion by the hospital to dismiss the lawsuit, the court struggled with the question of whether tort law requires informed consent when researchers are neither treating nor experimenting on their subjects but are merely using the subjects' tissues and medical data. It regarded the question as a "novel one in Florida."[30] Eventually, the court determined that the researchers did have a duty to the plaintiffs to obtain their informed consent, but it based its conclusion only on the ground that the defendants had conceded the point in oral argument.[31] Such an explanation can help a court resolve a difficult question in a particular case, but it hardly provides a ringing endorsement of a broad legal principle.

Although *Greenberg* provides no persuasive reasoning on the point, it reaches the right conclusion. A potential subject cannot make a decision to participate in research consistent with the core value of autonomy unless she is sufficiently informed of the costs and benefits involved. It is the usual information disparity between researcher and research subject that justifies the imposition of a duty to obtain informed consent rather than the adoption of the usual rule of *caveat emptor.* This disparity is just as likely to exist whether the subject is merely a tissue donor or the object of study in a therapeutic or nontherapeutic experiment. Further, the application of this principle should not depend on whether the donation requires a physical intrusion, such as when the researcher extracts eggs or draws blood from the donor, or is simply a donation with no physical intrusion, such as when a subject provides a previously drawn blood sample. The informed consent requirement is not necessary to protect the subject's control over her body in the latter example, but it is just as necessary to protect her decisional autonomy.

## Disclosure of Financial Interests

A more difficult issue to resolve is whether the doctrine of informed consent requires researchers to disclose not only the possible harms that a subject might suffer as a result of participation in a research project but also the financial benefits potentially available to the researchers. This question is likely to be particularly important in the context of stem cell research—and more so as the basic science advances and gives way to the development of marketable tests and treatments. The possibility that scientists will benefit financially from the fruits of their research is hardly unique to stem cell research, so it would seem likely that courts would be quite familiar with the question. In fact, it arises in published judicial opinions quite rarely.

The landmark case on the topic is *Moore v. Regents of the University of California.* UCLA physician Dr. David Golde obtained consent from a patient, John Moore, who suffered from hairy cell leukemia, to remove Moore's spleen along with blood and bone marrow.[32] The consent form, however, failed to mention that Dr. Golde and others intended to use the excised tissues for research purposes.[33] Within a few years of Moore's treatment, Dr. Golde established a cell line from Moore's T-lymphocytes—named the Mo cell line[34]—for which the Regents of the University of California obtained a patent.[35] The Regents subsequently licensed the cell line to Genetics Institute and Sandoz Pharmaceuticals, and the licensing earned the university and Dr. Golde substantial royalties.[36] Moore sued Dr. Golde, the Regents, Genetics Institute, and Sandoz, claiming, among other things, a "lack of informed consent."[37]

The California Supreme Court held that Moore's treating physicians had a duty to disclose any commercial interest they might have in the patient's biological tissue before removing the tissue.[38] The court reasoned that patients expect their doctors' therapeutic recommendations to be based entirely on their professional judgment of the patients' best interests and that patients are entitled to know of any information that might undermine the physicians' apparent motive of beneficence.[39] In contrast, the court found that the Regents, Genetics Institute, and Sandoz had no fiduciary duty to Moore and thus owed him no duty to disclose their commercial interests.[40]

Because the defendants in *Moore* either had a therapeutic relationship with the plaintiff or had no direct relationship at all, the decision in that case does not squarely address the disclosure responsibilities of researchers who collect tissues directly from donors in a nontherapeutic research setting, as is likely to be the case when stem cell researchers wish to biopsy tissue or harvest eggs.

Invasive procedures carried out by a researcher with no therapeutic relationship to tissue donors was precisely the context of the *Greenberg* case. After finding that medical researchers must obtain informed consent from their subjects, the *Greenberg* court decided that this principle did not require the researchers to disclose any potential economic interests in the research. The *Greenberg* judge distinguished *Moore* on the basis of the difference between a therapeutic and a nontherapeutic relationship with a subject.[41] The court defended a more limited disclosure requirement in the nontherapeutic context by claiming that extending *Moore*-type duties to medical researchers would be "unworkable and would chill medical research." The *Greenberg* judge also distinguished the situation of research subjects in the two cases by describing subjects in nontherapeutic settings as "donors rather than objects of human experimentation" who participate "voluntarily" and thus should be accorded different treatment from that given to a patient seeking a therapeutic benefit.[42]

The first of these justifications is inapt, and the second exactly backwards. As to the first, there is no reason why disclosure of financial interests would chill research. Surely no reason exists why there would be a differentially chilling effect on *nontherapeutic* research. It is a small burden for researchers who hope to patent biotechnological products or processes and profit from doing so to disclose this possibility as part of the informed consent that they must secure anyway. Research progress would be impeded only if subjects do not wish to donate tissues to researchers who seek personal profits, and promoting research by disguising facts from donors clearly undermines the philosophy of informed consent.

The second justification is backwards because, if anything, research subjects in nontherapeutic settings should be given more, not less, information.[43] The informed consent doctrine exists to protect the autonomy of patients and subjects. The principle that should therefore guide disclosure is materiality. That is, patients and research subjects should be given all information likely to be material to their decision as to whether to participate in research. Possible risks to subjects' health are clearly material, so they must be disclosed. A researcher's favorite color is not material, so there is no need to disclose this information; in fact, disclosure of immaterial facts should be discouraged because it can often create confusion.

The *Moore* court probably was correct in asserting that most patients would want to know if their physician had an economic interest in their treatment in order to identify if there might be a lurking conflict of interest that would call into question the objectivity of the physician's recommendations. All other things being equal, however, subjects who hope to obtain a therapeutic benefit from participation in medical research would be less likely to consider the scientists' economic incentives as material because the potential gains to the subjects from participation are clear and often potentially very valuable. That is, if a patient believes that a particular therapeutic intervention is the best course of treatment, the researcher's potential also to profit from it would almost certainly not cause the patient to reject the treatment, just as the amount of payment a physician stands to receive from the patient's health insurance company is unlikely to be material to the patient's decision to undergo the treatment. In contrast, subjects who stand to gain few or no tangible benefits from research participation are more likely to find the financial interests of the researchers material to their decision as to whether to participate in a study.[44] To these subjects, the perceived social value of the research is likely to be central to their decision to participate. The extent of the researchers' financial stake might, rightly or wrongly, affect subjects' evaluations of whether they should rely on the researchers' demonstrated level of interest in the project as a proxy for such social value.

Financial incentives are especially likely to be relevant to potential subjects when a request for research participation comes from a treating physician who has no direct role in conducting the research. Scientists often pay clinicians for each subject the clinicians enroll in a research study.[45] This arrangement will be particularly common in the context of stem cell research because it will often be efficient for scientists to rely on physicians who treat specific genetic diseases to recruit somatic cell donors with those diseases and to rely on infertility specialists to recruit egg or embryo donors. A patient who believes his physician is requesting a donation of tissue for research without financial inducement is likely to interpret the physician's willingness to make the request as a signal of the importance of the research. In contrast, a patient who knows his physician receives a fee for each donation procured is less likely to make such an inference.

Some medical organizations believe that it is improper for treating physicians to make requests for tissue donation under any circumstances.[46] Others believe that it is unethical for treating physicians to receive compensation for such efforts.[47] It is clearly cost-effective, however, for scientists to use medical personnel who have contact with particular populations to recruit research study participants. An offer of compensation for successful recruitment no doubt encourages clinicians' cooperation in these efforts. Explaining research protocols to potential participants and obtaining their informed consent for participation can be a time-consuming activity. Physicians usually are not expected to work for free in other contexts, and there is no reason why ethics would demand that they do so in the recruitment context. But a proper understanding of the autonomy principle underlying the doctrine of informed consent requires that they disclose their incentives to potential subjects so that those individuals may incorporate that information into their decision-making process.[48]

## Tissues Previously Provided for Non-hESC Purposes

A clinical trial or other medical experiment with a therapeutic component requires, by its very nature, interaction between researchers and research subjects. This is not always the case when a subject's participation consists of providing tissue on which the researcher will then experiment. For experiments on tissues, researcher/subject interaction occurs only if a project requires the extraction of new tissues. A rich potential source of the raw material needed for stem cell research, however, is preexisting tissue collections. These include sperm or ova originally donated for IVF purposes, somatic cells collected in a therapeutic context and stored in tissue banks, and embryos cryopreserved in IVF clinics. In some instances, no consent was ever given to use these tissues for research purposes. In others, consent was obtained to use the tissues for a specific research project, for which the tissue is no longer needed, or for research generally, without specific mention of stem cell research. Whether and what type of consent is required for the use of preexisting tissues for research is an important and un-settled issue for stem cell science.

## THE ROLE OF IDENTIFIABILITY UNDER
## THE COMMON RULE

The relevant legal regime concerning informed consent for the use of preexisting tissue is complex. The common rule applies only to "human subjects," whom it describes as "living indi-vidual[s]."[49] However, the common rule's definition of human subjects includes not only living individuals from whom the researcher directly obtains "data through intervention or in-teraction" but also living individuals about whom a researcher obtains "identifiable private information."[50] This definition clarifies that the original donors of preexisting tissues consti-tute "human subjects" covered by the rule, but it then raises the question as to what constitutes "identifiable information."

The common rule provides that information is identifi-able if "the identity of the subject is or may readily be ascer-tained by the investigator or associated with the informa-tion."[51] According to a policy statement issued by the federal government's Office for Human Research Protections (OHRP), which is responsible for guaranteeing compliance with the common rule, biological samples do not count as being iden-tifiable under the regulations if the researchers cannot link the samples to specific individuals, even if the samples are coded and someone else possesses the key to the code.[52] So, for ex-ample, according to the OHRP's interpretation, if a fertility clinic were to provide stem cell researchers with excess human eggs, the common rule would apply and informed consent would thus be required if the individually identifying infor-mation were provided along with the ova. But the common rule would not apply if the ova were first anonymized (that is, stripped of all individually identifying information), or if the ova were given a code in place of individually identifying information, as long as the clinic agreed never to provide the key to the researchers. Further, the common rule itself exempts from IRB review research involving the "study of existing . . . pathological specimens or diagnostic specimens, if . . . the information is recorded by the investigator in such a manner that subjects cannot be identified."[53] This provision suggests that researchers can legally use, without first obtaining informed consent, tissues provided by third parties (such as tissue banks) that come with identifying information so long as the researchers do not record the identifying information themselves.[54]

There is an even broader loophole in the common rule as well. IRBs may waive the informed consent requirement if they determine that the proposed research poses "only a minimal risk to the subject" and that the research would be "impracticable without the waiver."[55] Because the use of tissues that already exist outside of the donors' bodies would pose no physical risk to subjects, this provision clearly suggests that if a study's purposes require the use of identified tissues and if going back to donors for specific informed consent is impractical, researchers can (with IRB approval) proceed without informed consent.

The common rule appears to exclude embryos from coverage as human subjects.[56] It appears, however, to classify as human subjects both donors of the gametes that have formed an embryo (at least for research that makes use of federal funds or is conducted by an institution that has pledged to follow the common rule in all research). As is the case for gametes and other tissues, there appears to be no federal bar to researchers using "deidentified" embryos for stem cell research without the informed consent of the gamete donors.

## AUTONOMY, NOT PRIVACY

The distinction made by the common rule, and by the OHRP interpretation of it, between identifiable and nonidentifiable tissues is inappropriate because it is not based on the autonomy principle that underlies informed consent requirements. The same is true of the common rule's waiver provision. The identifiability rule protects donors' privacy and the possibility of discrimination or other consequences that a revelation of sensitive medical information might cause—sometimes called "psychosocial harms."[57] The waiver rule turns on the presence or absence of risk to subjects. Neither of these rules, however, makes any attempt to protect the rights of the donors as autonomous actors to decline to participate in research studies for any reason or for no reason at all.

This distinction became salient in the recent case of *Washington University v. Catalona*.[58] When Dr. William Catalona changed employers, he wished to take with him tissue samples from prostate cancer patients that he had collected over many years of treating that condition. A substantial number of the patients asked Washington University, Catalona's former employer, to transfer the tissues to Catalona's custody. To the extent that Washington University and not Dr. Catalona was the legal repository of the tissues, these patients asserted their right to withdraw consent for any further use of their tissues by the university. Although the issue in the case concerned the right to control the tissues as distinct from the right to use them for research, the victorious university contended—and the court did not contradict it—that the common rule permitted it to go right on using the plaintiffs' tissues for research purposes against their wishes so long as it anonymized them.[59]

Perhaps because of the inconsistency between the common rule and the autonomy principle, the National Research Council's 2005 *Guidelines for Human Embryonic Stem Cell Research (NRC Guidelines)* propose that informed consent be required before any gametes, somatic cells, or embryos are used for stem cell research.[60] The approach of the *NRC Guidelines*, however, fails to take the autonomy principle seriously. When researchers must collect tissue specimens from donors, requiring them to obtain informed consent protects the autonomy of all potential human subjects: those who consider all relevant information and subsequently agree to participate in the research endeavor and those who consider the information and decide not to participate. When researchers wish to make use of preexisting tissues originally collected for other purposes, however, it will often be too costly or too burdensome to trace the original donors, such that requiring specific informed consent for use of the tissues for a particular research project will effectively preclude the conduct of the research.[61] This outcome preserves the autonomy of those who would have declined to participate, but it undermines the decisional autonomy of those who would have wished to participate.

How to balance the needs of both groups requires a subtle analysis, not the blunt prohibition proposed by the *NRC Guidelines*. The proper question to ask is whether the use of preexisting tissues for stem cell research without consent would support or undermine what would have been the autonomous choice of most tissue providers had it been feasible to make research-specific individual requests. Answering this question requires a consideration of the type of tissue involved, the circumstances under which the tissue was collected, and whether the tissue is identified or deidentified (because privacy concerns would affect the participation decisions of many subjects).

If a donor provided consent to general research use of his tissue at the time of the donation—often called "blanket assent"—it is appropriate to use the tissue for stem cell research. If the consent was limited to the use of deidentified tissue, then obviously it should be used only if deidentified. If the original consent had no such limitation, no such limitation should be necessary when it is used in stem cell research.

A cogent argument can be made that blanket consent is never truly "informed" consent because the tissue donor lacked all of the information necessary to make an informed decision about whether to permit the use of his or her tissue in the research at issue.[62] The problem with this argument is that it loses sight of the fact that informed consent is not an end in itself but rather a means of satisfying the ultimate goal of protecting the autonomy of research participants. The vast majority of people who provided blanket consent would have provided consent even for stem cell research if researchers had been able to make a specific request at the time of tissue collection. The autonomy of these individuals is enhanced by a less restrictive rule. There is little doubt that some prior tissue donors who provided blanket consent to research use would object to their tissues' aiding stem cell research, especially hESC research. The less restrictive rule admittedly compromises their autonomy, although it does not undermine it completely. Such individuals should be permitted to contact the repository of their tissue and withdraw or amend their consent.

The problem is more difficult when no consent to research use was requested or provided at the time of tissue procurement—for example, if adult tissue was retained after treatment for potential therapeutic purposes or if in vitro embryos were cryopreserved for possible future IVF use and then abandoned by the gamete donors. For most tissues, the identifiable-deidentifiable distinction made by the common rule is appropriate when it is impractical to seek informed consent retrospectively. As long as privacy is protected, it is likely that most individuals would not object to the research use of their banked tissues, but this presumption seems far less likely to be correct if the tissue can be traced to the donor. In contrast, the use of embryos for stem cell research should never be permitted without consent, even if the embryos are deidentified. Empirical research shows that when given the choice, remarkably few couples—fewer than 3 percent according to one study—choose to donate their excess IVF embryos to research. It is not well understood why most IVF patients apparently would prefer to see their excess embryos destroyed than used for medical research, and it doubtlessly would benefit society if these doomed embryos were put to scientific use. It is clear, however, that the principle of supporting autonomy requires the opposite presumption, at least in light of the available empirical evidence concerning the preferences of potential donors.

## Special Embryo Consent Issues
### THE DUAL DONOR PROBLEM

Informed consent is more complicated in the case of embryos than it is for somatic cells or gametes because there are two individuals from whom consent potentially could be obtained. Imagine that a married couple that created embryos for IVF gets divorced and that one spouse wants to donate the cryopreserved embryos for research and one does not. Who controls the disposition of the embryos? This issue could prove quite important in the future if certain embryos—for example, those with rare genetic mutations—have unique value to researchers.

This precise issue arose in *Kass v. Kass,* in which the parties earlier had agreed that if they could not decide how to dispose of their frozen embryos, the unused embryos would be donated to research.[63] Upon divorce, Mrs. Kass sought possession of the embryos for implantation. The New York Court of Appeals (New York's highest court) relied on contractual principles to uphold the parties' contingent agreement to donate the spare embryos to research.[64] In other cases in different jurisdictions, courts have been called upon to resolve disputes in which one spouse wished to use existing embryos for procreation (for his or her own use or for donation to another couple) and the other objected. In all such cases to date, courts have ruled that the interests of the spouse seeking to avoid procreation outweighed the interests of the spouse seeking procreation, whatever the content of prior agreements.[65]

The judicial decisions concerning the disposition of stored embryos have appropriately recognized, more or less, both the foundational principle of freedom of contract and the limitation of that principle when constitutional values are implicated. Contracts to procreate should be unenforceable on public policy grounds because the interest in avoiding procreation has been recognized by the Supreme Court's privacy decisions as being constitutional in nature. When procreation is not at issue, however, a couple's pre-IVF decision about the future disposition of excess embryos should bind them unless they mutually agree to change their instructions. This means that if the Kasses had entered into an agreement at the outset of their IVF treatment that excess embryos would be donated to research, Mr. Kass should be permitted to direct the disposition of the embryos in that way.

It is important to recognize, however, that the issue of control over disposition is distinct from the question of whether scientists may use embryos directed to them for research purposes. Just because Mr. Kass is entitled to turn the Kasses' embryos over to scientists, it does not necessarily follow that those scientists should be permitted to use them for research purposes. Similarly, if a couple legally abandons excess embryos, thus giving the IVF clinic the right to dispose of them, this does not necessarily mean that scientists should be allowed to conduct research on those embryos. The issue of control over the embryos—a question of property rights—needs to be separated from the question of whether research use should be permitted; this question, in turn, properly depends on autonomy concerns.

Federal law is clear on this point, at least for research that falls under the common rule. Because excess embryos are not implanted, they lack standing as "human subjects" under the federal regulations. The two gamete donors (assuming that they are still alive) would both be considered human subjects if the embryos are not deidentified, and the consent of both would be required before the excess embryos could be used for research purposes. As discussed in detail in the previous section, when embryos are at stake, the legal need for informed consent turns on whether they are identifiable, a distinction that confuses privacy and autonomy interests. However, to the extent that dual consent is required, the law resolves the issue correctly.

The autonomy principle that underlies the concept of informed consent requires dual consent, whether or not the common rule applies to the research in question and whether or not the gamete donors are identifiable to the researchers. In this instance, the positions taken by the *NRC Guidelines* and the guidelines promulgated by the American Society of Reproductive Medicine's ethics committee *(ASRM Guidelines)* are appropriate.[66] If one gamete donor would like to see excess embryos used for stem cell research and the other objects, protecting the autonomy of one party requires compromising the autonomy of the other. This conflict obviously cannot be resolved by asking which decision would protect the autonomy of more individuals because the scorecard is even at one to one. In this situation, the relevant question is whose autonomy would be compromised to a greater extent by protecting the autonomy of the other gamete donor. The answer is that disallowing the use of the excess embryos for research would cause less damage. Permitting the use would completely sacrifice the autonomy interest of the donor who does not want to have his or her tissues employed in stem cell research. Not permitting the use would burden the other donor's autonomy interest, but to a far lesser degree: he or she could still choose to participate in stem cell research by donating other gametes.

Even more complex problems would arise if one or both gamete donors were not the same individuals who created the embryos at issue. Assume, for example, that an infertile couple uses donor eggs and sperm to create a number of embryos for implantation into the wife's uterus, the first implantation cycle is successful, and the parents want only one child, making excess embryos available for other purposes. Whose consent is needed before the excess embryos could be used for stem cell research? The courts would almost certainly find that the infertile couple has dispositional control over the embryos. Under the common rule, however, the consent of the gamete donors and not the infertile couple would be necessary before scientists could use the embryos for research purposes.

Here the common rule's identified-deidentified distinction is a sensible proxy for the hypothetical choices of gamete donors when it is impractical to seek their actual choices. If the embryos are deidentified, research use should be permitted. Most individuals willing to allow their gametes to be used for another couple's reproductive purposes would not object to the research use of embryos created from those gametes, so long as there was no risk that such use would violate their privacy. (To be sure, not all gamete donors would feel this way.) This prediction would seem less certain if the genetic information contained in the embryo could be traced back to the donors.

## THE TIMING OF THE INFORMED CONSENT PROCESS

Another unsettled question in the context of excess embryo disposition is when it is proper to obtain informed consent for research use. The *ASRM Guidelines* provide that the process should take place only after a couple attempting IVF has decided to discontinue storing excess embryos.[67] The justification is that postponing a discussion of research use until that time protects couples who are just beginning the IVF process from facing any pressures to donate.[68] The implicit assumption is that patients will believe the physician seeking informed consent would prefer to see excess embryos donated to research or to another couple rather than destroyed and that they will hesitate to choose an option that could disappoint their treating physician. The law in some jurisdictions, however, requires earlier presentation of all options for disposition. The California Code, for example, requires that fertility treatment providers obtain advanced written directives from patients concerning the disposition of excess embryos and that one of the options offered be donation for research.[69]

In this conflict of views, it is easy to side with California and against the ASRM. The approach of the former reinforces the autonomy principle underlying informed consent, and that of the latter undermines that principle. In addition, being informed about the possible uses of excess embryos—including but not limited to research—and being able to direct their disposition prior to the beginning of IVF treatment might make some couples more comfortable with the IVF process. In addition, pre-IVF choice reduces the costs of obtaining informed consent for donation by saving the patients and the clinic staff from having to arrange a meeting after treatment has ended. For all these reasons, it is unsurprising that the vast majority of IVF clinics ask their patients to designate what should be done with their excess embryos prior to treatment.[70]

The ASRM's concern with the possibility of patients' expressing choices that do not express their true preferences can be addressed by ensuring that the informed consent process include an explanation that the couple is free to change its decision at any time. This requirement is already found, in fact, in the common rule.[71] So long as the donors can notify their IVF clinic at any time after they are finished using its services that they have changed their minds and no longer wish to have excess embryos donated to research, any fears of subtle pressure to donate at the beginning of the process are alleviated. Couples who feel pressured to give the "right answer" prior to receiving treatment can simply notify the treating clinic of a "change" in preference when treatment ends.

# 7

# Buying and Selling Human Tissues

The 2005 National Research Council's *Guidelines for Human Embryonic Stem Cell Research* includes the following recommendations:

> No cash or in kind payments may be provided for donating blastocysts in excess of clinical need for research purposes.[1]

> No cash or in kind payments should be provided for donating oocytes for research purposes. Similarly no payments should be made for donations of sperm for research purposes or of somatic cells for use in nuclear transfer.[2]

Among scientific organizations that provide ethical advice, the NRC position is hardly unique. The NIH guidelines for hESC research provide that "no inducements, monetary or otherwise" should be offered for embryo donation.[3] The American Association of Pediatrics is in agreement.[4] In fact, it is hard to find any group in the scientific research or public policy advocacy communities that questions the appropriateness of a no-compensation rule.

This policy consensus has begun to infiltrate the legal regulation of stem cell research, as well as the recommendations of expert panels. President Bush's decision to permit the NIH to fund research on hESC lines created prior to August 2001 came with the caveat that such lines would be eligible for federal funding only if they had been derived from embryos obtained without the payment of compensation.[5] The SCREA, had it avoided the president's veto pen, would have expanded federal funding of hESC research significantly but maintained the no-compensation requirement for embryo donations.[6]

California's Proposition 71 authorized $3 billion in state bonds to fund stem cell research, but it prohibits the payment of a single penny of that money to any tissue donors—including but not limited to gamete and embryo donors—although the direct expenses of donation may be reimbursed.[7] In the summer of 2006, the California legislature expanded this restriction by enacting a law that prohibits any compensation to donors of eggs for purposes of medical research, whether or not state funds are involved.[8] A handful of other states that are supportive of hESC research, including Massachusetts, Connecticut, Maryland, and New Jersey, have enacted targeted no-compensation laws as well, focused on embryos or gametes and on stem cell research specifically or medical research more generally.[9] The pro–stem cell initiative narrowly enacted by Missouri voters in November 2006, which made national headlines as a result of the advertisements featuring actor Michael J. Fox (who suffers from Parkinson's disease) that were criticized by Rush Limbaugh, explicitly precludes compensating any tissue donors.[10]

The breadth of opposition to the idea of compensating donors of tissues for stem cell research is surprising in light of several observations. First, there is widespread belief that fulfilling the potential of regenerative medicine will require a great deal of raw material, be it blastocysts from which hESC lines can be created, sperm and egg cells to create blastocysts, egg cells and adult cells for therapeutic cloning, or other adult tissues for research on hASCs.

Second, there is no vocal opposition to scientists, universities, biotech companies, pharmaceutical companies, state governments, lawyers, or health care providers profiting from stem cell research and regenerative medicine. It is only the potential providers of the raw material, without which the research cannot be done and new medical treatments cannot be developed, who are singled out for remuneration prohibitions.

Third, it is common for medical research subjects to be compensated for their research participation, although the amounts are usually small and often framed as payments for the subjects' time, not the use of their bodies.

Fourth, the remuneration so broadly opposed today was perfectly legal in most cases prior to the start of the recent trend that singles out stem cell research for specific regulatory prohibitions. With one narrow exception, no federal law prohibits compensating individuals for tissues, and the minority of states that regulate tissue sales in general do so haphazardly. In fact, there are thriving markets for some human tissues—most notably sperm and eggs—throughout most of the nation.

## The Law of Tissue Sales

The primary federal law relating to the purchase or sale of human tissues is the National Organ Transplant Act (NOTA). NOTA, enacted in 1984, specifically prohibits—on pain of fine or imprisonment—the buying or selling of human organs, which it defines to include the kidneys, liver, heart, lungs, pancreas, bone marrow, cornea, eye, bone, and skin or any subpart thereof, and any other human organ (or any subpart thereof, including that derived from a fetus).[11] The inclusion in the statute's scope of any "subpart" of any listed organ suggests that even a single skin cell, which conceivably could be used in therapeutic cloning, would fall under the prohibition on sales. However, its scope does not encompass renewable tissues, including blood or sperm.[12] More important, NOTA's reach is limited, on its face, to organs "for use in human transplantation."[13] This language indicates that researchers may buy and donors may sell for research purposes the organs covered by NOTA without running afoul of the statute.[14]

The Uniform Anatomical Gift Act (UAGA) is a state law, but its adoption in all fifty states gives it national scope.[15] The UAGA provides that individuals may donate their entire body or "body parts" for transplantation, therapy, research, or education.[16] The act prohibits the purchase or sale of body parts for use in transplantation or therapy but notably omits research purposes from this prohibition.[17] In addition, the sale prohibition applies only "if removal of the part is to occur after the death of the decedent," so it does not cover transactions involving live donors.[18] For both reasons, this statute appears inapplicable to transactions of the type that might be relevant for obtaining raw materials for use in stem cell research.

Furthermore, neither the NOTA nor the UAGA appears to apply, under any conditions, to gametes, which—especially ova—are likely to be needed in large numbers for stem cell research if the practice of therapeutic cloning becomes widespread. In fact, a federal law criminalizes the donation or *sale* of *HIV-positive* gametes, which seems, by implication, to recognize the validity of purchases involving uninfected gametes.[19]

There is only one federal statute that interferes with the right to buy or sell human tissues for research purposes, and, as noted, its scope is limited. As part of the NIH Revitalization Act of 1993, which provided federal support for fetal tissue research, Congress criminalized any purchase or sale of human fetal tissue procured from induced or spontaneous abortions.[20]

Many states have enacted legislation prohibiting the sale of organs and/or tissues in particular circumstances. Most of these, like NOTA, are specifically limited to organs and tissues for transplant. A minority of states—at least nine—have broader statutes that either clearly prohibit tissue sales for research purposes or appear to do so.[21] A few of these exempt from coverage renewable tissues, such as blood and sperm.[22] At least one state (Virginia) has enacted a sales ban that is broad enough to cover scientific research purposes but that groups eggs with renewable tissues and excludes them from the ban.[23] (Eggs, unlike blood and sperm, are, strictly speaking, not renewable, although the number with which each woman is born is so substantial there is no realistic possibility of running out.)[24] Louisiana, in contrast, does not generally ban tissue sales for research purposes,[25] but it bans the sale of ova for all purposes.[26]

The anomalous nature of the Louisiana egg sales law and the new California statute prohibiting payment for eggs for stem cell research is indicated by the fact that in most states (California included), gametes are actively bought and sold for reproductive purposes. Agencies recruit women as potential egg donors and actively market them to infertile couples who wish to purchase their ova for IVF and, hopefully, the creation of a baby. Typically, potential purchasers can view photos of donors and learn about their physical attributes, health history, and life accomplishments. Some agencies allow the purchasers to conduct live interviews.

Donors who are selected, or hired, typically receive between \$2,500 and \$10,000 for one ovulation cycle, although advertisements in college newspapers routinely offer \$50,000– \$100,000 or more for ova from women with certain physical characteristics or intellectual achievements. (The donation requires that the donor be injected with hormones for 7–10 days, resulting in the hyperstimulation of her ovaries. The eggs are then harvested directly from the ovaries with a needle inserted through the vagina.)[27] The agencies that match purchasers with donors usually receive a service fee from the purchasers above and beyond the payments to the donors. A similar market exists for sperm, although the dollar figures are far lower— \$25–\$100 per donation—and the market is structured slightly differently. Rather than waiting for a purchaser to select a sperm donor, sperm banks that serve as intermediaries usually pay donors directly to provide sperm for the bank.

It is not surprising that more states prohibit the sale of embryos than the sale of other tissues for research purposes. But at approximately thirteen, the number of states with prohibitions is still relatively small.[28] Although some foreign nations prohibit cash payments to embryo donors, there is no federal law in the United States that does so.

To summarize briefly, the full range of human tissues likely to be useful in stem cell research can be bought and sold freely for that purpose in approximately 75 percent of U.S. jurisdictions. The tissues that are prohibited in the remaining jurisdictions vary, and at least some of the state regulations include somewhat ambiguous language that has never been interpreted by courts. Following NOTA's rules concerning the transfer of organs for transplants, many jurisdictions that prohibit tissue sales often explicitly permit payment to donors to compensate for costs incurred in making the donation, including indirect costs such as travel, housing, and lost wages, in addition to the direct cost of tissue extraction.[29]

# Prohibitions of Monetary Inducements

There are several arguments for prohibitions of monetary compensation for the donation of tissues for stem cell research, but none of them bear up under careful scrutiny. Ultimately, there is no convincing reason to use law to interfere with paid transactions between scientists in need of tissues for stem cell research and willing donors who are sufficiently informed concerning the consequences of donation.

## INVOLUNTARINESS AND COERCION

The most widespread argument within the medical research establishment for a no-compensation rule is that payment undermines the voluntariness of the donation decision and, similarly, can be coercive. This view clearly animates the recommendations of the *NRC Guidelines* that no cash or in-kind payments be made to donors of eggs, sperm, or any other cells for stem cell research, with the exception of reimbursement for direct expenses of the donation procedure.[30] It also lies behind the position of the *ASRM Guidelines,* which acknowledge the need to compensate egg donors for IVF but argue that ethics demands a ceiling be placed on payment—specifically, that compensation should never exceed $5,000.[31] A closely linked concern is that payments will result in a greater rate of donation by the economically disadvantaged as a result of their greater need for money.[32]

This argument relies on definitions of what constitutes a "voluntary" decision and what constitutes "coercion" that are unusual, to say the least. A voluntary decision is generally understood as one made of free will. On this definition, a decision to provide tissue is no less voluntary if financial compensation is offered than if it is not. If no material compensation is offered, a potential donor must decide whether the gratification of participating in potentially important research outweighs the risks and inconvenience of undergoing whatever procedure is necessary for donation. If compensation is offered, a potential donor must conduct the same calculation, but an additional factor—the amount of compensation—is added to the positive side of the ledger. The psychic benefits of altruistic donation will appeal to some, cash payments will appeal to others, and these two benefits together will entice still others. As long as the donor is fully informed of the risks and inconveniences involved and may choose to make the donation or not, the decision is an equally voluntary one in both cases.

An action is usually understood to be coerced if the actor is threatened with a negative consequence or penalty relative to a baseline condition of what he otherwise could reasonably expect.[33] On this definition, convincing a person to take an action by offering an enticement to which he would not otherwise be entitled is not any more coercive than it is inconsistent with voluntariness. Providing people with positive options that they might be tempted to accept can create decision stress, and consequently it is not always the case that it is desirable to have more choices rather than fewer, as economists usually assume. But offering people money to do something that they might not choose to do in the absence of compensation is definitely not coercive. The amount of money offered similarly is irrelevant because the distance between the value of the donor's options—that is, the degree to which donating for compensation is favored over the status quo—is irrelevant to the issue of whether the donation is coerced.

Whether or not it is appropriate as a matter of linguistics to call tissue donations that are enticed by a large sum of money "involuntary" or "coerced," the important question is whether prohibiting such transactions is beneficial to the potential donors because it is they whom the involuntariness argument for no-compensation seeks to protect. To use a concrete example, consider a fully informed woman who would agree to donate a cycle of eggs for a fee of $5,000. The "involuntariness" justification for a no-compensation rule (although not necessarily other justifications) must stand or fall on whether a prohibition would help or hurt her.

Quite obviously, the fact that our hypothetical donor would choose to enter into the transaction if permitted to do so shows that she would consider a no-compensation rule to be harmful to her. Perhaps she would choose to enter into the transaction in order to raise funds for food or shelter. Perhaps she would do so in order to be able to afford IVF services to help her conceive her own child or to finance her college education.[34] One can claim that a rule that precludes her from making this choice is in her best interest only by assuming that she is incapable of making a reasoned decision that maximizes her utility given the constraints that she faces. This argument for paternalism is more than a little condescending to potential donors, especially if the requirements of informed consent are taken seriously and researchers clearly explain all of the risks associated with donation before accepting even altruistic donations. When the issue concerns donations that only women are in a position to make—in the stem cell context, the donation of eggs—the suggestion that donors are not capable of making a voluntary decision when money is at issue takes on the added connotation of gender stereotype and discrimination.

This is not to say that regulation for paternalistic purposes is always inappropriate. It is possible that a lack of information or education—or even just the routine operation of mental shortcuts that all people use when required to make decisions based on complex information—will lead individuals to make choices that are bad for them in the long run, even assuming that the quality of the choice is judged by reference to their individual, subjective preferences. When this is the case, paternalism, in the form of preventing people from making certain choices, can be justified. The federal "common rule" concerning government-funded research involving human subjects implicitly recognizes this possibility. Under the common rule, an IRB must independently determine that the potential benefits of any research project justify any risks to subjects. If the risks are too great, the IRB may not approve the research, regardless of whether researchers obtain the informed consent of subjects.

Whether paternalism is appropriate, however, logically does not depend on the availability of cash compensation. If the risks associated with making a particular tissue donation are so great that we, as a society, believe potential donors necessarily would be made worse off by taking the risk, even when taking into account the potential beneficial uses of compensation offered, it logically follows that the risks are certainly too great for an uncompensated donor to accept. Yet most proponents of no-compensation rules in the context of stem cell research believe that altruists should be allowed—and perhaps even encouraged—to serve as tissue donors. The *NRC Guidelines* attempt to defend a no-compensation rule on the ground that payment would "create an undue inducement that could compromise a prospective donor's evaluation of the risks or the voluntariness of her choice."[35] The problem with this claim is that while the offer of money no doubt changes the cost-benefit calculation of a potential donor, there is no good reason to believe that it blinds the donor to items on the cost side of the ledger that she would otherwise take into account.

Although some opponents of compensation who fear that payment undermines voluntariness are motivated by a paternalistic belief that potential donors do not know what trade-offs best serve their interests, others are no doubt motivated by an unstated belief that providing tissue for compensation might maximize the utility of donors (given the constraints they face) but that this should not be so. Women should not have to choose between selling their eggs for science and working in a menial job or feeding their children. Couples should not have to choose to donate excess embryos from IVF treatment in order to afford the IVF treatments they need to have children of their own. All people should be entitled to meaningful work, sufficient food and shelter, and the best medical technology.

The flawed, magical thinking that underlies this reasoning should be obvious. Wishing away difficult or unpleasant choices in no way assists the people who face the choices. In a capitalist society with an unequal distribution of resources, it is inevitable that the inducement of compensation will affect some people more than others and that people of lesser means will be more likely to donate at any given payment level than people of greater means. The well-to-do rarely accept dangerous, dirty, or unpleasant jobs, whereas the near-destitute often do. Society's usual response to this fact of life is not to prohibit the poor from accepting such employment and suggesting that the work should instead be done by altruists but by making conditions as safe as reasonably possible and allowing the market to provide a risk premium for such labor.[36] It is not clear why potential donors of human tissues, when such donors are needed for important medical research, should be treated differently from potential coal miners when such laborers are needed for energy production. Coal mining is unpleasant, often dangerous, and correlated with a reduction in lifespan. These facts rarely lead to suggestions that society should leave the task of coal mining to altruists willing to work for free.

Margaret Radin, who has argued forcefully that government should place limits on what can be bought and sold in the marketplace, concludes that it would be hypocritical to prohibit sales of items solely because monetary inducements create hard choices for some people in our society without simultaneously drastically reorganizing the social allocation of resources to create a far more egalitarian nation.[37] A person faced with a choice between two unpleasant options is not helped by a regulatory authority eliminating the preferred of the two without also offering a better one. Robert Veatch, long a proponent of no-compensation rules in the context of organ donation, now opposes them based on the same reasoning: "a society that [immorally] turns its back on the poor" would be "even more immoral . . . to withhold the right of the desperate to market the one valuable commodity they possess."[38]

Radin's and Veatch's pointed observations are correct, but even they fail to appreciate the full extent of the problem. It is not just the unequal distribution of resources (which in theory could be remedied) that often forces individuals to choose between two goods when they would prefer to have both. The cause of such hard choices is the unalterable fact of resource scarcity. Even if wealth were distributed equally among all citizens, no one would have everything he or she

would like to have in sufficient abundance. Monetary inducements would always tempt some people to barter what they
have for what they would prefer or what they would prefer in
greater quantities. Assuming that researchers obtain informed
consent before providing any monetary inducements, allowing compensation for tissue donations promotes the freedom
and expands the opportunities of potential donors.

Because compensation will most likely increase the
number of donors, its availability has the indirect benefit of reducing the overall risk of the type of donations most likely to
be actually coerced. Consider the following case: Just before
South Korean scientist Hwang Woo-suk's claims to have created human embryos using cloning technology were exposed
as fraudulent, a scandal erupted when word leaked out that
two of the junior members of his research team had donated
eggs for the effort as the result of a shortage.[39] The press reported that these donations raised the fear of coercion, and in
this context, use of that term was appropriate and the donations themselves troubling.[40] Permitting donations from the
subordinates of a researcher presents a serious risk of coercion
because the donor might be threatened, explicitly or implicitly,
with the loss of job benefits or advancement opportunities
that she otherwise would reasonably expect to receive. If Hwang
were able to avoid tissue shortages by offering cash compensation, his junior scientists would almost certainly never have
found themselves in a situation in which they felt compelled to
donate.

The greatest risk of coerced tissue contributions, outside
of the Hwang context, is likely to arise when family or friends
suffer from diseases under study and the number of volunteer
donors is insufficient to support the research. In this situation,
potential donors might perceive that a refusal to donate will be

punished with social ostracism. Again, the more people who are enticed by compensation to make voluntary donations, the lower the likelihood that coercion of this type, which is extremely difficult for researchers or policy makers to detect and police, will take place.

## ANTI-COMMODIFICATION

A second common argument in support of no-compensation rules is that treating tissues as marketable commodities is an affront to human dignity that harms society as a whole.[41] Implicitly, this argument suggests that no-compensation rules are justified not as an effort to paternalistically protect potential donors, but rather to protect the rest of us from the consequences of such transactions. Radin suggests that permitting gifts but prohibiting sales can be appropriate when the use of "market rhetoric" in the conception of the interrelationship between people and a good "creates and fosters an inferior conception of human flourishing."[42] In other words, treating an item that is fundamental to personhood in the realm of market transactions suggests a commensurability between personhood and money that devalues the former. Somewhat more bluntly, Leon Kass, the former chair of the President's Council on Bioethics, puts the point this way: "If we come to think about ourselves like pork bellies, pork bellies we will become."[43]

For Radin, the potential harms of commodification justify child adoption but prohibit baby selling: if babies could be sold for cash, both babies and the adults they would grow into—as well as their individual attributes—would be viewed as commodities, and a widespread perception of people as commodities would be socially destructive.[44] Even assuming that Radin's empirical claim is correct in this context, the question remains as to whether permitting compensation for *human tissues* would have the same negative social effects as permitting compensation for *human beings* themselves. For such an analogy to be persuasive, we would need broad social agreement—which almost certainly does not exist—on a theory of personhood that includes within its definition every individual human cell. Otherwise, to borrow Kass's analogy, although we might well come to view disembodied human tissues like pork bellies, there is no reason to fear that we will come to view persons like pork bellies.

## Adult Tissues

Of the types of tissues potentially needed for stem cell research, specialized adult tissues present the clearest example of the weakness of the anti-commodification argument. Suppose, for example, that a researcher wished to obtain skin cells from persons with a particular rare genetic mutation, with the hope of creating an hESC line containing the mutation via therapeutic cloning. An anti-commodification argument for prohibiting the scientist from compensating the stem cell donors would emphasize the potential psycho-social harms that such market transactions would create. But what social meaning is expressed by the sale of skin cells? One possible interpretation is that our society considers human beings to be mere commodities, commensurable with toasters and widgets. But this interpretation requires equating the moral worth of skin cells to that of human beings.

A far more plausible interpretation of the social meaning of such a transaction is that it reflects not at all on human dignity because what it means to be human transcends a handful of particular cells.[45] We all shed cells naturally every day, but few if any among us grieve for the loss of a portion of our humanity as a result, simply because we do not view particular cells as central to what makes us what we are. Organs that are necessary for survival might reasonably be viewed differently. Selling a heart (while alive) might be morally equivalent to selling a person because each of us requires our heart in order to flourish as a human. But this is the type of extreme exception that proves the rule.

### Embryos

On one view, embryo sales create the greatest risk of undermining human dignity and causing psycho-social harms and thus present the strongest case for a no-compensation rule. Since embryos could potentially become children, the sale of embryos seems most closely analogous to the selling of a person. It is thus not surprising that more states have prohibited the sale of embryos than the sale of somatic tissues or gametes.[46]

There are several problems with this view, however. First, as Chapter 2 discusses in detail, there are obvious differences between early-stage embryos and children—including, but not limited to, a lack of neural function and consciousness— and these differences undermine arguments that the former possess the attributes of personhood. In vitro embryos lack even the potential to become persons without severe human intervention, distinguishing them from in utero embryos.[47]

Second, for people who equate in vitro embryos with children, even the uncompensated donation of embryos for research purposes is inappropriate. Unlike the uncompensated adoption of children, which results in treatment of the children in a way that is appropriate to their status as persons, the donation of embryos for research results in the use of the embryos for the sole benefit of others. In other words, if the premise that embryos are persons is accepted, it is the use of embryos for research that is the fundamental problem, not the market rhetoric that might accompany such use if the compensation were to be permitted.

Third, a compelling argument can be made that given the primary role that the IVF process currently serves in the production of embryos, prohibitions on compensation for embryo donation could undermine society's special respect for the dignity and value of human life. IVF treatment can cost tens of thousands of dollars, and most people unable to conceive on their own are not fortunate enough to have health insurance that covers such costs.[48] With compensation for excess embryos created through the IVF process, many infertile couples could afford what would otherwise be prohibitively expensive. If the ability to procreate is an important element of personhood, permitting those in need of IVF to receive compensation for excess embryos, and thus to defray the cost of treatment, can promote human flourishing rather than undermine it.

### Eggs

The sale of human eggs presents the strongest case for a no-compensation rule, but the argument is ultimately unavailing. The problem is not, as is sometimes argued, that eggs are critical to giving life, which is in turn an important attribute of personhood.[49] Selling one's ovaries might be harmful to human dignity on this ground, but selling a cycle of eggs does not, in itself, interfere with the ability of the seller to fulfill an essential element of personhood, because every woman is born with far more eggs that she could ever actually need for reproductive purposes. The problem is that selling eggs, at least when not done in connection with the creation of embryos for IVF, also requires selling the right to conduct an intrusive bodily invasion to procure them. Bodily integrity, unlike eggs, might reasonably be viewed as necessary for human flourishing, such that permitting its commodification could undermine respect for human dignity.

As noted above, however, the sale of eggs in the IVF context is widespread. According to the Centers for Disease Control, more than 14,000 cycles of IVF and related procedures are attempted each year in the United States using donor eggs.[50] A recent Google search for "egg donation + compensation" returned 41,500 results.[51] There is no evidence that indicates this extraordinarily active tissue market undermines the dignity of either persons or women in particular. In fact, it is not even clear how we would measure or even recognize such effects. But even if we assume for the sake of argument that this example of tissue commodification causes the type of psychosocial harms that many proponents of no-compensation rules fear, permitting a slight expansion of the market to include egg donations for research purposes is unlikely to have much of a marginal effect—and certainly not enough of a marginal effect to justify the constraints on scientific progress.

The sale of eggs for IVF is in fact much more troubling from the commodification perspective than the sale of eggs for stem cell research because IVF donors routinely are selected, and compensated, on the basis of specific physical attributes or talents.[52] The clear social message of the IVF egg donation system, in which height, weight, high SAT scores, musical ability, or modeling experience often demand higher prices, is that prettier, smarter, thinner, or more accomplished women are more valuable than others. This message presumably would be absent in the research context, in which genetic diversity might be valued but no specific attributes would be prized over others. The fact that only members of one gender can contribute the large number of eggs that might eventually be needed for stem cell research renders theoretically possible the development of a dehumanizing view of women as inputs to scientific research. Not only does such a development seem far-fetched, however, but it is also unclear how the consequence would be less likely if altruistic donation were permitted and prohibitions were levied only on compensation.

## CROWDING OUT ALTRUISM

A completely different argument against compensation emphasizes the negative effect that the availability of compensation theoretically could have on the practice of altruistic donation. Two versions of the concern about the "crowding out" of altruism can be distinguished, although proponents often conflate the two. One version seeks to protect the ability of altruism to flourish in society. In the book that is the standard citation for the crowding out theory, *The Gift Relationship,* Richard Titmuss argues against paid blood donation by claiming that allowing the market to operate can "place men in situations in which they have less freedom or little freedom to make moral choices and to behave altruistically if they so will."[53] The other version is entirely consequentialist in nature: the availability of compensation might result in fewer donations to medical research because fewer potential donors would be induced by money than by the opportunity to be altruistic. The UAGA lists this concern among the reasons that it prohibits payment for posthumous organ donations for transplant purposes.[54]

The former concern seems implausible on its face in the stem cell research context. If some researchers offer compensation to donors of research tissues, this would not in any way preclude altruistic donation. Any donor motivated entirely by a desire to help the ill or promote scientific progress who wished not to be tainted by compensation would be perfectly free to decline payment. Of course, some, and perhaps many, people who would have been willing to provide uncompensated donations probably would accept payment if it were offered them. If so, however, the acceptance of compensation suggests that such individuals find compensation more attractive than the warm glow of altruism, not that the market has infringed the freedom of those who wish the opportunity to give altruistically.

The latter concern raises a serious empirical question: would the availability of compensation convince more potential altruists not to donate than it would persuade non-altruists to donate? To understand the theoretical problem, consider the following hypothetical example. Assume that (1) a research project requires one hundred women to donate ova; (2) in a world in which payment for ova donation were prohibited, one hundred altruists would donate, satisfying the project's needs; (3) women are routinely paid $5,000 to donate ova for other research projects. Because of the availability of payment, the one hundred would-be altruists might perceive ova donation as an inherently commercial activity in which they have no interest in participating, rather than as a charitable or humanitarian one that they find enticing, and consequently they might refuse to donate. Put slightly differently, commercialization might reduce the psychic benefit of volunteerism, thus reducing the desirability of altruism and reducing the amount of it. (Or viewed from the opposite perspective, a no-compensation rule might encourage altruism that otherwise would not exist.) Of course, for this to imperil the research project in question, there would have to be fewer non-altruists induced by the possibility of payment than altruists turned off by it.

There is no research that definitively demonstrates the empirical ratio between what might be called "offended altruists" and "non-altruistic sellers" in any particular context. However, two relevant studies suggest that compensation is likely to attract more research participants than it repels. A survey of blood donors in the United States, where cash payments for blood have been virtually nonexistent for more than three decades,[55] found that the number of donors who said they would be *encouraged* to donate in the future by various incentives minus the number who would be *discouraged* by those incentives was positive—and in most cases quite substantially so— for every race, every educational level, both genders, and every age group, with the exception of people over age fifty-five.[56] In a survey of blood donors in New Zealand, 76 percent of the respondents said that they would continue to give blood for free if other donors were paid, while only 6 percent said that they would not.[57]

As donation becomes more inconvenient, painful, or risky, the number of potential altruists is likely to decline, rendering any crowding out of offended altruists by the existence of a market less significant. Many altruists might be willing to donate sperm for stem cell research without monetary inducement, in the belief that helping the cause of science is reward enough. It seems plausible, although far from certain, that a significant number of these altruists might be dissuaded from donating if researchers were to pay for sperm, in which case donating sperm might appear indistinguishable from making a cash donation equal to the market price of sperm but would be significantly less convenient.

In contrast to sperm donation, there are likely to be far fewer altruistic egg donors. The donation procedure is painful, is accompanied by the risk of bleeding and infection, and carries a small but nontrivial risk of substantial medical complications, including hospitalization and, in extreme cases, infertility. So payment is likely to be necessary if the needs of stem cell researchers are to be met.

Press reports of the efforts of one company, Advanced Cell Technology, to recruit egg donors for therapeutic cloning research, although confined to a single anecdote, appear to support this hypothesis. That company's scientists reported that a six-month effort to recruit egg donors for no compensation failed because women who initially came forward declined to participate when they learned about what was involved.[58] Another relevant fact is that countries that prohibit the compensation of egg donors for IVF purposes face donor shortages that do not exist in the United States, and black markets prosper.[59] In the United Kingdom, where cash payments for IVF egg donations are prohibited (beyond a token amount and compensation for expenses), demand for egg donations substantially exceeds the supply of altruistic donors.[60] Certainly some women will choose to donate eggs solely for the progress of science and the benefit of humanity, just as some choose to donate ova for IVF solely for the privilege of helping an infertile couple achieve a dream. But the number is likely to be limited.

## INCREASING THE COST OF RESEARCH

A final argument against permitting compensation for research tissue is that doing so will increase the cost of conducting research and, consequently, reduce the amount of research and the number of medical advances. This concern is rarely articulated by scientists or bioethicists, but it has been raised by legal analysts in several different forms. Two versions of the claim—that permitting compensation will increase uncertainty over ownership of tissues and increase transaction costs— have little logic to support them in the context of stem cell research. A third version—that the direct costs of conducting research will increase—is likely to be true, but it does not provide a compelling basis for no-compensation rules.

In its landmark decision in *Moore v. Regents of the University of California,* the California Supreme Court addressed John Moore's claim that he was entitled to compensation from his physician and the University of California when leftover tissue from his splenectomy was used for commercial research purposes.[61] In ruling for the defendants on this claim, the court raised the concern that if it validated Moore's claim, biotechnological research would be hampered by "uncertainty about how courts would resolve [future] disputes between specimen sources and specimen users."[62]

This concern seems misplaced, at least for prospective tissue donations. Any potential uncertainty could be resolved by a clear specification by researchers and donors of the terms of their transactions and the future compensation, if any, due to the donors. If potential downstream users of tissues, such as biotechnology companies that purchase licenses to exploit patented stem cell inventions, find future obligations to donors (such as royalties based on commercial success) too constraining, researchers would most likely insist that any compensation be fixed and paid at the time the tissue is donated and that donors disclaim any interest in future inventions or developments.

A related concern, that increased costs of negotiating tissue donations will inhibit medical research, is also a red herring because the alternative to tissue sales is not the unimpeded right of researchers to claim any tissue that might advance their research.[63] The informed consent requirement ensures that researchers must communicate in a substantive way with potential donors prior to using their tissues. In practice, any negotiations over compensation probably would be conducted as part of this interaction.[64] Documenting the terms of a commercial arrangement conceivably could entail some marginal transaction costs, but these should be minimal.

A third concern, that the permissibility of compensation would increase the direct cost of research, requires a more detailed evaluation.[65] If the willingness (or lack thereof) of potential tissue donors to make uncompensated donations is static, allowing scientists the freedom to compensate donors would not increase the cost of any research project that would be conducted under a no-compensation regime. When tissue donations would involve little pain or risk and when a wide range of donors would be satisfactory—for example, donors of generic skin cells—researchers likely would be able to collect as much raw material as would be necessary for their purposes without offering compensation. Where there are enough altruists to satisfy all research needs, the market-clearing price will be $0.

For tissues that are difficult or risky to collect (such as human eggs) or for unique tissues (such as those from donors with unusual diseases or genetic mutations), the market-clearing price for the necessary quantity of tissue might be considerably greater. If so, the cost of research would be higher if compensation were allowed than if it were not, but this result cannot be counted as a strike against a system that permits compensation. Under a no-compensation regime, scientists would have no choice but to abandon the research; if compensation were permitted, they would have the option of pursuing the research if they (or their funding sources) believed that the potential benefits justified the costs.

Consider the following simple example: Assume that to develop a new treatment for disease X, researchers predict that they will need one thousand human egg donors in order to create embryonic stem cell lines via therapeutic cloning. Assume also that there are one hundred altruists willing to donate their ova to the research without compensation, but the remaining nine hundred donors can be recruited for the painful and somewhat risky procedure only if $5,000 per donor is offered as an inducement.[66] When egg sales are permitted, the researchers have four options: (1) they can collect eggs from the altruists for free and pay the non-altruists $5,000 each; (2) they can pay all one thousand donors $5,000 each if they believe equity requires that the altruists be compensated if others are compensated; (3) they can attempt to make do with one hundred donors; or (4) they can cancel the project. If egg sales are prohibited, however, the researchers have only options (3) and (4). Thus, having the *option* of purchasing the gametes strictly dominates not having the option.

The problem with this analysis is that the population of altruists is probably dynamic rather than static, and its number is likely to depend on whether compensation is permissible. As the crowding out concern suggests, if some tissue donations are compensated, the perception among potential donors of the social meaning of donation will change, and some potential altruists might exit the donor pool, making them unavailable even to researchers who choose not to offer compensation. Altruists might also exit the donor pool if and when the availability of compensation eliminates tissue shortages and leads them to believe that their altruism is unnecessary for scientific progress. A different but related effect—and probably a far more significant one—is that some portion of potential altruistic donors would remain in the pool but demand compensation. For these subjects the warm glow of altruism would be sufficient for them to make uncompensated donations if no other payment were allowed, but they would hold out for monetary compensation if they knew it was available. For this population, the possibility of compensation will not cause a shift in the perceived social meaning of donation, but it will cause a shift in the perceived social meaning of accepting a low price (that is, $0). Whereas accepting $0 when scientists can offer no more means that one is a good citizen, accepting $0 when more could be paid means that one is a chump.

For these reasons, it is probably the case that the research that could be conducted under a no-compensation regime would be more expensive to conduct if compensation were permissible. The question is whether this effect is sufficient to justify a no-compensation rule for research tissues.

The fundamental problem with prohibiting tissue sales based on this effect is that there is no clear basis for distinguishing between tissue donors and other individuals who provide socially useful goods or services—in the context of biomedical research or any other. Exactly the same type of argument could be made in favor of prohibiting compensation of stem cell researchers, to use just one of a near-infinite number of possible examples. If such compensation were prohibited, we would have many fewer researchers, of course, but some scientists would work for free, and a few individuals who are not now scientists might join the profession because they would find scientific research a more attractive pursuit if it were divorced from the realm of commerce. Not very much science would be done, but what science survived would be done for a lower monetary cost than society must pay for it now.

We permit the compensation of scientists because of our implicit determination that it is worth the extra cost of having to pay the few scientists who might work for free in order to ensure that more science (hopefully something close to the socially optimal amount) will be conducted. Proponents of a no-compensation rule for tissue donation on the grounds that it would increase the direct costs of research should bear the burden of demonstrating why tissue donation ought to be treated differently than the vast array of goods and services for which our society permits compensation. Proponents may not satisfy this requirement by claiming that such donations should not be treated like other goods or services because their source is the human body or by claiming that financial rewards might cause some people to feel undue pressure to donate. Such contentions would effectively shift the argument from an increase in the costs of research to anti-commodification or involuntariness, arguments that have already been considered and found wanting.

## Alternatives

For all the reasons described above, none of the arguments for prohibiting the compensation of tissue donors are convincing, whether their premise is that payment will harm donors, potential altruists, scientific progress, or society more generally. The most rational policy is to permit stem cell researchers to offer payment to tissue donors if and when doing so is necessary for useful research to proceed, with the caveat that informed consent requirements must be observed.

Although an intuitive distaste for the buying and selling of human tissues is difficult to justify with logic, especially given the potential medical value of stem cell research, no-compensation rules appear to be gaining rather than losing support in the early years of the stem cell century. If the medical research and policy-making communities remain unalterably opposed to cash compensation, it is important to realize that there are less restrictive alternatives to a complete compensation ban that might be acceptable to no-compensation advocates while at the same time minimizing the risk to scientific progress.

One possibility is to carefully structure how cash compensation is framed rather than ban it altogether. This approach might explain why many state laws that prohibit payment of "valuable consideration" for human tissue (and the federal NOTA, which prohibits payment for organs in the context of transplants) permit compensation of donors for costs incurred, time spent, and wages lost.[67] It also might help explain the ASRM's position that it is morally permissible to pay oocyte donors up to $5,000, but not more, in recognition of the fifty-six hours that the organization estimates are required for the donation process;[68] the position of a New York State Task Force on Life and the Law that "gametes and embryos should not be sold, but gamete and embryo donors should be offered compensation for the time and inconvenience associated with donation";[69] and the standard claims of egg donor agencies that this is precisely the basis on which they offer compensation to their donors.

In one sense, these distinctions are at best merely semantic and at worst dishonest.[70] Whether scientists say they pay egg donors for their time and inconvenience or for their ova does not affect any tangible aspect of the exchange. If payment amounts exceed the out-of-pocket costs of donating, the donors are reaping material gains in exchange for providing tissues, and a market price is implicitly set. But whether society is harmed by market transactions involving tissues certainly depends, at least in part, on the social framing of the exchange.

Another option is for researchers to provide in-kind compensation to donor groups. Although most supporters of no-compensation rules oppose in-kind compensation just as strongly as they do cash compensation, certain kinds of in-kind compensation can carry less of a connotation that tissue donation monetizes the value of human beings, and they can thus prompt less opposition. In the United Kingdom, the law prohibits cash payments above a token sum to women who donate ova for IVF, but clinics may provide discounted IVF treatment to egg donors as compensation.[71] In a recent decision, that country's Human Fertilisation and Embryology Authority agreed that researchers may offer the same in-kind benefit to women in return for their agreement to share harvested eggs with researchers rather than with other IVF patients.[72] Since IVF treatment has a market price, it is not difficult to calculate the implicit payment that any particular woman receives for providing eggs. But payment in infertility treatment rather than in cash probably weakens the public perception that bodily tissues are being traded in the market as if they were widgets.

The way blood commonly is procured in the United States exemplifies this point. About half of blood donors in this country receive some kind of compensation for their contributions.[73] In some cases, such as the gift of a T-shirt, the compensation is minimal and might not encourage many people who otherwise would not donate blood to do so. In other cases, the compensation is more significant and undoubtedly provides a participation incentive. Many companies offer their employees time off of work to give blood, a clear inducement to any workers who mind giving blood less than they mind working.[74] In other cases, donors are promised preferential treatment if they ever need a blood transfusion in return for their contributions.[75] In these cases, blood donation is a barter transaction. Yet because cash compensation is virtually nonexistent, most Americans perceive the blood donation regime to be entirely altruistic and outside of the market.

In 2001, a group representing patients with pseudoxanthoma elasticum (PXE), a genetic disease that affects the connective tissue, negotiated with researchers for a share of future patent rights and licensing control in return for identifying and soliciting tissue donations from families affected with the disease, along with fund-raising assistance.[76] The group pledges to use these rights to ensure screening tests, and treatments are available to all who need them at an affordable cost. This type of arrangement also might strike many as a compensation method more compatible with the nature of the human person than cash payments to individual tissue donors.

## Consistency with Organ Transplantation Rules

The argument for permitting the compensation of tissue donors in the stem cell research context has obvious implications for the governing law of tissue transplants, which—between NOTA and the UAGA—clearly prohibits sales for the purpose of transplantation. The no-compensation rule for organ transplants is commonly defended with the same arguments criticized in this chapter, and these arguments suffer most of the same shortcomings in the transplant context as they do in the research context. More than 94,000 Americans are currently on waiting lists for transplant organs, and approximately 6,500 die each year because demand so far outstrips supply.[77] Only a minority of Americans agree to make a cadaveric donation of their organs without compensation, even though agreeing to serve as a donor after one dies quite obviously requires no effort, inconvenience, or pain to the donor. Against this background, it is overwhelmingly likely that thousands of lives could be saved and thousands more greatly improved every year if the law were reformed to permit compensation for cadaveric transplantation organs.[78] This said, however, there are arguments for a no-compensation rule in the organ transplant context that do not apply to the stem cell research context. In other words, a case for permitting tissue sales in the research context is stronger. This is an important point to recognize because it indicates that the principles of consistency and coherence in public policy do not necessarily require that the prohibitions on the sale of transplant organs be lifted if tissue sales for research are permitted.

Transplant organs are a private good in a way that research tissues are not. If all prohibitions on buying and selling organs for transplant were lifted, significant changes in the distribution of those organs would result, with those willing and able to pay the most jumping to the front of the queue rather than those who are the sickest or have been on the waiting list for the longest time. There are arguments for such changes, and, to be sure, there are also ways the law could be structured to avoid or minimize the problems. However, there are serious issues of equity across economic classes that generally cut against eliminating no-compensation rules for transplant organs.

Such concerns are not implicated in the research context. Of course, "richer" researchers—that is, those with more funding—might have better access to tissues than others. This disparity does not raise serious equity concerns, however, because the distribution of research funds is correlated, at least broadly speaking, with the worthiness of the research. Government research funding is allocated based on the perceived social importance of a research topic and the quality of the researchers and their grant proposals. Commercial funding is allocated on the basis of what research capital markets believe has the greatest chance of leading to the creation of commercially useful tests and treatments.

# 8

# Default Rules for
# Tissue Donations

Recall John Moore's lawsuit against the University of California. As Chapter 6 explained, Moore prevailed in his claim that his physicians failed to inform him of their financial interests in using his tissue for research purposes. His case received celebrity, however, primarily for a portion of the lawsuit that he lost. Moore claimed his doctors had stolen his spleen.[1]

The thirty-two-year-old Moore was working on the Trans-Alaska Pipeline in 1976 when his gums began to bleed and his body became covered with bruises. He was diagnosed with hairy cell leukemia, a rare blood cancer in which malignant blood cells that appear hairy under a microscope flood the spleen. The average spleen weighs about half a pound; Moore's weighed at least fourteen pounds and considerably more than that according to some sources. Given six months to live, Moore sought treatment at UCLA from hematologist Dr. David Golde. Under Golde's supervision, UCLA performed a splenectomy that saved Moore's life: the patient would go on to live another twenty-five years. Unsurprisingly, when Moore left the hospital, he did not ask for his spleen, and no one offered it to him.

For the next seven years, at Golde's instruction, Moore traveled from his home in Seattle to UCLA from time to time so that the doctor could obtain samples of the patient's blood, sperm, and semen. Moore's trips to Los Angeles for lab work had a therapeutic purpose, as they allowed Golde to physically examine Moore in addition to drawing fluids. But it was clear that Golde's interest in drawing and maintaining the fluids himself went beyond a concern for Moore's health. When a healthy Moore complained about the expense of the travel and asked if he could have a physician in Seattle collect the tissue samples and send the results to Golde, the doctor started paying Moore's travel expenses from his research funds, including lodging at a posh Beverly Hills hotel.

By the early 1980s Golde had discovered that the unusual blood cells in Moore's spleen could be used to produce potentially valuable proteins. In 1981, Golde and UCLA agreed to a three-year deal (later extended to four) with a Massachusetts biotech firm called Genetics Institute. Under the deal, the institute would have exclusive use of the "Mo" cell line—that is, the line Golde developed from Moore's T-lymphocytes—would pay UCLA $110,000 a year to fund Golde's research, and would give Golde 75,000 shares of the private company's stock in return for the doctor's consulting services. When Genetics Institute held an initial public offering in 1986, its stock became worth nearly $2,250,000.[2] In 1983 Golde sought patent protection for the Mo cell line, and a patent was granted the following year. Just after Golde filed the patent application, he asked Moore to sign a consent form granting the University of California "all rights . . . in any cell line or any other potential product which might be developed from the blood and/or bone marrow obtained from me." Moore refused and then avoided several increasingly desperate attempts by Golde to obtain his signature.

Ultimately, Moore sued Golde and the university. The California Superior Court dismissed Moore's claim on all counts, and that decision was appealed. The California Supreme Court issued a split decision of sorts. It ruled that Golde had an obligation under the informed consent doctrine to reveal his financial interests to Moore, thus permitting a trial to go forward on whether Golde had breached this duty. (This claim was then settled out of court.) But it held that the facts alleged by Moore, even if true, could not support his claim for the conversion—or theft—of the spleen.[3] This portion of the *Moore* decision is quite significant to understanding the law relating to tissue sales, although not for the reasons usually assumed.

## Property Rights in Tissues

The *Moore* court's refusal to recognize the theft of John Moore's spleen is widely misinterpreted in academic journals and the popular press as standing for the proposition that the law recognizes no property rights in human tissues or, at a minimum, that the law recognizes no property rights in disembodied tissues.[4] This understanding of the landmark decision is far broader than what the court's reasoning can support, and it is clearly inconsistent with a wide range of accepted legal principles.

The usual metaphor for property among contemporary legal theorists is that of a bundle of sticks.[5] A full bundle of property rights includes the ability to use the item as the owner sees fit, to exclude others, and to transfer freely or dispose of the item for any reason. But in any society, property rights are rarely absolute. The law regulates our enjoyment of much of what we commonly think of as property. The law often limits our dominion over property or, to follow the popular metaphor, deprives us of some of the sticks in the bundle. For example, if you own a parcel of land in an urban area, tort law and zoning restrictions will prevent you from building a dynamite factory on it. Such regulation does not mean that you do not own the land or that you lack property rights in it. It means only that there are some limitations on your use rights, and, thus, you lack all of the sticks that might possibly be found in the bundle. With this understanding of property, even a cursory glance at a range of statutes and judicial decisions reveals that individuals possess substantial property rights in their own tissues and that it is possible to enjoy property rights in tissues of others that have been separated from the body.

As to the former point, we need to look no further than the common law doctrine of informed consent and its regulatory doppelganger, the common rule, for evidence that demonstrates we clearly enjoy a right to exclude others from using our tissue.[6] Similarly, the law provides us with the complete right to our tissues against the claims of others who need them, even if their need is great and ours is small. This principle is illustrated quite nicely by the case of *McFall v. Shimp*. McFall faced death without a bone marrow transplant, and the only potential donor with the right tissue match to minimize the likelihood of immune system rejection was his cousin Shimp. When Shimp declined to make the needed donation, which is briefly painful put poses virtually no long-term medical risks, McFall asked a court to order Shimp to provide the marrow. The court ruled for Shimp, citing his absolute right to exclude others from the use of his bodily tissues, no matter the circumstances.[7]

The UAGA provides individuals with the right to donate organs after death for transplants or research. It thereby recognizes an important property right to bequeath tissues.[8] Similarly, several judicial decisions have upheld the ability of decedents to bequeath their sperm to nonfamily members against challenges by unhappy relatives.[9] Federal law, in the form of the NOTA, provides us the right to donate for transplant tissues that are renewable or not necessary for survival even while we are alive.[10] As described in Chapter 6, courts have upheld the right of gamete donors to contract for the future disposition of embryos created for IVF but never used for that purpose, especially when there is no fear that procreation will be forced upon one of the donors against his or her will.[11] These examples of clear rights to make altruistic, testamentary, and contractual transfers of tissues and gametes, like the power to exclude others, indicates the existence of substantial private property rights in these items.

As to the potential for property rights in tissues emanating from others, Justice Broussard pointed out in dissent in *Moore* that if John Moore's spleen had been stolen from his physician's laboratory, there would have been little doubt that the intruder would be liable for conversion.[12] This is no doubt correct. One federal court found that a researcher who destroyed a rival's cell line was liable for conversion,[13] and more recently the University of California at Irvine settled civil lawsuits brought by infertility clinic patients when a physician there sold their eggs to other patients.[14] Clearly, then, the fact that a tangible item is a tissue that was extracted from the human body does not render it incapable of the status of private property in the same way that a chair, a silk scarf, or a Van Gogh painting can be private property.

## Discerning the Default Rules of Tissue Transactions

If individuals enjoy property rights in their bodily tissues and if the law in most states poses no obstacle to individuals' selling their tissues for use in stem cell research, a range of different terms could conceivably govern tissue donations. Notwithstanding the legal permissibility of compensation, individuals might agree to contribute their tissues for research without receiving any. The lack of a no-compensation rule certainly would not mandate payment, and for any particular research need, there might be a sufficient number of altruistic donors so that researchers would see no need to offer compensation. This case is especially likely when the tissues required are broadly available in the population—that is, scientists are not limited to donors with a specific and unusual genetic makeup—and the tissues can be procured with minimal physical discomfort.

When stem cell researchers choose to compensate donors, the compensation could take a variety of forms. The most obvious possibility is that donors could receive a fixed cash payment based on the desirability of their particular tissues. Consider, for example, Ted Slavin, a hemophiliac who developed unusually high concentrations of hepatitis B antibodies as a result of being exposed to the virus through repeated tainted blood transfusions. Slavin's antibodies were uniquely valuable for the creation of a hepatitis B vaccine, so he started a business selling his blood serum. According to an article in the *New York Times Magazine,* he charged up to $10 per milliliter.[15]

If the usefulness of an individual's tissue is less clear to researchers, they might choose to compensate donors with a percentage of future profits from licensing income, contingent on the tissue leading to a commercially viable product. Another possible approach would be to offer various forms of in-kind compensation, such as reduced-price IVF treatment for embryo donors (as is common in the United Kingdom) or medical treatments for donors with a particular genetic disease.

With many types and amounts of compensation possible— including no compensation at all—the law has an important role to play beyond determining whether the parties *may* negotiate compensation. It also must determine whether and what compensation will be due when the parties fail to agree on any type or amount of compensation. In legal jargon, such determinations are called default rules. The terminology is borrowed from computer technology: the computer user who does not affirmatively select computer settings will automatically work with the default settings chosen by the software vendor.

In addition to setting the legal default rule, the law must determine what amount of evidence will constitute an agreement by the parties to set their own terms, or "contract around" the default. A strong default rule requires that the parties make a clear contractual statement of a different allocation of resources before the rule is overridden. A "weak" default rule, in contrast, allows the courts to determine that the default rule has been overridden by the parties in the event of more ambiguous or implicit evidence that the parties wished a different resource allocation.

## THE REAL SIGNIFICANCE OF THE *MOORE* CASE

The *Moore* court's decision that Dr. Golde and UCLA did not steal Moore's spleen established a default rule that tissue donations are made altruistically and with no expectation of compensation. No agreement was ever reached between Moore and Golde. Moore never agreed to turn over his spleen and all its profit potential to Golde free of charge, but neither did he demand compensation for it. Golde never broached the subject with Moore one way or another. The dissenting justices, who would have ruled that Moore was the victim of conversion, implicitly favored a default rule in favor of compensation; the justices in the majority implicitly established just the opposite default.

When a donor allows physicians or researchers to take tissues without explicitly establishing terms of the transaction, *Moore* instructs courts to treat the absence of an explicit contract for compensation as if the donor had abandoned the tissue or made a gift of it to the researchers. Under this rule, the research establishment—whether it ultimately would mean the scientists, their academic institutions, funding sources, commercial biotech firms, or some combination of the aforementioned—would be entitled to whatever commercial fruits it creates by mixing the tissue with its intellect and labor.

This reading of *Moore* is supported by a later California appellate court decision in *Hecht v. Superior Court,* which upheld the right of the decedent, Kane, to transfer sperm, held in a sperm bank, to his girlfriend.[16] The court determined that Kane had "an interest in the nature of ownership" in his sperm, and it ruled that Kane's situation was different from *Moore's* because Kane had an explicit contract with the depository recording both his expectation of control over the sperm and his intent to transfer it to his girlfriend at death.[17] Hence, Kane's actions sufficiently rebutted any presumption of a gift to the bank or an abandonment of the tissue in a way that Moore's actions did not.

## HOW STRONG IS THE DEFAULT RULE?

In 2003, the federal district court in Florida that decided *Greenberg v. Miami Children's Hospital Research Institute, Inc.* had an opportunity to weigh in on the question of the strength of the default rule enunciated in *Moore*—that is, on how specific and explicit a donor's intent must be *not* to bestow a gift upon the researchers to overcome the default presumption of altruism.[18] Unfortunately, the *Greenberg* court missed the opportunity, issuing an internally inconsistent ruling that fails to provide donors or researchers much useful guidance. This is quite unfortunate because *Greenberg* is the only published judicial decision that presents a set of facts necessary for a court to pass judgment on the strength of the *Moore* default rule.

Recall that the *Greenberg* plaintiffs were parents of children afflicted with Canavan disease who donated tissues (as well as time and money) to a medical researcher who was trying to identify the gene mutation that causes that disease. The researcher wanted to create a diagnostic test and a cure, as well as to form a nonprofit organization to promote further research on the disease.[19] The plaintiffs alleged that their donations were made "with the understanding" that any discoveries would benefit "the population at large," that any diagnostic tests developed would "be provided on an affordable and accessible basis," and that the research findings "would remain in the public domain."[20] When the defendants patented the genetic sequence that causes Canavan disease and began charging licensing fees for the use of any Canavan disease diagnostic test, the plaintiffs brought suit under a variety of legal theories.

The court dismissed the plaintiffs' claim for conversion of their tissue and genetic information. It did so not because the plaintiffs lacked property rights in these items but because "the property right in blood and tissue samples . . . evaporates once the sample is voluntarily given to a third party," and there were no allegations that the defendants had used any of the plaintiffs' materials for an "expressly unauthorized act" or in violation of any conditions of use.[21] This ruling suggests that the court was constructing a particularly strong default presumption in favor of altruistic donation, thus pushing the *Moore* decision one step further. In *Moore,* no conditions had been placed on the use of the plaintiff's spleen. In *Greenberg,* there apparently had been discussions about the purposes for which the plaintiffs' tissues would be used, but ultimately no clear agreement of terms had emerged. There appears to have been only a vague, inchoate "understanding," and the court appeared to rule that this was insufficient to overcome the presumption of altruistic donation.

Unfortunately for the sake of clarity, however, the court's ruling on another of the *Greenberg* plaintiffs' claims—one for "unjust enrichment"—implicitly contradicts its resolution of the conversion claim. The court listed as the elements of an unjust enrichment claim that the plaintiffs had conferred a benefit on the defendant, the defendant had voluntarily accepted and retained the benefit, and "under the circumstances *it would be inequitable for the defendant to retain the benefit without paying for it.*"[22] Then, concluding that the plaintiffs' allegations "paint a picture of a continuing research collaboration," the court held that the plaintiffs had sufficiently pleaded a cause of action for unjust enrichment and denied the defendant's motion to dismiss.[23] This meant that the plaintiffs would be permitted to proceed to a jury trial on that issue.[24]

The inconsistency of the dual conclusions stems from the fact that if the plaintiffs had in fact voluntarily transferred their property rights to the defendant without conditions, there would be nothing inequitable about the defendant's retaining all the benefits without paying for them. The unjust enrichment claim is viable only if the plaintiffs' donations had not been completely altruistic but rather had been made with the reasonable expectation of some consideration—presumably as a consequence of the vague "understanding" between the parties, if not an enforceable contract. The unjust enrichment portion of the *Greenberg* decision suggests that the default presumption in favor of altruistic donation is relatively weak. Even somewhat vague discussions of a partnership could overcome that presumption and establish that the donor was entitled to compensation.

The practical implication of the internally inconsistent *Greenberg* ruling is that, although researchers may negotiate for altruistic, uncompensated tissue donations, they should make certain that their consent documents clearly define or disclaim donor control over potential commercial activities and donor rights to present or future compensation. In the absence of clear contractual terms with donors, researchers risk future litigation. They also run the risk that potential downstream investors will determine that the researchers' property rights in the tissues are too uncertain to commercialize subsequent discoveries.

A potential complication with this analysis is raised by a "no-waiver" provision in the common rule. This portion of the rule bars researchers from including in informed consent forms "any exculpatory language through which the subject or the representative is made to waive or appear to waive any of the subject's legal rights, or releases or appears to release the investigator, the sponsor, the institution or its agents from liability for negligence."[25] Based on this provision, the OHRP has said that it would be improper for researchers to insert a clause in informed consent documents stating that subjects would give up all claims to personal benefits from their tissue samples.[26]

The OHRP's conclusion is incorrect. Such releases do not in fact violate the common rule, for two reasons. First, the "no-waiver" provision's use of the term "exculpatory language" suggests that the clause is best read as prohibiting waivers for tort liability on the part of the researchers. It does not address agreements concerning the allocation of financial gains derived from use of a subject's donated tissues. Second, even if the "no-waiver" clause is read more broadly, so long as the default rule is that tissue donors receive no compensation, a clause inserted in an informed consent document affirming this fact would not constitute the waiver of any legal rights that the subject has.

## Choosing the Best Default Rule

In the stem cell century, progress in medical research will become increasingly reliant on human tissue donations. As a result, not only will progress require that scientists be permitted to compensate tissue donors, as argued in Chapter 7, but also that the choice of a default rule concerning the compensation of tissue donors when researchers and donors remain silent on the matter will become increasingly important. As it turns out, the *Moore* decision provides the appropriate default rule.

### MAJORITARIAN DEFAULTS

There are three principled bases for selecting a default rule from among two or more rules among which contracting parties are privileged to choose to govern their particular transactions. One basis is to choose what contract law scholars call a "majoritarian" default rule.[27] A majoritarian default rule mimics what most silent parties would have agreed to had they explicitly addressed the issue in question.[28] This approach has two benefits. First, the courts most often provide parties what they would have explicitly negotiated for, which makes them jointly better off than any other allocation of rights. Second, the parties who are satisfied with the default rule need not explicitly memorialize these terms in a contract, which saves them transaction costs.[29]

In a simple world, selecting a majoritarian default rule concerning tissue compensation would require only a determination of whether a majority of researchers and donors, if they were to expressly discuss the question of compensation, would agree to a compensated or an uncompensated donation. In the real world, the question is more complicated because parties who hypothetically would agree to compensated donations could agree to a variety of different compensation schemes—for example, a flat fee, a flat fee contingent on the usefulness of the tissue donated, a flat fee contingent on the commercial success of the research, or a percentage of profits from commercial innovations—and the amount of compensation under each scheme could be set at a nearly infinite range of levels.

It is difficult to predict whether an actual *majority* of donation agreements that are silent on the issue of compensation would have called for no compensation if the researchers and donors had expressly discussed the issue. It might be the case that even if compensation was explicitly considered in every tissue donation, most donations would be altruistic. Many tissues will have little unique financial value to researchers, and researchers will be able to find enough altruists who are willing to make uncompensated donations to satisfy the needs of science. Even when potential donors have a genetic mutation that makes their tissue particularly valuable, they will often have enough interest in helping researchers to develop treatments, cures, or diagnostic tests for their conditions that they would be willing to donate without any direct compensation.[30]

But even if this is the case, it is safe to predict that at a minimum, a plurality of donation agreements that would result from explicit discussion and consideration of the compensation issue would include a "no-compensation" term as opposed to any other specific compensation agreement. Thus, the majoritarian default—or perhaps it more accurately should be called the "pluralitarian" default—in the context of tissue donation would be one of no compensation. That is, because uncompensated donors all would receive the same amount of compensation (that is, nothing), whereas compensation could take many forms and be set at various amounts, the default rule that would mimic the express agreements of the greatest number of silent researchers and tissue donors would almost certainly be no compensation.

## INFORMATION-FORCING DEFAULTS

A second basis for choosing a default rule is to provide an incentive for better-informed parties to share information with those who possess less information in order to increase the likelihood that all parties will make informed decisions. This is done by selecting as the default a rule unattractive to better-informed parties, thus encouraging them to explicitly request an alternative contract term and, in so doing, disclose information. Default rules selected with this goal in mind are often called information-forcing defaults or penalty defaults.[31]

In the tissue donation context, an information-forcing default rule would provide that donors are due compensation for their tissues. Researchers, with their ready access to legal counsel and administrative support, have the wherewithal to make the terms of the donation explicit, whereas individual donors often will not realize the financial consequences of their donation.[32] An information-forcing default rule gives researchers an incentive to inform subjects about these consequences. Specifically, if researchers intend not to compensate donors, they have to state this rather than remaining silent.

To best serve their purpose, information-forcing defaults should be strong defaults. For example, in order to secure an uncompensated donation under an information-forcing default rule, researchers would be required to procure a signed agreement, probably incorporated as part of the informed consent process, that provides something akin to the following: "The parties agree that the donor will not receive any compensation whatsoever as a result of this donation, regardless of whether it is used for commercially profitable innovations." Failure to state this agreement clearly would subject the researcher who produced a commercially viable product to future financial liability under an implicit contract for "reasonable" remuneration or under a theory of unjust enrichment, as per the *Greenberg* case (either for the market value of the tissue or the amount of value that tissue created for the researcher). Alerted to the facts (1) that the researcher believes that the donated tissue might help in the development of a commercially profitable test or treatment, and (2) that it is the researcher's intent not to compensate the donors for the tissue regardless of its usefulness, a potential donor could either accept the proposed no-compensation term knowingly or attempt to negotiate a different term with the researcher.

Whether a potential donor would be successful in negotiating a different term would depend on market conditions. If there are many altruistic donors whose tissue would provide a perfect substitute, the researcher presumably would refuse a request for payment. If the donor's tissues would be uniquely useful for a particular research project, the researcher would be more likely to agree to compensation. Either way, the default rule would ensure that donors possessed clear information about the financial consequences of their decision to donate.

### POLICY-SUPPORTING DEFAULTS

A third basis for selecting a default rule is to encourage, without requiring, private contractual choices that are consistent with the larger public interest. Defaults chosen for the purpose of encouraging socially desirable private agreements can be called policy-supporting default rules.[33]

Individuals' preferences are constructed rather than inherently fixed, and they are based, at least in part, on external cues.[34] One consequence of these facts is what is called the "status quo bias": all other things being equal, people tend to prefer the status quo to alternative states of the world.[35] Research has demonstrated that in many contexts default rules can be perceived as reflecting the status quo, even when opting out of the default is easy to do.

Consider the following findings from experimental and real-world studies: Given a choice among investment funds with different objectives, people who inherit or receive money tend to prefer the fund in which the money was invested when they received the money.[36] Automobile drivers prefer no-fault insurance if state law makes that the default and fault-based insurance if state law makes that the default, even if they may freely choose the alternative type.[37] More workers choose to invest in workplace-sponsored 401K plans if they must opt out of participation than if they must opt in, even when opting in or out is simple and costless.[38] Contract negotiators are not willing to pay as much money to override an undesirable default term in favor of a more desirable term as they would demand before agreeing to the undesirable term if the desirable term were the default.[39]

The research on the general bias in favor of default options suggests that if the law makes no compensation the default rule for tissue donations, we should expect to see relatively more uncompensated donations. In contrast, if the law makes compensation a default rule, we should expect to see more compensated sales. If the default is no compensation, researchers will be less likely to offer compensation and donors less likely to request it than if compensation is the default because what is viewed as standard or normal carries with it a certain amount of desirability.

Stem cell research is a socially desirable goal, so selecting default rules in a way that will tend to make research less expensive is "policy supporting." Regardless of the default rule, some donors will demand compensation and some will not. But for a third group, the default is likely to have an effect on the strength of their preference to demand payment. The percentage of potential donors who fall into this category is not known, but for them a no-compensation default might suggest that demanding compensation would be greedy, whereas a pro-compensation default might imply that people who donate for free are rubes. The choice of defaults is likely to have an even greater impact on the preferences of researchers who, after all, are more likely than donors to know the content of the default rule. Whereas a no-compensation default is likely to suggest that seeking uncompensated donations is thrifty, a pro-compensation default might cause more members of the research community to perceive such behavior as exploitative.

Because the choice of default rules is likely to have at least some effect on the proportion of tissue donations that are altruistic rather than compensated, a no-compensation default supports the policy goal of keeping the cost of stem cell research as low as possible within a broader legal framework that permits compensated donations.

## WEIGHING THE PRINCIPLES FOR STEM CELL RESEARCH

When choosing between majoritarian and information-forcing default rules, two critical considerations are the degree of information disparity between the relevant parties (greater disparities favor information-forcing rules) and the transaction costs that would burden parties who wish to agree on terms other than the default (greater costs favor majoritarian rules).

In regard to the first factor, research scientists have far easier and greater access to the legal rules governing the rights to compensation of tissue donors than do potential donors. Most researchers have university or company lawyers available to help them clearly delineate compensation arrangements, including a term that specifies no compensation regardless of tissue value. In contrast, most potential donors, excepting the few who are part of organized disease advocacy groups, are far less sophisticated.[40] That said, an information-forcing default rule is unlikely to alter information asymmetries in any meaningful way. Most donors will not expect payment to be forthcoming if none is offered or discussed, so a default rule that would force researchers to say expressly that they are not willing to compensate donors would have little practical benefit.

This is not to say that information asymmetries between researchers and tissue donors are unimportant or even that the law should not try to level the informational playing field. Recall that Chapter 6 argued that the law of informed consent should be interpreted to require that researchers disclose personal financial interests to potential donors. This goal is better accomplished, however, by imposing an affirmative disclosure requirement on researchers than by using the choice of default rules to encourage information disclosure. The crux of John Moore's complaint was not that he thought Dr. Golde was planning to pay him for his spleen—a problem that an information-forcing default rule might solve—but that Dr. Golde never told him how valuable the spleen might be.[41]

In regard to the second factor, transaction costs are unlikely to be significant for parties who would wish to avoid the default rule, regardless of the choice of defaults, when the issue is research tissues procured specifically for stem cell research. In very few cases (the facts of *Greenberg* are perhaps an exception that proves the rule) are researchers and donors likely to bargain over the terms of tissue donations. The overwhelmingly likely scenario is that researchers will determine, based on the supply of altruistic donors, whether and how much compensation to offer for particular types of tissues and then present donors with what effectively is a take-it-or-leave-it proposal. Notwithstanding current federal funding limitations, the vast majority of stem cell research will fall under the requirements of the federal common rule, discussed in Chapter 6, which requires that researchers disclose a substantial amount of information to their subjects as part of the informed consent process.[42] Because it would be both cheap and easy for researchers to specify their compensation policies as part of or adjunct to the informed consent process, requiring them to specify their policy to avoid the effects of a default rule would add very little marginal cost to any research endeavor.

The choice of the default rule will have an important effect on total transaction costs, however, when stem cell scientists wish to use tissues already housed in tissue banks for research purposes. A recent study conducted by the Rand Corporation estimates that more than 300 million human tissue samples reside in tissue banks in the United States alone.[43] Most of these samples were obtained either as part of therapeutic interactions or for research projects long since completed. In some cases, researchers long ago obtained general consent to use the tissues for research purposes; in others, no consent for research was ever sought. It is probably the very rare case that there is documentation of an explicit discussion concerning compensation between a tissue's donor and the physician or researcher who procured the tissue.

A no-compensation default would almost certainly be the majoritarian rule concerning all varieties of banked tissues. That is, the vast majority of tissue donors, if specifically approached, would be willing to permit the research use of their banked tissues, usually long forgotten, without compensation. And when banked tissues are at issue, the transaction costs associated with contracting around a pro-compensation default would be extremely high. In order to avoid paying compensation under such a regime, researchers would be forced to locate and contact the donors and seek explicit permission to use the tissues without charge. In many cases, perhaps most, this process would be infeasible or extremely costly, and it could stifle research progress, for very little purpose.[44] It was probably with an eye to this problem of preexisting banked tissues accompanied by consent forms silent on the question of compensation that the *Moore* court claimed biotech research would be hampered by "uncertainty about how courts would resolve [future] disputes between specimen sources and specimen users" if it were to rule that John Moore was due compensation for his spleen.[45]

The case for a no-compensation default on majoritarian grounds is reinforced by the policy-supporting principle, which points in the same direction. As argued in Chapter 7, it is important to permit researchers to compensate tissue donors in order to ensure that stem cell research is not impaired by a shortage of necessary raw materials. But a no-compensation default rule can help reinforce a social norm that favors altruistic donation and, in so doing, convince some potential donors to give without compensation, thus reducing the cost of research. A legal system that permits compensation for research tissues but treats donations that are silent on the issue of compensation as altruistic provides the optimal combination of rules.

## WEAK OR STRONG DEFAULTS?

When a default rule is selected on the basis of its presumed hypothetical appeal to the greatest number of parties—that is, based on the majoritarian principle—the default should be interpreted relatively weakly. If there is any evidence that the parties intended some other arrangement, that alternative arrangement should be enforced. Since majoritarian default rules achieve their legitimacy because they are presumed to reflect the terms that silent contracting parties would have chosen had they not been silent, any indication that parties actually prefer a different term must be recognized. This point suggests that under the majoritarian principle, the *Greenberg* court should have permitted the Canavan patients to proceed to a jury trial and attempt to prove their allegations that they had an inchoate understanding with Dr. Matalon. Although the details of the arrangement between the plaintiffs and Dr. Matalon were unclear, if the plaintiffs' allegations are believed, it is clear that both researcher and subjects understood that participation was not expected to be entirely altruistic.

When a default rule is selected based on the policy-supporting principle, in contrast, the default should be strong. Because such a rule derives its legitimacy not from presumed party approval but from the social benefits it can provide in cases in which it is operative, it should be interpreted to be operative in unclear cases. The policy-supporting principle suggests that the *Greenberg* court should have dismissed the conversion and unjust enrichment claims of the Canavan patients, ruling that allegations of a hazy agreement to provide some sort of compensation for tissue donations are legally insufficient to overcome the presumption of the no-compensation default.

Because the two grounds for selecting a no-compensation default for tissue donations point toward opposite approaches, the choice between interpreting the default rule strongly or weakly is not clear-cut. Ultimately, however, the balance of practical concerns suggests a weak default rule is most appropriate. Because donors will usually be far less sophisticated than researchers, contradictory or vague assurances that could reasonably be interpreted as offers or promises of cash or in-kind compensation should be interpreted as such. As discussed above, except when banked tissues collected in the past are concerned, the cost to researchers of avoiding confusion or misunderstanding concerning compensation will be low—at worst, they can avoid the problem by placing clear language in their consent documents—so there is little reason not to place the burden of avoiding such misunderstandings on them.[46]

It is when banked tissues are at issue that interpreting the no-compensation default weakly could create some unavoidable problems for researchers who wish not to pay compensation. If preexisting consent forms are silent on the issue of compensation, researchers could use the tissues without payment. If consent forms suggest (but do not clearly promise) some type of compensation and the cost of recontacting and "reconsenting" the donors is high, however, researchers might have to forego using those tissues to avoid, as the *Moore* court feared, "purchas[ing] a ticket in the litigation lottery."[47] With hundreds of millions of banked tissue samples available, however, this limitation is unlikely to substantially slow research progress.

# 9

# Looking Forward:
# Stem Cell Treatments

I n 1994, Molly Nash was born with a genetic disorder called Fanconi Anemia (FA), which causes bone marrow failure. Children with FA have compromised immune systems and usually die before the end of childhood from leukemia or other resulting complications.[1] Although people afflicted with most gene-linked diseases can only hope that stem cells might provide a cure at some time in the distant future, FA sufferers, along with people afflicted with other blood- and bone-marrow-related diseases, are an exception: treatment with a transplant of healthy hematopoietic stem cells, a multipotent type of adult stem cell that produces blood cells, has a high success rate. For Molly Nash, such a stem cell treatment offered the best—and indeed the only—hope for a cure.

Molly faced two significant obstacles to treatment. First, hematopoietic stem cell transplants are most likely to succeed when the donor is a sibling of the patient, and Molly was an only child. Second, not just any sibling would do. Molly needed the stem cells of a histocompatible sibling—that is, one with the same HLA profile. Transplants from unrelated donors are possible, but patient survival rates are much lower as a result of increased risk of subsequent infection and of GVHD, the syndrome in which healthy transplant cells recognize the patient's cells as foreign and attack them.[2]

In an effort to save Molly's life, her parents, Jack and Lisa Nash, set out to create an HLA-compatible sibling who could serve as a stem cell donor.[3] Using standard IVF technology, they would use Jack's sperm and Lisa's eggs to create embryos. Then, putting the technology of preimplantation genetic diagnosis (PGD) to a unique use, they would select for implantation into Lisa's uterus only embryos that both did not carry the mutation for FA and were an HLA-match with Molly.

FA is an autosomal recessive disease, meaning that a child will suffer from it if a recessive gene is inherited from both parents.[4] Because Jack and Lisa both carry the gene, each of their offspring would have a 25 percent chance of contracting the disease. In addition, there is only a 25 percent chance that any sibling of Molly's would have a compatible HLA profile. When these probabilities are combined, each embryo created with Jack and Lisa's gametes would have an 18.75 percent chance of being both disease-free and histocompatible with Molly.

Reproductive technology is almost completely unregulated in the United States, so no legal restrictions interfered with the Nashes' ability to pursue their strategy. And fortunately, the Nashes possessed sufficient means to afford the IVF and PGD services involved. Still, they struggled to find a PGD expert who would work with them. Even though Jack and Molly had no fertility problems, it is common for carriers of gene-linked disorders like FA to use IVF combined with PGD to select embryos for implantation that are not affected by the disease in question. But many PGD providers were uncomfortable with the part of the Nashes' plan that called for the selection of embryos with a particular HLA profile to the detriment of other, perfectly healthy, embryos. Eventually, the Nashes identified a PGD lab in Chicago and a physician at the University of Minnesota willing to assist in their quest to harness modern medical technology in an effort to cure their daughter.

In 2000, Lisa gave birth to Adam Nash, who was both free of FA (although he has one FA gene and is thus, like each of his parents, a carrier) and an HLA match for Molly.[5] Adam's umbilical cord blood—a rich source of hematopoietic stem cells—was preserved, and a month after he was born, the cord blood was used for an infusion for Molly. The transplant was successful, and within one month Molly's bone marrow was functioning normally.[6] Molly remains a healthy child, although there is no guarantee that other complications related to FA will not one day appear.

The Nashes' story helps to illuminate a number of legal and policy issues that appear to be on the horizon as we look forward into the stem cell century—issues that are almost certain to become broadly significant as the progress of laboratory scientists enables physicians to treat a broader range of maladies with stem cells. One set of questions concerns the ethics of using reproductive technology to create stem cell donors who, like Adam Nash, obviously cannot give informed consent to their participation in the treatment plan and whether the law should create rules for resolving such moral quandaries. A second set of questions concerns how our country's regulatory apparatus should approach the use of stem cells as direct medical treatments. Molly's doctors could not have attempted to cure her FA with a pill before the pill had obtained FDA approval. Should stem cell treatments be subject to the same preapproval requirements? Finally, in a future world of stem cell treatments, firms will collect, preserve, store, treat, and manipulate the stem cells used for treatment. If the hopes of stem cell research backers come to fruition, in fact, stem cell preparations are likely to become a relatively common commercial product. What liability burdens should be imposed on the commercial entities involved? Consider the possibility, for example, that rather than curing FA, hematopoietic stem cells infused into the body of someone like Molly Nash caused a fatal cancer. Under what circumstances, if any, should an intermediary that collected and treated the donor's cord blood be legally responsible for such consequences?

With the observation that each of these topics could justify a book of its own, this chapter provides a brief discussion and analysis of these issues, which are likely to dominate debates over stem cell technology a decade from now.

## Creating Stem Cell Donors

Adam Nash was not the first child conceived with the hope that he could provide stem cells that would save a sibling's life—there are earlier documented cases of parents who conceived a child in the hope that he or she could serve such a purpose—but Adam was the first child arguably "designed" for such a purpose.[7] Prior to the widespread use of PGD, parents of children afflicted with FA or similar diseases could not guarantee that a second child would be histocompatible with the first. If they chose to conceive a second child in an effort to save the first, they had to take their chances in the genetic lottery. Adam's case was different in that the lottery was rigged by technology.

Not only does this difference arguably affect the ethical appropriateness of Adam's conception, but it also has a great deal of practical significance when it comes to evaluating whether the government should regulate such reproductive practices. Even if society thought it inappropriate to conceive a child to serve as a stem cell donor for another, the government could not prevent Jack and Lisa Nash from producing a second child through sexual intercourse without unconstitutionally and intolerably intruding in their most private affairs. But the government could have prevented the conception of Adam Nash in a much less intrusive way. It need only have prohibited the use of PGD to screen for histocompatibility.

Unlike the United States, the United Kingdom requires a government agency that regulates the use of reproductive technology, the Human Fertilisation and Embryological Authority (HFEA), to approve proposed new uses of PGD. In one controversial decision in 2001, the HFEA approved the use of PGD for a family identically situated to the Nashes. Two-year-old Zain Hashmi suffered from beta thalassemia rather than FA, but his chance of survival, like that of Molly Nash, depended on receiving a histocompatible hematopoietic stem cell transplant, which could come from the umbilical cord blood of a sibling. Like Jack and Lisa Nash, Zain's parents, Raj and Shahana Hashmi, wished to use PGD to select embryos for implantation that would be both free of the genetic disease that afflicted their child and HLA-compatible with him. The case spawned litigation, but the HFEA's decision was finally upheld on appeal in 2005.[8]

In 2002, however, the HFEA denied an application to use PGD to screen embryos for histocompatibility with three-year-old Charlie Whitaker, who suffered from a blood disorder called Diamond-Blackfan Anemia. Like Molly Nash and Zain Hashmi, Charlie Whitaker also needed a hematopoietic stem cell transplant from a histocompatible donor. Charlie did not inherit his disease from his parents, however. Instead, his illness was caused by an unpredictable genetic mutation that was no more likely to afflict him than any other child. This meant that it was not necessary to use PGD to screen his parents' embryos for the same disease that afflicted him. That is, in the Whitaker case, PGD, if employed, would benefit only the living child, whereas in the Hashmi and Nash cases PGD would benefit the embryo and the living child simultaneously.[9]

The distinction drawn by the HFEA is implicitly grounded in both a view that embryos enjoy the same moral value as do persons and a strict version of the Kantian imperative that one person should not be used solely for the benefit of another—the same set of beliefs that causes some people to oppose any embryo research.[10] When PGD, a process that requires the removal of a blastomere from a three-day-old embryo, was performed on the Nash embryos, it had the dual purpose of helping the future child itself (by its avoiding FA) and helping Molly (by assuring an HLA match). Performing PGD on the Whitaker embryos would have been solely for the benefit of Charlie.

This analysis raises two types of questions: Does the Kantian imperative in fact require that a line be drawn between Zain Hashmi and Charlie Whitaker, and is the Kantian imperative the proper principle to apply in this circumstance? As to the former, it is difficult to sustain the claim that performing PGD on a particular embryo is ever for the benefit of that embryo because if the test reveals a genetic disease the consequence is that the embryo will not be implanted. This result is clearly disastrous for the embryo in question unless one wishes to argue that some people would be better off never being born than being born—a conclusion that arguably borders on discredited eugenic theory. When PGD is performed to detect FA, the intended result is not to repair the genetic defect but to select for implantation a disease-free embryo. This is good for the disease-free embryo but bad for the embryo with FA. Indeed, it seems that a faithful application of the Kantian imperative's strict version would counsel against PGD in any case because PGD is never conducted on an embryo that would otherwise be implanted for that embryo's own benefit: all benefits will accrue to other embryos (that might be implanted and thus be given a chance to become a person that otherwise would have been denied to them) and to the potential parents (who will have a disease-free child).

The point here is not to argue that PGD should never be performed to avoid birth defects but rather to demonstrate how inappropriate a strict Kantian analysis is for analyzing this problem. A disease-free child will have a longer and less painful life expectancy than a child with a severe genetic birth defect, and good health is undoubtedly beneficial to the child, to the parents, and to the family unit. It is therefore neither unethical nor inappropriate for prospective parents to use PGD to maximize the likelihood that embryos selected for implantation will be disease-free, even if one assumes that embryos have heightened moral status. Notice, however, that this conclusion requires abandoning a strict version of the Kantian imperative as the touchstone and adopting a utilitarian form of analysis that requires a balancing of costs and benefits.

Assuming that a couple whose child needs a stem cell transplant from an HLA-compatible sibling has decided to conceive one new child for this purpose, exactly one new child will be born, regardless of its HLA profile. Given that one and only one child will be created, there is no compelling reason to prefer that it be a child that is not an HLA-match for the sibling who requires treatment. It follows that it is morally acceptable to use PGD to ensure that the child who is born possesses the HLA type that could potentially save the life of the diseased sibling.

What about the appropriation of stem cells from an HLA-compatible child who is not old enough to provide informed consent for the procedure for the benefit of a sibling? This step would always seem to violate the Kantian imperative, even if embryos are not assumed to possess elevated moral status. Using Adam Nash's umbilical cord blood for Molly's benefit can be justified on the ground that cord blood is usually disposed of as medical waste, so Adam is not placed at risk.[11] The problem with this reasoning, however, is that today it is possible to store cord blood, and there is some possibility that future advances in stem cell technology will make that blood useful for curing future ailments contracted by its donor. Thus, using Adam's cord blood to benefit Molly presents some risk to Adam and provides him no direct benefits. This problem can be solved either by proposing a *de minimis* exception to the Kantian imperative, under which it is acceptable to use Adam for Molly's benefit if the risk to Adam is small, or by considering it a psychological benefit to have a sister and observing that this "benefit" will accrue to Adam if his cord blood is used to save Molly's life.[12] In either case, these justifications seem to recognize that as a practical matter, at least some utilitarian balancing of benefits and burdens, rather than a strict adherence to the Kantian imperative, needs to inform our ethical judgments in these cases.

The Nash case will strike all but the most unreconstructed Kantians as relatively untroubling, but more difficult cases can arise today, and even more problematic cases are likely to arise in the future as stem cell technology improves. If the hematopoietic stem cells from Adam's umbilical cord had failed to cure Molly, the next step would have been to attempt another transplant using Adam's bone marrow. This would have required subjecting Adam to a painful procedure that, in an infant, would not be entirely risk-free.[13] Would this procedure have been ethically justified? What if a future Molly Nash has an ailment that can be treated with a transplant of a different variety of stem cell that is more difficult to obtain? To how much pain or risk is it appropriate to subject a future Adam Nash, and on what principled basis can we resolve these questions?

One way for society to approach these very difficult problems is to abdicate decision-making authority to parents like Jack and Lisa Nash. This could be justified either as a mechanism for preserving their autonomy or on the grounds that they are in the best position to make decisions for children who are not old enough to exercise personal autonomy on their own—an approach often referred to by courts as "substituted judgment." But these arguments prove too much. Although parents should be offered great latitude to make choices for their children, few among us would argue that the government should place absolutely no limits on parental control over their children.

In fact, the government places limits on the choices parents can make for their children, not only to prevent the most extreme cases of physical abuse, but also to prevent some relatively benign cases of irresponsible parenting. For example, Jack and Lisa Nash could expect a visit from child protective services if they failed to enroll young Adam in school when he reached the appropriate age unless they substituted a suitable home-school curriculum, and in most states they could be ticketed if they transport him about town without a child car seat. Against this regulatory background it is clear that some government-imposed limits on the Nashes' ability to provide consent on Adam's behalf for nontherapeutic medical procedures would be appropriate. When the potential beneficiary is the Nashes' other child, Molly, the inherent conflict of interest heightens the need for society to set some boundaries.

The best approach to drawing such boundaries requires adopting a version of the "veil of ignorance" heuristic famously proposed by philosopher John Rawls.[14] Rather than focusing solely on the potential harms to Adam, we should construct the following thought experiment: Imagine that Adam and Molly know that they are siblings but know nothing about their personal health status or birth order. Would they be willing to enter into an agreement with one another according to which, if one were to have a life-threatening illness that could be best treated only if the other submitted to a particular procedure, the healthy sibling would so submit?

If we believe that the answer would be yes, then the Nashes should be permitted to authorize the conduct of that procedure on Adam for Molly's benefit. After all, their situation could have been reversed. Adam could have been the first-born child suffering from a serious health condition, and Molly could have been the younger, healthy sibling. In that case, there is no doubt Jack and Lisa Nash would have sought to procure Molly's stem cells for Adam.

Judged from beyond the veil of ignorance, it appears that Adam receives no benefit from donating his cord blood or bone marrow to Molly. But this is too narrow a perspective. By virtue of having a histocompatible sibling, Adam (situated behind the veil of ignorance) actually enjoyed what can be viewed as stem cell donation insurance provided by Molly, just as she possessed identical insurance provided by Adam. That Molly needed to call on her insurance and Adam did not need to call on his does not mean Adam's insurance was itself valueless.[15]

Like many of the other issues addressed in this book, these difficult questions do not arise solely in the context of stem cell research. The very same issue raised by the Nash case, for example, would have been present if Molly Nash needed a solid organ transplant from an HLA-compatible donor rather than a stem cell transplant. Courts have struggled mightily with just this question, reaching inconsistent conclusions. Some have approved organ donations from minor or incompetent siblings either on the ground that the psychological value to the donor child of saving his sibling outweighs the risk or on the ground of parental autonomy.[16] Others have blocked proposed donations on the ground that there was no benefit (or too little benefit) to the donor.[17] But although the issues are not unique to stem cell treatments, they are likely to become more prevalent and urgent as the stem cell century progresses, assuming that stem cell treatments become as widespread as scientists hope. Unless and until therapeutic cloning technology can enable scientists to create individually tailored hESC lines for use in treatment, histocompatibility is likely to be a significant issue in stem cell treatments.

## FDA Oversight

Before a physician can provide a patient with a prescription drug that will hopefully cure an ailment, that drug must earn premarket approval of the federal FDA. This demanding process requires the manufacturer to demonstrate both the safety and efficacy of the drug in humans.[18] The usual procedure begins with the filing of an investigational new drug application (IND), which provides results of tests of the drug on human cells and animals. If the IND is approved, the pharmaceutical must undergo three sets of clinical trials. Phase I trials test the safety of the drug on a small number of human subjects. Phase II trials test whether the product is effective in treating disease in a small number of human subjects and further assess the drug's safety by tracking short- and long-term side effects. Phase III trials assess the product's safety and efficacy on a much larger scale, usually in controlled experiments conducted at several different sites.[19] At that point, the manufacturer may file a new drug application (NDA) or a biological license application (BLA) seeking FDA permission to market the substance. Should all stem cell treatments be made to satisfy these extensive requirements, or should exceptions be made in some cases?

Current law provides the FDA with the authority to require premarket approval of stem cell treatments. The Food, Drug, and Cosmetics Act allows the FDA to regulate any "drug," which is defined as an "[article] intended for use in the diagnosis, cure, mitigation, treatment, or prevention of disease."[20] The Public Health Services Act provides the FDA authority over any "biological product," defined to mean "a virus, therapeutic serum, toxin, antitoxin, vaccine, blood, blood component or derivative, allergenic product, or analogous product . . . applicable to the prevention, treatment or cure of a disease or condition of human beings."[21] These definitions are sufficiently broad that stem cell treatments could qualify as both drugs and biological products and be regulated under either statute.

Whether and when the FDA should exercise this statutory authority to require premarket approval is a different question. Requiring product manufacturers to demonstrate safety and efficacy before unleashing potential risks on an unsuspecting public seems commonsensical when considered in the abstract. But the FDA premarket approval process takes more than seven and a half years on average, from the submission of an IND to final approval, and it costs applicants, on average, more than a quarter of a billion dollars. Because fewer than one out of four drugs for which an IND is filed ever obtain FDA approval and because of the time lag between the research expenditures and the ultimate approval, the expected capitalized cost of ushering one successful drug through the FDA approval process is more than $800 million.[22] Two obvious consequences of requiring new medical products to run this gauntlet are that (1) patients who could have benefited from a useful drug die (or needlessly suffer) before the drug finally wins approval, and (2) manufacturers must charge significantly higher prices to patients and health insurers to recoup the large and risky preapproval costs.

A less obvious consequence of the premarket approval process is that its high cost acts as a disincentive to the creation of drugs with limited market potential because companies fear that sales will not earn back the start-up costs even if the drug is successful. This problem could prove to be even more significant in the case of many stem cell treatments than it is for most drugs, especially in the case of treatments for uncommon conditions. A successful stem cell treatment, such as Molly Nash's transplant, might require only a single administration, whereas most pharmaceuticals are continuously prescribed to patients over long periods of time. Much like an appliance that never wears out, a treatment that can cure a patient with a single application gives its manufacturers fewer expected sales over which to spread the product's research and development costs.

Some critics of the FDA argue that the regulatory approval process should depend on the type of illness that a medical product is designed to treat and the condition of patients. The D.C. Circuit Court's decision in *Abigail Alliance*, discussed in Chapter 3, can be read as a reflection of this view.[23] In that case, plaintiffs sought—with partial success— expanded access to unapproved treatments for their otherwise terminal illnesses. The FDA's "compassionate use" program, which allows drug makers to provide unapproved pharmaceuticals to the terminally ill under some conditions, likewise reflects the realization that ironclad guarantees of safety and efficacy are luxuries that provide cold comfort to people for whom access to an experimental treatment represents the only hope for survival.[24]

Even in circumstances of terminal illness, however, the optimal balance between access and regulation is difficult to pinpoint. If treatments are made available prior to large-scale clinical studies of effectiveness, it can be difficult to recruit patients for randomized trials at all. If a patient can obtain an experimental treatment from his physician, there is little incentive for him to participate in a trial in which half the subjects are assigned to a "control" group and receive either a placebo or an approved standard treatment that probably has already failed to improve the patient's condition. The treatment of solid cancers with a combination of high-dose chemotherapy and autologous bone marrow transplants serves as a cautionary tale in this respect. In the 1980s and 1990s, physicians widely provided this course of treatment to patients with solid tumor cancers, such as breast cancer, that failed to respond to other treatments, even though there was no clinical evidence of its effectiveness for this purpose. As a result, it took nearly two decades to recruit enough patients for large-scale clinical trials aimed at determining whether the treatment actually worked on such tumors.[25] The results of those studies strongly suggested that the treatment was, in fact, completely ineffective.[26]

The FDA's current policy concerning stem cell treatments is to waive premarket approval requirements if the stem cells meet three criteria: first, the cells are no more than "minimally manipulated" and are not combined with any product that raises clinical safety issues; second, they are for "homologous" use, meaning that they are for use in the bodily system in which they naturally arise; and third, they are for use in either the donor or a first- or second-degree relative of the donor. Any stem cell treatment not meeting these requirements is subject to premarket approval requirements.[27]

The FDA's underlying concept is sensible enough: require premarket approval for stem cell treatments most likely to be dangerous in unpredictable ways and waive the requirement for the treatments least likely to be dangerous in order to usher them into clinical use faster and at less cost. But the categories seem ill fitted to the goal in several ways. The "minimally manipulated" criterion seems appropriate because it draws a rough line between hASCs and hESCs. Scientists are particularly worried about the possibility that hESCs might morph into uncontrollable cancerous tumors under some conditions, so it is appropriate to require a preparation of hESCs manipulated to differentiate into, say, hematopoietic stem cells to receive greater regulatory scrutiny than a preparation of hematopoietic stem cells prepared using only umbilical cord blood.

The criterion of use in a close relative, however, seems unrelated to the potential of stem cell treatments to cause harm as such. This rule allows a patient like Molly Nash to receive umbilical cord stem cells from her brother but would require premarket approval before she could access the same type of cells from a nonrelative.[28] The relationship between donor and recipient might matter for the risk of transferring a

communicable disease, but this risk can be managed independently under the FDA's "Current Good Tissue Practice" requirements for treating, testing, and handling cellular products.[29] It does not suggest the need to prove the safety and
efficacy of the product itself as required by the premarket
approval process. The relationship between donor and patient might also affect the likelihood of immune system rejection or GVHD, but these risks are identical to those that occur
in solid organ transplants, for which there is no premarket approval process. It is not clear under what theory stem cells emanating from a stranger would have any greater risk of causing
unexpected harms than stem cells donated by a second-degree
relative.

The requirement of homologous use creates a different
problem. The medical profession has long demanded, and the
FDA has conceded the point, that doctors be permitted to prescribe pharmaceuticals for "off-label" uses.[30] This means that
once the FDA approves a drug for one purpose, physicians may
use it for any purpose, even if it has not been proven to be safe
and effective for other purposes. In the context of the FDA rules
applicable to stem cells, this practice means that manufacturers
can essentially avoid premarket approval requirements by marketing stem cell products for homologous use. For example, a
preparation of minimally manipulated retinal stem cells must
earn premarket approval before it can be explicitly marketed as
a treatment for brain damage, but a manufacturer could conceivably avoid the approval requirements by marketing it only
for the purpose of reversing retinal damage and leaving the
question of whether it should be used to reverse neuron damage to the judgment of individual physicians.

Where to draw the line between stem cell treatments that
require premarket approval and those that do not is funda-

mentally a policy choice that must balance the desire for safety and efficacy, which the FDA's arduous process is designed to provide, with the competing objective of moving biomedical innovations from the laboratory into clinical use quickly and cost effectively. The proper balance, however, depends on the medical risks of stem cell treatments. Herein lies the problem: at this early point in the stem cell century, even medical researchers understand only dimly the type and extent of these risks. In light of this basic fact, it would be quite uncharitable to criticize the FDA's current approach too severely. It seems fair to say, however, that the question of how much regulatory scrutiny should be provided to stem cell treatments should be continually revisited as basic scientific knowledge of how stem cells work advances.

## Products Liability

The law utilizes two primary methods to protect consumers from harm caused by potentially dangerous products and to provide manufacturers with incentives to minimize product risks to the extent possible. The first method is government regulation of the production and sale of products, represented in the context of medical treatments by the FDA. The second method is the tort system, which redresses harms after they occur by allowing injured parties to sue in court for monetary compensation. As attractive as it is to focus attention on the tremendous medical benefits that stem cell treatments will (hopefully) provide, the reality is that in some cases the treatments will cause harm. The law needs to adopt rules to determine when, and under what circumstances, the makers of stem cell treatments will be held legally liable.

One approach would be to hold producers of stem cell treatments liable for any and all harm that they cause, irrespective of whether any fault on their part caused the harm. Lawyers call this approach "strict liability," and one familiar example of it in the U.S. economy is the workers' compensation system. Employers are held liable for workplace injuries, regardless of fault. This rule gives employers the maximum incentive to minimize accidents, and it also creates a system of insurance for accidents that are beyond anyone's control. Employers purchase workers' compensation insurance to cover the harms resulting from accidents, and much of the cost is passed on to customers in the form of higher prices and, in some cases, to workers in the form of lower wages.

A benefit of strict liability is that, in theory, it prevents an industry from producing goods or services when doing so would be socially inefficient—that is, when the total costs of production would exceed the total benefits produced. For example, imagine it costs a farmer $100 in direct costs (such as water, fertilizer, and seeds) to produce an acre of lettuce; that consumers are willing to pay a total of $150 for the lettuce; and that producing the lettuce causes fertilizers to leach into the local water supply, causing $80 worth of damage to the community. Growing the lettuce would be socially inefficient because the total costs of doing so ($180) exceed the total benefits produced, as measured by consumers' willingness to pay for the lettuce ($150). Without liability for the harm caused to the water supply, the farmer would have a private incentive to farm the lettuce because he could earn a $50 profit by so doing. Under a strict liability regime, the farmer has the incentive to put the land to an alternative use or let it lie fallow, either of which would be socially preferable, because growing lettuce would end up costing him $30 per acre.

One problem with strict liability, however, is that it can undermine the incentives of potential victims to take prudent steps to avoid or minimize injury. Because they know they will be fully compensated for any injury suffered on the job, workers might not be as careful as they otherwise would be, and they might not take all possible steps to recuperate and return to work as quickly as possible. If product makers were liable for all accidents caused by their product, consumers might be more careless, and more rather than fewer injuries might result. For example, a right to collect damages for any slip of a knife might cause consumers to use less caution when wielding a cleaver. In addition, more careful consumers would be forced to subsidize the incautious behavior of the careless in the form of higher product prices.

A second problem with strict liability is that it can encourage litigation-averse sellers to take precautions that are too expensive, in either dollars or inconvenience, given the amount of safety the precautions would provide. Kitchen knives would be safer if their blades were duller or they came in locked cases, but most consumers would rather assume the risk of a sharp knife than use a dull one or pay the added cost of installing a locking mechanism on each individual knife.

For these reasons, the manufacturers of products that operate as intended are generally liable for harm caused only in the case of a "design defect." Most courts consider a product's design to be defective only when a safety improvement would be justified under a cost-benefit test—that is, when the benefits of an alternative design would outweigh higher product costs or reduced functionality.[31] Substantively, this approach eschews strict liability and instead assigns liability based on fault, meaning that producers are liable for harms caused by their products only if they have behaved unreasonably under the circumstances.

This legal standard has two important qualifications: First, a producer is strictly liable for harms caused by manufacturing defects. For example, if, as the result of a malfunction in the production process, a knife blade is not firmly attached to its handle, the producer is liable for harm caused when the blade becomes detached and injures its user. Liability for manufacturing defects is strict rather than fault-based, in the sense that it attaches regardless of whether the victim can prove the manufacturer failed to take reasonable precautions to prevent defects. Second, the manufacturer can also be liable for failing to provide reasonable warnings along with products that present inherent dangers.

Courts treat prescription drugs in much the same way as other products. Manufacturers must provide adequate warnings of known risks, and they are strictly liable for manufacturing errors that result in an adulterated version of the product that varies from design specifications. Proof of unreasonable behavior, however, is required before the law will impose penalties for harms caused by a properly manufactured version of the drug (that is, one that meets design specifications).[32]

This narrowing of legal responsibility relative to strict liability can be justified in three ways. First, as described above, the narrower rule might encourage consumers to exercise more caution than would a rule of strict liability. Doctors and patients can reduce drug-induced harms by heeding product warnings and using drugs only when they are most clearly indicated. Because of the traditional grant of professional autonomy to physicians, as noted, doctors may prescribe FDA-approved drugs for any purpose. Limiting product liability to instances in which the manufacturer behaved unreasonably effectively means that doctors (who can be sued for malpractice) and patients assume the inherent risks of dangerous drugs.

Second, consumers may prefer to bear some risk of low-probability harms rather than to pay the higher costs that a strict liability rule would predict. Under truly strict liability, a drug that cures ninety-nine out of one hundred severely ill patients but kills one will be extremely expensive to market because the producer will have to include the cost of liability payments to the one in the price charged to all. Patients might prefer to go without the insurance that strict liability effectively provides rather than pay its cost. This is especially true because implicit insurance provided by the tort system includes coverage for "pain and suffering" in addition to economic losses—a necessarily expensive type of insurance that individuals rarely purchase on their own in the market.

Third, if companies cannot estimate in advance a product's possible harm and its resulting costs, they may be unwilling to venture into the market, fearing that their pricing will be insufficient to cover the liability costs.

The second and third of these justifications are even stronger for emerging stem cell treatments than they are for traditional prescription drugs. Because stem cell technology is new and will entail transplanting live biological material into the bodies of patients, it is likely that the risk of harm associated with stem cell treatments will be more difficult to predict than it is for other types of treatments, even when FDA premarket approval requirements ensure that evidence of safety will be gathered and presented before a treatment (that is, the product) may be made commercially available. Liability for unknown and unknowable risks would be likely to deter market entry by companies appropriately cautious with their shareholders' money. And because stem cell treatments are likely to be most commonly used, at least initially, in the treatment of diseases or conditions for which there are no other effective treatments, patients with limited means would likely prefer the option of assuming the risk of the treatment rather than being priced out of the market entirely by product prices that include a significant implicit insurance premium. Similarly, most Americans whose medical benefits are paid for with health insurance probably would prefer access to new treatments without implicit insurance against all of the risks to the alternatives of (1) no coverage for stem cell treatments or (2) significantly higher health insurance premiums.

This analysis suggests that makers of stem cell treatments should be held to a lower legal standard than strict liability for all harms caused by their products. But should they be treated precisely the same as the makers of most prescription drugs, or should the law afford them even greater protection from lawsuits? Even in the early years of the stem cell century, some commentators argue that stem cell treatments should be granted special protection from tort liability in order to encourage their production.[33]

There are examples of legislatures enacting special protections from liability for specific biomedical products that could serve as models for the legal treatment of stem cell therapies. One model is to create an insurance system that provides compensation similar to that of a strict liability regime but outside of the litigation system. In 1986, in response to a dramatic increase in litigation over vaccines, the withdrawal from the market of several vaccine makers, and the fear of shortages,[34] Congress enacted the National Childhood Vaccine Injury Act (NCVIA).[35] The NCVIA discourages lawsuits against vaccine makers by offering compensation from a government-run insurance fund to any child harmed by a vaccine on the condition that the victim forego litigation.[36] (The vaccine makers pay into the fund predictable insurance premiums based on the number of doses sold.)[37] The law also provides vaccine makers with enhanced substantive protection against lawsuits by specifying that product warnings need be provided only to physicians (rather than directly to patients) and by prohibiting awards of any punitive damages as long as the manufacturer complied with relevant FDA requirements.[38] The Centers for Disease Control calls the act "a key component in stabilizing the U.S. vaccine market" and lists "providing liability protection" as one of its chief virtues.[39]

Stem cell treatments are likely to be similar to vaccines in the sense that products effective for the many will harm the few, and it will be difficult to determine in advance which people will fall into each category. In addition, both types of products involve introducing biological materials into the body, and these are far more difficult to manufacture with precise consistency than are chemical-based pharmaceutical products.[40] For these reasons, when stem cell treatments are introduced in large numbers, uncertainty about their risks could cause insurers to shrink from providing manufacturers with product liability coverage.

But there are two significant differences between stem cell treatments and vaccines that suggest the NCVIA model is not appropriate for the former. First, harms induced by childhood vaccines are extremely rare.[41] This means that even though the average award issued by the insurance fund exceeds $800,000, its costs are funded with a tax of only 75 cents on each vaccine administration.[42] When stem cell treatments arrive on the market, their risks are likely to be greater and more uncertain; thus, establishing an insurance system that would compensate for all injuries would be likely to raise the price of those treatments substantially. Second, vaccinations are required as a condition of school enrollment.[43] This means that patients have no ability at all to exercise caution when deciding whether to subject themselves to the inherent risks of treatment. Consequently, providing guaranteed compensation for injuries does not undermine an existing incentive to act with care. Stem cell treatments, in contrast, will be voluntary, so an NCVIA-type approach could reduce patients' incentives to study the risks and potential benefits of a treatment and choose to undergo it only if the latter outweighed the former for them.

Another model for reducing the litigation exposure of manufacturers is to place statutory limits on tort liability. Forty-eight states have enacted what are known as blood shield laws, which effectively exclude the makers of blood products from any product-based liability.[44] The laws do not put the purveyors of blood and related items completely above the law, but the makers can be held liable for any harms caused, including from manufacturing defects, only on a showing that their behavior was negligent. Like the NCVIA, blood shield laws minimize without completely eliminating the liability risk of manufacturers. Unlike the NCVIA, blood shield laws shift all of that displaced risk to patients rather than substituting a government-sponsored insurance system funded by the manufacturers.

Much like the NCVIA, blood shield laws were originally justified, and continue to be justified, as an attempt to ensure that there will be both a sufficient number of producers in the market and reasonable prices for blood products—noble goals, to be sure. But the laws also should serve as a cautionary tale. According to a report by the Institute of Medicine (IOM), in the late 1970s it was technologically possible to apply a heat treatment to certain plasma products relied on by hemophiliacs that would have prevented the spread of blood-borne hepatitis, but the industry did not move quickly to develop that technology because it considered hepatitis to be a manageable complication of blood transfusions.[45] That inertia proved fatal when the AIDS epidemic emerged and the HIV virus, transmitted via blood transfusions, ravaged the hemophiliac population because the same process that would have destroyed the hepatitis virus would have killed the HIV virus as well. The IOM concluded that "the absence of incentives, as well as the lack of a countervailing force to advocate blood product safety, contributed to the plasma fractionation industry's slow rate of progress toward the development of heat treatment measures earlier."[46] Hemophiliacs who contracted HIV through tainted transfusions in the early years of the AIDS epidemic were largely unsuccessful in lawsuits against the makers of blood products. It is at least possible (although by no means certain) that a greater risk of legal liability would have induced manufacturers to adopt more sophisticated processing practices earlier.[47]

Products liability, like FDA regulation, is a double-edged sword. On one hand, liability encourages more precaution and provides compensation for the injured. On the other hand, these benefits come at the cost of higher product prices, delays in bringing products to market, and—especially if liability is unpredictable or uninsurable—fewer innovators willing to enter the market, all other things being equal. The right balance for emerging stem cell treatments is difficult to strike because no one knows whether there will be more Molly Nashes who will be saved from harm by more expansive liability rules or more who will die as an indirect result of such rules because rising health insurance prices or producer unwillingness to even enter the market have put the life-saving treatment beyond their reach.

In the early years of the stem cell century, when risks posed by stem cell treatments are likely to be more unknown and unpredictable than those of other pharmaceuticals, the best balance is probably to make compliance with all relevant FDA regulations—including manufacturing standards and warning requirements—a complete defense to tort claims, at least for the broad class of stem cell treatments for which the FDA will require premarket approval. By statute, Congress has effectively provided at least a partial regulatory compliance defense to the makers of some medical devices, but not to the makers of drugs or biologics.[48]

There are problems with this approach, to be sure. First, the FDA does not investigate whether a new drug is as safe as is reasonably possible, only whether the benefits of a particular product outweigh its risks.[49] An FDA compliance defense would undermine an incentive created by tort liability for manufacturers to make a useful product even safer when doing so is relatively easy to do. Additionally, manufacturers will often know of—or have the ability to learn about—adverse events that occur after a product receives FDA approval before the agency knows. A regulatory compliance defense would undermine a manufacturer's incentive to provide new warnings or even withdraw dangerous products from the market before the FDA, with its limited staff and budget, can learn of the problems, examine them carefully, and order appropriate action.[50]

The benefits that a regulatory compliance defense would provide, however, outweigh the costs. By enabling manufacturers to both manage and, more important, predict their tort law exposure, the availability of the defense would provide some cost containment and encourage more and faster commercialization of revolutionary treatments.

# 10

# Conclusion

The stem cell century presents our society with a variety of complex and controversial policy challenges in addition to those we face in the realm of science and technology. At root, there are two basic, related questions with which to grapple: how do we maximize the likelihood that stem cell research and regenerative medicine will achieve their full therapeutic potential, and how do we balance that worthy goal against other moral and ethical values with which it might come into conflict? This book has critically analyzed a broad range of issues with these questions in mind and, in so doing, has reached the following conclusions.

There is no logically defensible basis for viewing human embryos as possessing the same moral value as persons and, consequently, no justification for disfavoring hESC research in funding policy when the research has the potential to save and improve millions of lives. Further, the federal government's current stem cell research funding policy is logically inconsistent with its basic premise—which is to avoid causal complicity in embryo destruction—because it permits funding of

some hESC research that will encourage future embryo destruction, because it forbids funding of some hESC research
when embryo destruction is already inevitable, and because it
relies upon the tool of spending limitations when its premise,
if accepted, would call for a complete legal prohibition.

The congressional alternative, stymied to date by the
presidential veto, would be an improvement, but it is also
flawed. It rests on a logically indefensible distinction between
discarded embryos and those created specifically for research
purposes. This distinction, if ultimately enshrined into law,
would slow the progress of research without providing any significant offsetting benefits.

Congressional attempts to prohibit therapeutic cloning—
SCNT—are undesirable because they would impede medical
progress and undermine several independent constitutional
values while doing little to achieve any legitimate policy goal.
Although its medical value is still unproven, therapeutic
cloning is currently the most promising theoretical approach
to overcoming the problem of immune system rejection likely
to be triggered by hESC-based treatments. It is also likely to
have other benefits, such as enabling the creation of disease-
specific cell lines that can be used to test new pharmaceuticals.
Criminalizing SCNT would have the additional negative consequences of undermining the value of federalism, which counsels toward allowing states rather than Congress to legislate
moral judgments, and interfering with individual liberty interests in seeking medical treatments and in exercising reproductive freedom.

Prohibiting the investigation of SCNT technology because it strikes many as unnatural would be improvident because such reactions are often a consequence of social con-
ditioning and cannot be considered reasons in themselves.

Banning the technology to avoid a slippery slope toward reproductive cloning—the creation of babies who are a genetic copy of adults—is unlikely to be very useful because it is not clear how a ban on SCNT in the United States alone would significantly reduce the risk of reproductive cloning. In any event, less restrictive steps could be taken to minimize the likelihood of reproductive cloning, such as altering genes in cloned blastocysts so as to prevent implantation.

Patent policy must carefully balance the benefits of encouraging the invention of primary technologies against the benefits of encouraging secondary innovations. The need for this balance counsels for providing patents to scientists who create innovative *methods* of producing sustainable hESC lines and substances used to sustain and maintain such lines, but not issuing *product* patents on hESCs themselves or on any other cell type. Such a policy would encourage innovation in the field without creating such broad property rights that using stem cells to create new treatments would become unduly cumbersome, constrained, or costly.

Whether patent law will achieve this delicate balance remains uncertain. An assertive interpretation of the products of nature, moral utility, or enablement doctrine by the PTO or the federal courts could be used to reach the appropriate results, but doing so would mean reversing the Federal Circuit Court of Appeals' narrow, excessively pro-patent jurisprudence. An expansive interpretation of patent law's nonobviousness doctrine or of the safe harbor protection against infringement claims provided by the Hatch-Waxman Act, on the other hand, potentially could shift policy too far in the other direction and result in too little patent protection to encourage investment in risky new technology.

While patent rights are necessary to encourage socially beneficial scientific research, the need is reduced when public funding underwrites the costs of innovation. Typically, funding for scientific research by federal agencies like the NIH or, now, state agencies like California's CIRM, supports basic laboratory research, while the costs of commercialization are borne by private industry. In this situation, the incentive of patent protection is unnecessary to encourage the production of basic science, but it remains necessary to encourage private industry to invest the enormous sums of money necessary to create manufacturing processes and achieve regulatory approval. Both the federal Bayh-Dole Act and CIRM's intellectual property policies are inattentive to this subtlety because they allow grantees to patent all government-funded inventions, rather than just the types of inventions for which the incentive is necessary to assure that the innovation reaches the market.

California's innovative new approach does improve on Bayh-Dole, however, by requiring publicly funded stem cell inventors to share revenues earned from patents with the state. This will create some return on the public's investment while posing little risk of discouraging scientific research. It is true that California is unlikely to earn an enormous windfall, but every dollar recaptured by funders is one dollar that can be used on additional research or other public needs.

Stem cell research requires not only scientific freedom, carefully calibrated intellectual property rules, and public funding, but also human tissues: blastocysts for hESC research, eggs for therapeutic cloning, and adult tissues for adult stem cell research as well as therapeutic cloning. This means the future of the enterprise depends on the recruitment of donors. Tissue donors are somewhat differently situated than typical research subjects, such as clinical trial participants, who are the objects of experimentation. Nonetheless, donors' interests in making autonomous decisions concerning the use of their bodily tissue are just as important as the autonomy interests of traditional research subjects because the informational asymmetries between researcher and lay participant are just as great. This observation counsels for courts to apply the common law doctrine of informed consent to interactions between researchers and tissue donors even in circumstances in which federal informed consent regulations do not apply. It also counsels that, as part of the informed consent process, scientists should be required to disclose any financial interests they have in the research results.

It is essential that informed consent rules balance the autonomy interests of those who might wish not to donate with those who do wish to have their tissues used for important, possibly path-breaking research. This means that researchers should be permitted to use most preexisting banked tissue samples for stem cell research when donors originally provided general or "blanket" assent but were not informed at that time that stem cell research was a possible use for their tissues. When banked tissues are at issue, it is probable that most donors would wish to consent, but obtaining specific informed consent is often impractical. On the other hand, when one of the two individuals whose genetic material is involved wishes to donate a blastocyst to research and the other does not, usage should not be permitted, even when the research supporter has a preexisting contractual right to control the disposition of the blastocyst. In this circumstance, the interests of the dissenter should be given priority because the person who favors donation has the ability to contribute other gametes to research.

Notwithstanding the recent passage of state laws that prohibit payment to tissue donors, there is no persuasive justification for "no-compensation" rules. Such rules risk slowing

the progress of research, and the alleged countervailing benefits prove illusory on careful examination. Prohibitions on
payment harm potential donors by depriving them of valuable
options rather than, as is often claimed, protecting them from
coercion. And there is no empirical or theoretical basis for
thinking that tissue sales harm the rest of society by commod-
ifying human beings: tissues are not the essence of personhood, and, in fact, compensation earned can be put to use in
ways that promote human flourishing.

In addition, compensation prohibitions will not provide
a net benefit to medical research, as is sometimes asserted. The
legality of cash compensation might dissuade some "offended
altruists" from donating, but it will encourage a far greater
number of individuals to provide tissues. Although the legal
permissibility of cash payments will increase demand for payments, and thus modestly increase the cost of research, this
effect will be far outweighed by the increase in the amount of
research that payment for tissues will facilitate.

While payment for tissues should be permitted, no compensation should remain the default position of the law. That
is, when donors provide researchers with tissue and no mention of compensation is made by either party, no financial obligation should be presumed. This default rule will not result
in an unfair surprise to many tissue donors—most will assume
that if no mention is made of payment, none will be forthcoming—and it will provide support for an ethic of altruistic
donation that is beneficial to medical research as long as it is
not insisted upon.

When we transition into an era in which stem cell treatments are widespread, new policy issues will emerge and increase in importance. Current therapeutic success with
hematopoietic stem cell transplants highlights a problem that

arises when one person's treatment requires the HLA-compatible stem cells of another and the potential donor is legally incapable of providing informed consent. This issue is best addressed not by demanding that the donor receive an actual benefit before donation is permitted, but by asking whether the donor could have counted on a tissue donation from the patient had their circumstances been reversed.

Whether the FDA should regulate stem cell products in the same way it regulates other drugs and biologics is a critical issue but one that is extremely difficult to resolve because it requires balancing the values of access, timeliness, and cost effectiveness against that of safety. The FDA's current approach of regulating stem cell products in which the cells are "minimally manipulated" less stringently than other stem cell products is sensible. However, the distinctions the agency has drawn based on whether a product is intended for the use of a relative or nonrelative of the stem cell source, and based on whether the labeled use is homologous or nonhomologous, are suspect.

Finally, it is a near certainty that stem cell treatments will cause harm in some cases, even if they promote healing and reduce suffering in many more. What recourse through the tort system should be available to the victims of the inevitable mishaps? Although not a perfect solution, the best balance between promoting safety and encouraging the development and production of uncertain new technologies is to shield manufacturers of new stem cell treatments from legal liability if they fully comply with all applicable FDA regulatory requirements.

These policies will not guarantee that stem cell medicine will ultimately achieve its promise, but they will help to set us on a course in the right direction.

# Notes

## Chapter 1.
## The Promise and the Hype

1. Hans S. Keirstead et al., *Human Embryonic Stem Cell-Derived Oligodendrocyte Progenitor Cell Transplants Remyelinate and Restore Locomotion after Spinal Cord Injury*, 25 JOURNAL OF NEUROSCIENCE 4694 (2005).

2. Connie Bruck, *Hollywood Science*, NEW YORKER, Oct. 18, 2004.

3. *See* Terri Somers, *Investors Wanted—Must Have Vision, Passion*, SAN DIEGO UNION-TRIBUNE, Dec. 17, 2006.

4. Barbara Demick, *Faith in "Miracle Cures" Is Fading in South Korea*, LOS ANGELES TIMES, March 5, 2006, at A10; Kim Tae-gyu, *Korea Tightens Rules on Stem Cell Therapy*, KOREA TIMES, January 23, 2006.

5. *Stem Cell Research: Hearings before the Subcommittee on Labor, Health and Human Services, Education and Related Agencies of the Senate Committee on Appropriations*, 105th Congress 9–10 (1998).

6. Joseph Martin, dean of the Faculty of Medicine at Harvard University; *available at* http://www.news.harvard.edu/gazette/2004/04.22/99-StemQuotes.html.

7. On NPR's *Morning Edition*, Feb. 13, 2004.

8. Letter to President Bush, principal authors Rep. Cal Dooley (D-Cal.) and Rep. Randy "Duke" Cunningham (R-Cal.), Apr. 28, 2004.

9. *Hype over Experience: Stem Cells and Business*, ECONOMIST, Sept. 24, 2005, at 90.

10. For a concise description, see Christopher Thomas Scott, STEM CELL NOW: FROM THE EXPERIMENT THAT SHOOK THE WORLD TO THE NEW POLITICS OF LIFE 15–22 (2006).

11. *See, e.g.,* Douglas A. Melton & Chad Cowen, *"Stemness": Definitions, Criteria, and Standards, in* ESSENTIALS OF STEM CELL BIOLOGY xxv (Robert Lanza et al. eds., 2006).

12. *See* President's Council on Bioethics, MONITORING STEM CELL RESEARCH 7 (2004) [hereinafter PCB MONITORING].

13. *See, e.g.,* Melton & Cowen, *supra* note 11, at xxvi.

14. Scott, *supra* note 10, at 27; PCB MONITORING, *supra* note 12, at 167.

15. *See* R. L. Gardner, *Present Perspective and Future Challenges, in* ESSENTIALS OF STEM CELL BIOLOGY 1, 2 (Robert Lanza et al. eds., 2006) (noting that the "widely adopted convention is to describe ES cells as pluripotent").

16. *See* Melton & Cowen, *supra* note 11, at xxviii (stating that "no totipotent stem cell has been isolated from the early embryo"). Trophectoderm stem cells have been isolated, but these differentiate only into cells of the trophectoderm lineage. *Id.*

17. *See* PCB MONITORING, *supra* note 12, at 168.

18. The development process the embryo undergoes in the two months following fertilization is described clearly and concisely in PCB MONITORING, *Appendix A: Notes on Early Human Development. Id.* at 157–79.

19. *Id.* at 173.

20. *Id.*

21. *Id.* at 172. President's Council on Bioethics, HUMAN CLONING AND HUMAN DIGNITY: AN ETHICAL INQUIRY 136 (2002) [hereinafter PCB CLONING]. Twinning is very rare, although possible, after this point and can lead to the birth of conjoined twins. PCB MONITORING, *supra* note 12, at 172.

22. *See* Darwin J. Prockop, *Embryonic Stem Cells versus Adult Stem Cells: Some Seemingly Simple Questions, in* ESSENTIALS OF STEM CELL BIOLOGY xxiii (Robert Lanza et al. eds., 2006).

23. Some scientists suggest that unipotent stem cells be referred to as "progenitor cells" to distinguish them from multipotent stem cells. *See, e.g.,* Melton & Cowen, *supra* note 11, at xxvi.

24. Ann B. Parson, THE PROTEUS EFFECT 62 (2004).

25. Martin Evans & Matthew Kaufman, *Establishment in Culture of Pluripotential Cells from Mouse Embryos,* 292 NATURE 154 (1981).

26. James A. Thomson et al., *Embryonic Stem Cell Lines Derived from Human Blastocysts,* 282 SCIENCE 1145 (1998).

27. Scott, *supra* note 10, at 5.

28. PCB MONITORING, *supra* note 12, at 128; PCB CLONING, *supra* note 21, at 65. On mitochondrial DNA, *see id.* at 58–59.

29. *See generally* PCB CLONING, *supra* note 21, at 59–60 (describing the steps in the SCNT process).

30. PCB Cloning, *supra* note 21, at 65–66.

31. *See* Gina Kolata, *Scientist Reports First Cloning Ever of Adult Mammal,* New York Times, Feb. 23, 1997, at A1. A decade earlier, the Danish veterinarian Steen Willadsen produced a live-born sheep after fusing the nucleus of a sheep embryonic stem cell (rather than a somatic cell) with a sheep's egg. *See* Scott, *supra* note 10, at 45.

32. *See, e.g.,* Gardner, *supra* note 15, at 8 ("therapeutic cloning has been widely advocated as a way of tailoring grafts to individual patients, thereby circumventing the problem of graft rejection").

33. *See* W. M. Ridout et al., *Correction of a Genetic Defect by Nuclear Transplantation and Combined Cell and Gene Therapy,* 109 Cell 17 (2002).

34. *See* Nicholas Wade & Choe Sang-Hun, *Human Cloning Was All Faked, Korean Reports,* New York Times, Jan. 10, 2006, at A1.

35. M. J. Shamblott et al., *Derivation of Pluripotent Stem Cells from Cultured Human Primordial Germ Cells,* 95 Proceedings of the National Academy of Sciences of the United States of America 13, 726 (1998).

36. *See* Behrouz Aflatoonian & Harry Moore, *Human Primordial Germ Cells and Embryonic Germ Cells, and Their Use in Cell Therapy,* 16 Current Opinion in Biotechnology 530, 531 tbl. 1 (2005).

37. *See* Yuval Dor & Douglas A. Melton, *Pancreatic Stem Cells, in* Essentials of Stem Cell Biology 245, 250–51 (Robert Lanza et al. eds., 2006) (pancreatic beta cells, necessary to treat Type 1 diabetes, appear to be maintained in the adult body by self-duplication rather than stem cell differentiation); *see also* Scott, *supra* note 10, at 82–85 (describing the research of Dor and Melton).

38. *See* Parson, *supra* note 24, at 182–83.

39. *Id.* at 207.

40. *See, e.g.,* John C. Fletcher, *Deliberating Incrementally on Human Pluripotent Stem Cell Research, in* National Bioethics Advisory Commission, Ethical Issues in Human Stem Cell Research Vol. II (Commissioned Papers), at E6–E7 (2000); National Institutes of Health, *Stem Cell Basics; available at* http://stemcells.nih.gov/info/basics/.

41. In August 2006, Nature published an important study in which scientists were able to create two hESC lines using cells from three-day-old embryos made up of 8–10 cells each; the result suggests that it might be possible to create such lines without destroying embryos. Irina Klimanskaya et al., *Human Embryonic Stem Cell Lines Derived from Single Blastomeres,* 444 Nature 481 (2006). To date, this result has not significantly dampened opposition to hESC research. The reasons for the continued opposition are explored in detail in Chapter 2.

42. *See* Scott, *supra* note 10, at 101 (describing the procedure); Parson, *supra* note 24, at 64–65 (reporting this procedure is now more common than traditional bone marrow transplants).

43. This is also the response provided on the Web site of the National Institutes of Health to the question of why scientists do not use only hASCs in research. See National Institutes of Health, *Stem Cell Information; available at* http://stemcells.nih.gov/info/faqs.asp.

44. *See* Dor & Melton, *supra* note 37, at 250–51.

45. PCB MONITORING, *supra* note 12, at 135–36.

46. *See* Prockop, *supra* note 22, at xxiii; Gardner, *supra* note 15, at 8.

47. *See* Parson, *supra* note 24, at 240.

48. *See* Melton & Cowen, *supra* note 11, at xxix.

49. *See* Parson, *supra* note 24, at 200–201. The dominant opinion in the scientific community today is that hASCs that appear to have transdifferentiated have really only fused with other types of cells. *See, e.g.,* Gardner, *supra* note 15, at 8.

50. Paolo De Coppi et al., *Isolation of Amniotic Stem Cell Lines with Potential for Therapy,* 25 NATURE BIOTECHNOLOGY 100 (2007).

51. *See* Rick Weiss, *Scientists See Potential in Amniotic Cells,* WASHINGTON POST, Jan. 8, 2007, at A1; Karen Kaplan, *Stem Cells in Amniotic Fluid Show Promise,* LOS ANGELES TIMES, Jan. 8, 2007, at A1.

52. Keisuke Okita et al., *Generation of Germline-Competent Induced Pluripotent Stem Cells,* NATURE advance online publication, June 6, 2007 (doi: 10.1038/nature05934); Marius Wernig et al., *In Vitro Reprogramming of Fibroblasts into a Pluripotent ES-cell-like State,* NATURE advance online publication, June 6, 2007 (doi: 10.1038/nature05944); Nimet Maherali et al., *Directly Reprogrammed Fibroblasts Show Global Epigenetic Remodeling and Widespread Tissue Contribution,* 1 CELL STEM CELL 55 (2007).

## Chapter 2.
## The Embryo Wars

1. Matthew C. Nisbet, *Public Opinion about Stem Cell Research and Human Cloning,* 68 PUBLIC OPINION QUARTERLY 131, 133 & tbls. 1, 3 (2004).

2. *See* Christopher Thomas Scott, STEM CELL NOW: FROM THE EXPERIMENT THAT SHOOK THE WORLD TO THE NEW POLITICS OF LIFE 9 (2006) (quoting a Bush campaign speech).

3. Balanced Budget Downpayment Act of 1996, Public Law No. 104–99, § 128, 110 STATUTES AT LARGE 26, 34:

None of the funds made available by Public Law 104–91 may be used for—

(1) the creation of a human embryo or embryos for research purposes; or

(2) research in which a human embryo or embryos are destroyed, discarded, or knowingly subjected to risk of injury or death greater than that allowed for research on fetuses in utero under 45 CFR 46.208(a)(2) and 42 USC 289g(b).

For purposes of this section, the phrase "human embryo or embryos" shall include any organism not protected as a human subject under 45 CFR 46 as of the date of enactment of this Act that is derived by fertilization, parthenogenesis, cloning, or any other means from one or more human gametes.

4. *See* O. Carter Snead, *The Pedagogical Significance of the Bush Stem Cell Policy: A Window into Bioethical Regulation in the United States,* 5 YALE JOURNAL OF HEALTH POLICY, LAW, & ETHICS 491, 494 (2005).

5. Memorandum of Harriet S. Raab, Gen. Counsel, Dept. of Health and Human Servs., to Harold Varmus, Dir., Nat'l Insts. of Health (Jan. 15, 1999), *in* Lori B. Andrews et al., GENETICS, ETHICS, LAW & POLICY 138 (2002); *see also* LeRoy Walters, *Human Embryo Research: Lessons from History,* 293 SCIENCE 1401, 1401 (2001).

6. *See Stem Cell Research: CRS Report for Congress,* 840 PLI/Pat 351, 363–64 (2005).

7. Katharine Q. Seelye, *A Long Process That Led Bush to His Decision,* NEW YORK TIMES, Aug. 11, 2001, at A1.

8. *See* Scott Lindlaw (Associated Press), *Bush Allows Some Stem Cell Funding,* Aug. 9, 2001, 9:33 p.m. EDT.

9. Address to the Nation on Stem Cell Research from Crawford, Texas, 37 WEEKLY COMPILATION OF PRESIDENTIAL DOCUMENTS 1149 (Aug. 9, 2001) [hereinafter Address to the Nation]; *available at* www.whitehouse.gov/news/releases/2001/08/20010809-2.html; *see also* National Institutes of Health Guidelines for Research Using Human Pluripotent Stem Cells, 65 FEDERAL REGISTER 51,976 (Aug. 25, 2000), *withdrawn by* 66 FEDERAL REGISTER 57,107 (Nov. 14, 2001).

10. Nisbet, *supra* note 1, at 137 & tbl. 17.

11. There is a utilitarian argument that embryo research could be justified even if embryos have equivalent moral value to persons if the poten-

tial gains from the research are sufficiently great, but this argument is left to one side here.

12. See President's Council on Bioethics, MONITORING STEM CELL RESEARCH 76–78 (2004) [hereinafter PCB MONITORING].

13. For example, *see* British Human Fertilisation and Embryology Act, 1990, c. 37, §§ 3(3)(a), (3)(4) (Eng.).

14. Committee on Guidelines for Human Embryonic Stem Cell Research, National Research Council, GUIDELINES FOR HUMAN EMBRYONIC STEM CELL RESEARCH 8 (2005) [hereinafter NRC GUIDELINES].

15. This hypothetical is adapted from similar versions in Michael J. Sandel, *The Ethical Implications of Human Cloning,* 48 PERSPECTIVES IN BIOLOGY & MEDICINE. 241 (2005), and George J. Annas, *A French Homunculus in a Tennessee Court,* 19 HASTINGS CENTER REPORT 20 (1989)

16. Uniform Determination of Death Act § 1. The National Conference of Commissioners on Uniform State Laws counts forty states, the District of Columbia, Puerto Rico, and the U.S. Virgin Islands as having adopted the model law either verbatim or with only minor variation. See www.nccusl .org/Update/uniformact_factsheets/uniformacts-fs-udda.asp.

17. Pope John Paul II, THE GOSPEL OF LIFE [EVANGELIUM VITAE], 1995, paras. 58–63.

18. *See* Aaron L. Mackler, INTRODUCTION TO JEWISH AND CATHOLIC BIOETHICS 127–130 (2003) (citing examples).

19. John A. Robertson, *Extracorporeal Embryos and the Abortion Debate,* 2 JOURNAL OF CONTEMPORARY HEALTH LAW & POLICY 53, 63 (1986); Michael J. Sandel, *Embryo Ethics: The Moral Logic of Stem-Cell Research,* 351 NEW ENGLAND JOURNAL OF MEDICINE 207, 208 (2004).

20. For an argument that for this reason the blastocyst lacks a "valuable future" and thus lacks moral status, see Bonnie Steinbock, *The Morality of Killing Human Embryos,* JOURNAL OF LAW, MEDICINE & ETHICS, 26, 33 (2006).

21. *See, e.g.,* Stephen S. Hall, *The Good Egg,* DISCOVER, May 2004, at 30, 34 (discussing rates of implantation and miscarriage).

22. *Cf.* John A. Robertson, *Causative vs. Beneficial Complicity in the Embryonic Stem Cell Debate,* 36 CONNECTICUT LAW REVIEW 1099, 1101–02 (2005).

23. *See, e.g.,* Lucinda L. Veeck et al., *High Pregnancy Rates Can Be Achieved after Freezing and Thawing Human Blastocysts,* 82 FERTILITY & STERILITY, 1418, 1418 (2004).

24. *See* Bruce L. Wilder, *Assisted Reproduction Technology: Trends and Suggestions for the Developing Law,* 18 JOURNAL OF THE AMERICAN ACADEMY

OF MATRIMONIAL LAWYERS 177, 191–92 (2002) (noting that the embryos rather than the eggs are frozen because embryos withstand the freezing process better than eggs do, and freezing the embryos prevents a woman from having to go through another egg harvesting procedure).

25. One recent study of an IVF clinic found that the average number of eggs harvested per patient was 16.1 and the average number of zygotes successfully created, 10.2. Evelyn Neuber et al., *Sequential Embryo Assessment Outperforms Investigator-Driven Morphological Assessment at Selecting a Good Quality Blastocyst,* 85 FERTILITY & STERILITY 794, 794 (2006).

26. *See id.* at 795 (an embryologist recommends which of the embryos to use, and the physician discusses the recommendations with the patient).

27. *See* Tarun Jain et al., *Trends in Embryo-Transfer Practice and in Outcomes of the Use of Assisted Reproductive Technology in the United States,* 350 NEW ENGLAND JOURNAL OF MEDICINE 1639, 1642 tbl. 1 (2004).

28. Andrea D. Gurmankin et al., *Embryo Disposal Practices in IVF Clinics in the United States,* 22 POLITICS & THE LIFE SCIENCES 4, 6 (August 2004).

29. *See, e.g.,* Susan C. Klock, *Embryo Disposition: The Forgotten "Child" of In Vitro Fertilization,* 49 INTERNATIONAL JOURNAL OF FERTILITY & WOMEN'S MEDICINE 19, 19 (2004); American Academy of Pediatrics, *Human Embryo Research,* 108 PEDIATRICS 813, 814 (2001).

30. *See generally* Ronald M. Green, *Benefiting from Evil: An Incipient Moral Problem in Human Stem Cell Research,* 16 BIOETHICS 544, 548–50 (2002) (discussing the ways in which making use of goods created through the commission of evil acts can encourage such acts).

31. Address to the Nation, *supra* note 9.

32. *See* Richard W. Momeyer, *Embryos, Stem Cells, Morality and Public Policy: Difficult Connections,* 31 CAPITAL UNIVERSITY LAW REVIEW 93, 99–102 (2003).

33. Alan Cooperman, *Catholics Split on Embryo Issue,* WASHINGTON POST, May 31, 2005, at A1; Nina J. Easton, *Stem Cell Vote May Challenge President,* BOSTON GLOBE, May 24, 2005, at A2.

34. Sheryl de Lacey, *Parent Identity and "Virtual" Children: Why Patients Discard Rather than Donate Unused Embryos,* 20 HUMAN REPRODUCTION 1661, 1666 (2005).

35. David I. Hoffman et al., *Cryopreserved Embryos in the United States and Their Availability for Research,* 79 FERTILITY & STERILITY 1063, 1066, 1068 (2003).

36. *See* Momeyer, *supra* note 32, at 103; *but see* Leon E. Rosenberg, *Exceptional Economic Returns in Investments in Medical Research,* 177 MEDICAL JOURNAL OF AUSTRALIA 368, 369 (2002) (reporting that in 1999 the biophar-

maceutical industry sponsored 55 percent of the total U.S. investment in medical research, while the federal government's contribution was only 33 percent of the total).

37. *See Gonzales v. Oregon,* 545 U.S. 243 (2006).

38. See Dept. of Labor, Health and Human Services, and Education, and Related Agencies Appropriations Act, 2006, Public Law No. 109–149, § 507, 119 STATUTES AT LARGE 2879, 2880.

39. Stem Cell Research Enhancement Act of 2005, H.R. 810, 109th Congress § 2 (2005).

40. *CBS News: Arlen Specter's Stem Cell Battle* (CBS television broadcast June 3, 2005); *available at* www.cbsnews.com/stories/2005/06/03/evening news/main699633.shtml.

41. Statement of Administration Policy, Executive Office of the President (May 24, 2005) (warning that if "H.R. 810 were presented to the President, he would veto the bill"); *available at* www.whitehouse.gov/omb/ legislative/sap/109–1/hr810sap-h.pdf.

42. Carl Hulse, *Senate Approves a Stem Cell Bill; Veto Is Expected,* NEW YORK TIMES, July 19, 2006, at A1.

43. Sheryl Gay Stolberg, *First Bush Veto Maintains Limits on Stem Cell Use,* NEW YORK TIMES, July 20, 2006, at A1.

44. *Id.*

45. *See also* John A. Robertson, *Embryo Culture and the "Culture of Life": Constitutional Issues in the Embryonic Stem Cell Debate,* 2006 UNIVERSITY OF CHICAGO LEGAL FORUM 1, 2–3. Although it is not binding on a court that might be called on in the future to interpret the SCREA, Rep. DeGette (D-Colo.), one of the bill's sponsors, explained on the floor of the House of Representatives that she does not interpret the bill as overturning the limitations imposed by the Dickey Amendment. *See* 151 CONGRESSIONAL RECORD H3824–25 (daily edition, May 24, 2005).

46. *See* Stem Cell Research Enhancement Act, *supra* note 39, at § 2 ("Human embryonic stem cells shall be eligible for use in any research conducted by the Secretary if . . . the stem cells were derived from human embryos that have been donated from in vitro fertilization clinics, were created for the purposes of fertility treatment, and were in excess of the clinical need of the individuals seeking such treatment.")

47. *Id.* at 55.

48. Gareth Cook, *Harvard Provost OKs Procedure: Key Approval Moves Project Closer to Launch,* BOSTON GLOBE, Mar. 20, 2005, at A29.

49. Kutluk Oktay et al., *Efficiency of Oocyte Cryopreservation: A Meta-Analysis,* 86 FERTILITY & STERILITY 70 (2006) (concluding that "in vitro fertilization success rates with slow-frozen oocytes are significantly lower when

compared with the case of IVF with unfrozen oocytes"); *see also* Victoria Clay Wright et al., *Assisted Reproductive Technology Surveillance: United States, 2003,* 55 MORBIDITY & MORTALITY WEEKLY REPORT 1, 1 (2006); *available at* www.cdc.gov/mmwr/preview/mmwrhtlm/ss5504a1.htm; SOCIETY FOR ASSISTED REPRODUCTION TECHNOLOGY, 2004 CLINIC SUMMARY REPORT; *available at* www.sartcorsonline.com/rptCSR_PublicMultYear.aspx?ClinicPKID=0.

50. Telephone interview by Brad Flood with Dr. Jeffrey Steinberg, U.S. Institutes director, Fertility Institutes, Los Angeles, California (July 25, 2006).

51. *See* Terri Somers, *Stem Cell Work Steps Forward in San Diego,* SAN DIEGO UNION-TRIBUNE, Mar. 7, 2006, at A1.

52. *See* Jon Entine & Sally Satel, *Inserting Race into the Stem Cell Debate,* WASHINGTON POST, Sept. 9, 2001, at B1 (lamenting "the lack of genetic and 'racial' diversity" among the embryonic stem cell lines approved for federally funded research and the fact that most of them "were harvested from embryos at U.S., Swedish and Israeli fertility clinics, where patients are overwhelmingly white").

53. A survey of 80,196 assisted reproduction cycles from 1999 and 2000 has shown the following breakdown of IVF users by race: Caucasian (85.6 percent), Hispanic (5.4 percent), African American (4.6 percent), and Asian American (4.5 percent). There is also a clearly pronounced effect of age and higher income. Married women over forty with incomes higher than three times the federal poverty level were significantly more likely to seek IVF than younger, unmarried, and less affluent women. *See* D. A. Grainger et al., *Racial Disparity in Clinical Outcomes from Women Using Advanced Reproductive Technology (ART): Analysis of 80,196 ART Cycles from the SART Database 1999 and 2000,* 82 FERTILITY & STERILITY S37 (2004); Elizabeth Hervey Stephen & Anjali Chandra, *Use of Infertility Services in the United States: 1995,* 32 FAMILY PLANNING PERSPECTIVES 132 (2000).

54. *See, e.g.,* Barry D. Bavister et al., *Challenges of Primate Embryonic Stem Cell Research,* 7 CLONING & STEM CELLS 82, 84–85 (2002); Gina Kolata, *Researchers Say Embryos in Labs Aren't Available,* NEW YORK TIMES, Aug. 26, 2001, at A1.

55. *Cf.* R. L. Gardner, *Present Perspective and Future Challenges, in* ESSENTIALS OF STEM CELL BIOLOGY 1, 6–7 (Robert Lanza et al. eds., 2006) (raising the question of whether the fact that excess IVF embryos are of relatively low quality for IVF purposes will undermine the therapeutic potential of their embryonic stem cells).

56. The NIH maintains a registry to identify lines eligible for federal funding and identifies which ones are actually available for use. *See* http://stemcells.nih.gov/research/registry.

57. *The Promise of Embryonic Stem Cells: Hearing before the Senate*

*Special Committee on Aging,* 109th Congress (2005) (statement of John D. Gearhart, Professor, Johns Hopkins University School of Medicine) [hereinafter Gearhart, Testimony] (explaining that "the 22 lines now eligible for federally funded research are contaminated with animal cells, lack genetic diversity, are not disease-specific, and are not adequate for researchers to apply to a wide variety of diseases"); *see also* PCB MONITORING, *supra* note 12, at 5.

58. NRC GUIDELINES, *supra* note 14, at 15 (stating that "the roughly 22 lines now available were grown on mouse-feeder cell layers" and that "the presence of animal feeder cells increases the risk of transfer of animal viruses and other infectious agents to humans that receive the hES cells and in turn to many others").

59. *See* Gearhart Testimony, *supra* note 57; Robertson, *Causative vs. Beneficial Complicity, supra* note 22, at 1109; Andis Robeznieks, *Embryonic Stem Cell Line Found to Be Contaminated,* AMERICAN MEDICAL NEWS, Feb. 14, 2005.

60. *See* Tom Abate, *UCSF Stem Cell Expert Leaving U.S.: Scientist Fears That Political Uncertainty Threatens His Research,* SAN FRANCISCO CHRONICLE, July 17, 2001, at A1.

61. Associated Press, *Singapore Woos Top Biotechnology Scientists with New Labs, Research Money,* April 14, 2006; *see also* Christopher Thomas Scott & Jennifer McCormick, *Vantage Point: United States Losing Competitive Edge in Stem Cell Research,* STANFORD REPORT, May 3, 2006.

62. *See, e.g.,* Eve Herold, STEM CELL WARS: INSIDE STORIES FROM THE FRONT LINES 204 (2006); Wayne Arnold, *Luring Top Stem Cell Researchers with Financing and Freedom,* NEW YORK TIMES, Aug. 17, 2006, at C1.

63. Jason Owen-Smith & Jennifer McCormick, *An International Gap in Human ES Cell Research,* 24 NATURE BIOTECHNOLOGY 391 (2006); Christopher Thomas Scott & Jennifer McCormick, *Falling Behind on Stem Cell Research,* BOSTON GLOBE, Apr. 18, 2006, at A1.

64. Owen-Smith & McCormick, *supra* note 63.

65. These estimates are derived from THE UK STEM CELL INITIATIVE: REPORT AND RECOMMENDATIONS, §§ 4.1, 4.2 (2005) (pages 28–54); *available at* www.advisorybodies.doh.gov.uk/uksci/uksci-reportnov05.pdf.

66. *See* Department of Health, *Government Responds to the UK Stem Cell Initiative Report and Recommendations* (Dec. 2, 2005); *available at* www.dh.gov.uk/PolicyAndGuidance; *UK Stem Cell Drive* (News in Brief), 24 NATURE BIOTECHNOLOGY 11 (2006).

67. *See* National Institutes of Health, *Estimates of Funding for Various Diseases, Conditions, and Research Areas* (updated March 10, 2006); *available at* www.nih.gov/news/funding.pdf.

68. Carl Hall, $16 *Million Gift for UCSF Research Center,* SAN FRAN-CISCO CHRONICLE, May 12, 2006, at B9; Press Release, University of Southern California, *Broad Foundation Donates $25 Million to Create New Stem Cell Institute at Keck School of Medicine* (Feb. 23, 2006); *available at* www.usc.edu/uscnews/stories/12094.html; Winnie Hu, *Metro Briefing/New York: Bloomberg Donates $100 Million to University,* NEW YORK TIMES, Feb. 3, 2006, at B4; Antonia Regalado, *Embryo Stem-Cell Research Spreads Despite Curbs,* WALL STREET JOURNAL, Apr. 4, 2006, at D3.

69. *See* Lori B. Andrews, *State Regulation of Embryo Stem Cell Research, in* 2 ETHICAL ISSUES IN HUMAN STEM CELL RESEARCH A1, A4, & A10 n. 11 (2000).

70. *See id.* at A4–A5.

71. ARIZONA REVISED STATUTES ANNOTATED § 35–196.04; NEBRASKA REVISED STATUTES § 71–7606; VIRGINIA CODE ANNOTATED § 23–286.1.

72. MISSOURI REVISED STATUTES § 196.1127 ; *id.,* § 196.1127.2(6).

73. INDIANA CODE §§ 36–7–32–7, –11, –18; MICHIGAN COMPILED LAWS §§ 207.801–207.803; 211.9j; VIRGINIA CODE ANNOTATED §§ 2.2–2233.2; 58.1–3506.

74. CALIFORNIA HEALTH & SAFETY CODE § 125115.

75. For a review of these statutes, see Susan Stayn, *A Guide to State Laws on hESC Research and a Call for Interstate Dialogue,* MEDICAL RESEARCH LAW & POLICY REPORT, vol. 5: 21, at 1 (Nov. 1, 2006) (identifying statutes enacted in Connecticut, New Jersey, Maryland, Massachusetts, and Rhode Island). More recently, Iowa also enacted a statute explicitly protecting stem cell research in that state. Iowa Legislative Service S.F. 162 (2007).

76. CALIFORNIA CONSTITUTION article XXXV.

77. *See* Russell Korobkin, *The Stem Cell Initiative, Sabotaged,* LOS ANGELES TIMES, Mar. 3, 2006, at B13.

78. Letter from Arnold Schwarzenegger, Governor, California, to Mike Genest, Director of Finance, California (July 20, 2006) (on file with author).

79. *See* Bill Ainsworth, *Charities to Fund Stem Cell Research,* SAN DIEGO UNION-TRIBUNE, Apr. 5, 2006, at C1.

80. *Id.*

81. Laura Mansnerus, *New Jersey Faces Tough Competition for Stem Cell Scientists,* NEW YORK TIMES, Jan. 17, 2005, at B1.

82. *See* William Hathaway, *Stem Cell Grants Now Available,* HARTFORD COURANT, May 10, 2006, at 39.

83. *See* Press Release, Office of Governor Rod R. Blagojevich, *Gov. Blagojevich, Comptroller Hynes Announce $10 Million in State Stem Cell Research Grants* (April 24, 2006); *available at* www.illinois.gov/PressReleases/ShowPressRelease.cfm?SubjectID=1&RecNum=4799.

84. Christine Vestal, *Stem Cell Wars Rage in State Capitols,* Stateline .org, July 20, 2006; *available at* www.stateline.org/live/ViewPage.action?site NodeId=137&languageId=1&contentId=128323).

85. *See* Nicholas Confessore, *Spitzer Wants New York to Enter the Stem Cell Race,* New York Times, Jan. 16, 2007, at B1.

86. For examples of the steps scientists are taking to avoid improperly intermingling funds, see Karen Kaplan & Erin Cline, *Stem Cell Limits Have Scientists Seeing Double,* Los Angeles Times, Aug. 9, 2006, at A19; Charles C. Mann, *U.S. Stem Cell Researchers Confront Uncertain Financing and Arcane Restrictions,* Technology Review, Sept. 2005, at 44, 48–49.

87. Claudia Dreifus, *At Harvard's Stem Cell Center, the Barriers Run Deep and Wide,* New York Times, Jan. 24, 2006, at F2.

88. The survey for the *Wall Street Journal Online* was conducted by Harris Interactive: Harris Interactive, *Public Support for Stem Cell Research Remains High, but Differences Widen between Supporters and Detractors,* June 7, 2005; *available at* www.harrisinteractive.com/news/allnewsbydate.asp? NewsID=935.

89. Harris Interactive, Harris Poll #78, October 20, 2005; *available at* http://www.harrisinteractive.com/harris_poll/printerfriend/index.asp? PID=608.

90. *See* Matthew C. Nisbet, *The Competition for Worldviews: Values, Information, and Public Support for Stem Cell Research,* 17 International Journal of Public Opinion Research 90, 104 fig. 1 (2005).

91. Lydia Saad (Gallup Poll News Service), *Stem Cell Veto Contrary to Public Opinion,* July 20, 2006; *available at* poll.gallup.com/content/Default .aspx?ci=23827&VERSION=p.

92. Pew Research Center, *Pragmatic Americans Liberal and Conservative on Social Issues,* Aug. 3, 2006; *available at* http://people-press.org/reports/ display.php3?ReportID=283.

93. Harris Interactive, Harris Poll #1, Jan. 3, 2007; *available at* http:// www. harrisinteractive.com/harris_poll/index.asp?PID=717.

94. Irina Klimanskaya et al., *Human Embryonic Stem Cell Lines Derived from Single Blastomeres,* 444 Nature 481 (2006).

95. Young Chung et al., *Embryonic and Extraembryonic Stem Cell Lines Derived from Single Mouse Blastomeres,* 439 Nature 216 (2005).

96. *See* Yuri Verlinsky, *Over a Decade of Experience with Preimplantation Genetic Diagnosis: A Multicenter Report,* 82 Fertility & Sterility 292 (2004).

97. *See, e.g.,* Jeremy Manier, *Stem Cell Find May Not End All Concerns,* Chicago Tribune, Aug. 24, 2006, at 1.

98. *See* Nicholas Wade et al., *In New Method for Stem Cells, Viable Embryos,* NEW YORK TIMES, Aug. 24, 2006, at A1.

99. Klimanskaya et al., *supra* note 94, at 4.

100. *See* Nicholas Wade, *Clarification Issued on Stem Cell Work,* NEW YORK TIMES, Sept. 2, 2006, at A13.

101. *Quoted in* Wade et al., *New Method, supra* note 98.

102. *See* Rick Weiss, *Stem Cells Made with No Harm to Embryos,* WASHINGTON POST, Aug. 24, 2006, at A3.

103. *Quoted in* Wade et al., *New Method, supra* note 98.

104. Weiss, *supra* note 102.

105. *Quoted in* Wade et al., *New Method, supra* note 98.

# Chapter 3.
## Cloning, Congress, and the Constitution

1. Gina Kolata, *Scientist Reports First Cloning Ever of Adult Mammal,* NEW YORK TIMES, Feb. 23, 1997, at A1.

2. S. 368, 105th Congress § 1 (1997) (introduced Feb. 27 by Senator Bond); Human Cloning Prohibition Act, H.R. 923, 105th Congress § 1 (1997) (introduced Mar. 5 by Representative Ehlers); Human Cloning Research Prohibition Act, H.R. 922, 105th Congress § 1 (1997) (introduced Mar. 5 by Representative Ehlers).

3. Memorandum on the Prohibition on Federal Funding for Cloning of Human Beings, 1 PUBLIC PAPERS 233 (Mar. 4, 1997); Letter to National Bioethics Advisory Commission Chair Harold Shapiro on Cloning Technology Issues, 1 PUBLIC PAPERS 196 (Feb. 24, 1997).

4. National Bioethics Advisory Commission, CLONING HUMAN BEINGS: REPORT AND RECOMMENDATIONS (1997).

5. President's Council on Bioethics, HUMAN CLONING AND HUMAN DIGNITY: AN ETHICAL INQUIRY (2002) [hereinafter PCB CLONING].

6. *See* Bert Vogelstein et al., *Please Don't Call It Cloning,* 295 SCIENCE 1237 (2002).

7. ARKANSAS CODE ANNOTATED § 20–16–1002; INDIANA CODE §§ 16–18–2–56.5, 16–21–3–4, 16–34.5, 25–22.5–8–5, 35–46–5–2, 35–46–5–3; MICHIGAN COMPILED LAWS §§ 333.16274-333.16275; NORTH DAKOTA CENTURY CODE § 12.1–39–02; SOUTH DAKOTA CODIFIED LAWS §§ 34–14–26 to 34–14–28.

8. ARKANSAS CODE ANNOTATED § 20–16–1002 (class C felony); INDIANA CODE § 35–46–5–2 (class D felony); NORTH DAKOTA CENTURY CODE §

12.1–39–02 (class C felony); SOUTH DAKOTA CODIFIED LAWS §§ 34–14–27 (class 6 felony); MICHIGAN COMPILED LAWS § 333.16275 ($10,000,000 fine); VIRGINIA CODE ANNOTATED § 32.1–162.22 ($50,000 fine for each cloning incident).

9. CALIFORNIA HEALTH & SAFETY CODE § 125300; MASSACHUSETTS GENERAL LAWS chapter 111L, § 1; NEW JERSEY STATUTES ANNOTATED § 26:2Z-2; RHODE ISLAND GENERAL LAWS § 23–16.4–2; VIRGINIA CODE ANNOTATED § 32.1–162.22.

10. CALIFORNIA HEALTH & SAFETY CODE § 24185; MASSACHUSETTS GENERAL LAWS ch. 111L, § 8; NEW JERSEY STATUTES ANNOTATED § 2C:11A-1; RHODE ISLAND GENERAL LAWS § 23–16.4–1; VIRGINIA CODE ANNOTATED § 32.1–162.22.

11. *See, e.g.,* Consolidated Appropriations Act of 2005, Public Law No. 108–447, § 509, 118 STATUTES AT LARGE 2809, 3163–64 (2004). The limitation of the Dickey Amendment's language to "research purposes" might suggest that a federal agency could legally fund a human cloning project with a goal of developing cloned embryos for implantation. In 1997, President Clinton issued a directive barring the federal funding of any cloning research. *See* 33 WEEKLY COMPILATION OF PRESIDENTIAL DOCUMENTS 281 (Mar. 10, 1997). This directive was integrated into the 2000 Research Guidelines for Research on Pluripotent Stem Cells, 65 FEDERAL REGISTER 51,976 (Aug. 25, 2000), *withdrawn by* 66 FEDERAL REGISTER 57,107 (Nov. 14, 2001).

12. Human Cloning Prohibition Act of 2001, H.R. 2505, 107th Congress (2001); Human Cloning Prohibition Act of 2003, H.R. 534, 108th Congress (2003).

13. The vote in 2003 was 241–155; the vote in 2001 was 265–162. See Jeffrey Brainard, *After Heated Debate, U.S. House Votes Again to Ban Cloning,* CHRONICLE OF HIGHER EDUCATION, Mar. 14, 2003, at A24.

14. Human Cloning Prohibition Act of 2005, H.R. 1357, 109th Congress § 302(b).

15. *Id.* at § 302(c).

16. For the text of the Address, *see* http://www.whitehouse.gov/state oftheunion/2006/index.html# (visited January 12, 2007).

17. *See* Alexander Morgan Capron, *Placing a Moratorium on Research Cloning to Ensure Effective Control over Reproductive Cloning,* 53 HASTINGS LAW JOURNAL 1057, 1064 (describing the "stalemate" in Congress over cloning legislation).

18. President's Council on Bioethics, MONITORING STEM CELL RESEARCH 132–33 (2004) [hereinafter PCB MONITORING].

19. *See, e.g.,* Paul R. McHugh, *Zygote and "Clonote": The Ethical Use of Embryonic Stem Cells,* 351 NEW ENGLAND JOURNAL OF MEDICINE 209, 210 (2004).

20. *See* PCB CLONING, *supra* note 5, at 161–63 (stating the moral hazards of the "complete instrumentalization of nascent human life").

21. *See* Leon Kass, *The Wisdom in Repugnance,* NEW REPUBLIC, June 2, 1997, at 17–26.

22. *See Loving v. Virginia,* 388 U.S. 1, fn. 5 (1967).

23. *See, e.g.,* Lori B. Andrews, *Regulating Reproductive Technologies,* 21 JOURNAL OF LEGAL MEDICINE 35, 35, 40 (2000).

24. *See* Capron, *supra* note 17, at 1061–62 (claiming that therapeutic cloning "would greatly increase the risk of reproductive cloning, just the way the availability of guns greatly increases the risk of homicide").

25. *See generally* Eugene Volokh, *The Mechanisms of the Slippery Slope,* 116 HARVARD LAW REVIEW 1026 (2003).

26. *See* PCB CLONING, *supra* note 5, at 165 (warning that "if we accept even limited uses of cloning-for-biomedical research, we significantly increase the likelihood of cloning-to-produce-children. The technique will gradually be perfected and the cloned embryos will become available, and those who would be interested in producing cloned children will find it much easier to do so").

27. Rudolf Jaenisch, *Human Cloning: The Science and Ethics of Nuclear Transplantation,* 351 NEW ENGLAND JOURNAL OF MEDICINE 2787 (2004).

28. *Id.* at 2789–90.

29. *See* Alexander Meissner & Rudolf Jaenisch, *Generation of Nuclear Transfer-Derived Pluripotent ES Cells from Cloned Cdx2-Deficient Blastocysts,* 439 NATURE 212 (2006).

30. *See* Irving L. Weissman, *Politic Stem Cells,* 439 NATURE 145, 146 (2006).

31. *See* Nicholas Wade, *In New Method for Stem Cells, Viable Embryos,* NEW YORK TIMES, Aug. 24, 2006, at A1 (citing Richard N. Doerflinger, deputy director for pro-life activities).

32. Warren Hoge, *U.S. Drops Effort for Treaty Banning Cloning,* NEW YORK TIMES, Nov. 20, 2004, at A3.

33. United Nations Declaration on Human Cloning, General Assembly Resolution 59/280, ¶ a-c, UNITED NATIONS DOCUMENTS A/RES/59/280 (Mar. 23, 2005).

34. U.S. CONSTITUTION article I, § 8.

35. 514 U.S. 549 (1995).

36. 529 U.S. 598 (2000).

37. *Id.* at 617–18, 627.

38. 545 U.S. 1 (2005).

39. *Raich*, 545 U. S. 1, at 17–24.

40. *Id.* at 26.

41. *Id.*

42. *Id.* at 48–52 (O'Connor, J., dissenting), 58–60 (Thomas, J., dissenting).

43. *Lopez*, 514 U.S. at 564–68; *Morrison*, 529 U.S. at 611–19.

44. 379 U.S. 241 (1964).

45. U.S. CONSTITUTION amendment V ("No person shall . . . be deprived of life, liberty, or property, without due process of law"). The Fourteenth Amendment extends to state governments the proscription against depriving citizens of life, liberty, or property without due process of law. U.S. CONSTITUTION amendment XIV.

46. *Cruzan v. Director, Missouri Dept. of Health*, 497 U.S. 261 (1990).

47. *Roe v. Wade*, 410 U.S. 113, 163–64 (1973).

48. *Id.* at 173 (Rehnquist, J., dissenting) (observing there would be "little doubt" that the Texas anti-abortion statute at issue would be unconstitutional if it were to prohibit abortion even when the mother's life was in danger).

49. See Eugene Volokh, *Medical Self-Defense, Prohibited Experimental Therapies, and Payment for Organs*, 120 HARVARD LAW REVIEW 1813 (2007).

50. 505 U.S. 833 (1994).

51. *Id.* at 878.

52. 530 U.S. 914 (2000). The Court's recent decision in *Gonzales v. Carhart* found a similar ban facially constitutional where it is uncertain that the procedure at issue is ever necessary to protect the health of the patient. 127 S.Ct. 1610, 1635–37 (2007).

53. *Id.* at 937.

54. 445 F.3d 470 (D.C. Cir. 2006).

55. The full D.C. Circuit is reviewing the panel's decision as of this writing.

56. 521 U.S. 702 (1997).

57. *Id.* at 710–12.

58. *Id.* at 721 and 725.

59. *Abigail Alliance*, 445 F.3d at 479–83.

60. *See Rutherford v. United States*, 616 F.2d 455, 457 (10th Cir. 1980).

61. 316 U.S. 535, 541 (1942).

62. 381 U.S. 479 (1965).

63. 405 U.S. 438, 453 (1972).

64. 410 U.S. 113 (1973).

65. 505 U.S. 833 (1992).

66. *Loving v. Virginia*, 388 U.S. 1 (1967).

67. *Zablocki v. Redhail,* 434 U.S. 374 (1978).

68. *Meyer v. Nebraska,* 262 U.S. 390 (1923); *Pierce v. Soc'y of Sisters,* 268 U.S. 510 (1925).

69. 539 U.S. 558 (2003).

70. *See generally* William J. Brennan, Jr., *The Constitution of the United States: Contemporary Ratification, in* INTERPRETING THE CONSTITUTION: THE DEBATE OVER ORIGINAL INTENT 23 (Jack N. Rakove ed., 1990).

71. *Casey,* 505 U.S. at 851 (emphasizing that "these matters, involving the most intimate and personal choices a person may make in a lifetime, choices central to personal dignity and autonomy, are central to the liberty protected by the Fourteenth Amendment").

72. *Cf.* John A. Robertson, *Procreative Liberty in the Era of Genomics,* 29 AMERICAN JOURNAL OF LAW & MEDICINE 439, 453–55 (2003) (arguing that "one could reasonably view" Supreme Court decisions as supporting a right to reproductive cloning); Judith F. Daar, *The Prospect of Human Cloning: Improving Nature or Dooming the Species?* 33 SETON HALL LAW REVIEW 511, 551 (2003) (arguing that "deprivation of the right to reproduce in a manner one chooses strikes at the heart of the [constitutional] liberty interest").

73. One potentially could argue that a cloning ban differentially burdens women because only women could produce a clone without the contribution of biological material from another person. For a man to produce a clone, a donor egg would be needed.

74. In cases in which the Supreme Court has identified a "fundamental right," it has allowed that right to be proscribed only on the showing of a "compelling government interest." *See generally* John E. Nowak & Ronald D. Rotunda, CONSTITUTIONAL LAW § 11.4 (6th ed. 2000). However, when the Court has instead recognized only a "liberty interest," it has tended to set somewhat lower standards for how important government interests must be to justify interference.

75. *See* PCB CLONING, *supra* note 5, at 80 (claiming that "serious though nonfatal abnormalities in cloned animals have also been observed, including substantially increased birth-size, liver and brain defects, and lung, kidney, and cardiovascular problems").

76. *See id.* at 89 (warning that "cloning experiments in other mammals strongly suggest that cloning-to-produce-children is, at least for now, far too risky to attempt").

77. *Cf.* CLONING HUMAN BEINGS: REPORT AND RECOMMENDATIONS OF THE NATIONAL BIOETHICS ADVISORY COMMISSION 63 (1997) ("Virtually all people agree that the current risks of physical harm to children associated with somatic cell nuclear transplantation cloning justify a prohibition at this time on such experimentation").

78. *See generally* Matt Ridley, The Red Queen: Sex and the Evolu-
tion of Human Nature (1994).

79. *Cf.* Cass R. Sunstein, *Is There a Constitutional Right to Clone?* 53
Hastings Law Journal 987, 997 (2002) (rejecting this argument on the
grounds that it is implausible that cloning would become so popular as to
endanger genetic diversity).

80. *See, e.g.,* Kass, *supra* note 21; *see also* R. Alta Charo, *Cloning: Ethics
and Public Policy,* 27 Hofstra Law Rev. 503, 504–505 (1999) (reporting anti-
cloning arguments presented to the National Bioethics Advisory Commission).

81. *See, e.g.,* Michael J. Sandel, *The Ethical Implications of Human
Cloning,* 48 Perspectives in Biology & Medicine 241 (2005); *see also* PCB
Cloning, *supra* note 5, at 104–5 (worrying that "parents, with the help of
science and technology, may determine in advance the genetic endowment
of their children").

82. *See id.* at 102 (arguing that "our genetic uniqueness is an important source of our sense of who we are and how we regard ourselves" and
therefore "cloned children may experience concerns about their distinctive
identity").

83. *See id.* at 103–4 (expressing concern that a "cloned child . . . is at
risk of living out a life overshadowed in important ways by the life of the
'original'—general appearance being only the most obvious").

# Chapter 4.
# Stem Cell Patents

1. Frederic Golden, *Stem Winder,* Time, Aug. 20, 2001, at 26.

2. U.S. Constitution article I, § 8, cl. 8.

3. 35 United States Code §§ 1–376.

4. *Id.* § 154(a)(2).

5. *See id.* § 282. An accused infringer must show by clear and convincing evidence that the patent is invalid. *See, e.g., Tokyo Shibaura Electric Co. v.
Zenith Radio Corp.,* 548 F.2d 88, 93 (3d Cir. 1977).

6. Alternative ways of challenging a patent in the U.S. system are reexaminations and interferences. Reexamination proceedings can be either *ex
parte* or *inter partes.* §§ 301–07, 311–18. Reexaminations put the patent's validity at issue. An interference is a complicated administrative proceeding for
determining priority between two would-be patentees. *See* 35 United
States Code § 135. (The U.S. system awards a patent to the first to invent
rather than the first to file.) Usually, an interference does not challenge the

patentability of a claimed invention but only who is entitled to the patent. Some patent systems, such as that of the European Union, allow a much broader range of individuals and organizations to question whether a patent should be issued or to argue that an existing patent should be held invalid, in a so-called opposition proceeding. Convention on the Grant of European Patents art. 99(1), Oct. 5, 1973, 1065 U.N.T.S. 199 [hereinafter European Patent Convention] (stating that "any person may give notice to the European Patent Office of opposition to the European patent granted").

7. *See* Christopher Hazuka, *Supporting the Work of Lesser Geniuses: An Argument for Removing Obstructions to Human Embryonic Stem Cell Research,* 57 UNIVERSITY OF MIAMI LAW REVIEW 157, 172 (2002).

8. *See* U.S. Patent No. 5,843,780 (filed Jan. 18, 1996) (issued Dec. 1, 1998) (the '780 patent); U.S. Patent No. 6,200,806 (filed June 26, 1998) (issued Mar. 13, 2001) (the '806 patent); U.S. Patent No. 7,029,913 (filed Oct. 18, 2001) (issued April 18, 2006) (the '913 patent). The actual patent claims define the scope of the patent in terms of markers found on cells that fall within the claim, but because all hESCs have these markers, this definition does not limit the claims. WARF's former general counsel, Elizabeth Donley, described the breadth of her organization's claims in the following way: "Our patents claim . . . a composition of matter characterized by the characteristics that most scientists agree define hES cells. Therefore, we would assert that in order to be an hES cell it must have those characteristics and [the unpermitted use of such cells] would then infringe the composition of matter claims." E-mail from Elizabeth Donley, General Counsel, Wisconsin Alumni Research Foundation, to Russell Korobkin, Professor of Law, University of California, Los Angeles, School of Law (July 5, 2006) (on file with author). *See also* Peter Yun-hyoung Lee, *Inverting the Logic of Scientific Discovery: Applying Common Law Patentable Subject Matter Doctrine to Constrain Patents on Biotechnology Research Tools,* 19 HARVARD JOURNAL OF LAW & TECHNOLOGY 79, 90 (2005) (arguing that the Thomson '806 patent claims "[encompass] virtually all hESCs of significant research value").

9. *See* University of Wisconsin–Madison, *Stem Cell Deal Reached,* Jan. 9, 2002; *available at* http://www.news.wisc.edu/6949.html.

10. *See id.;* Andrew Pollack, *University Resolves Dispute on Stem Cell Patent License,* NEW YORK TIMES, Jan. 10, 2002, at C11.

11. *See* John Fauber, *UW Stem Cell Patents Face Challenge,* MILWAUKEE JOURNAL SENTINEL, July 19, 2006, at A6.

12. Memorandum of Understanding between WiCell Research Institute, Inc., and Public Health Service, Sept. 5, 2001; *available at* http://stemcells .nih.gov/staticresources/research/registry/MTAs/Wicell_MOU.pdf.

13. *See id.* § 1(c).

14. Meredith Wadman, *Licensing Fees Slow Advance of Stem Cells,* 435 NATURE 272, 273 (2005).

15. Among the companies that reportedly have licensed hESC technology from WARF are Becton Dickinson, Advanced Cell Technology, General Electric, Novartis, and Novocel. *See id.*

16. For a critique of this analysis, which places a far lower estimate on the likely value of revenue-sharing agreements, see Richard J. Gilbert, *Dollars for Genes: Revenue Generation by the California Institute for Regenerative Medicine,* 21 BERKELEY TECHNOLOGY LAW JOURNAL 1107 (2006).

17. Quoted in Lee Romney, *Out-of-State Facility Demands Part of Stem Cell Research Royalties,* LOS ANGELES TIMES, Mar. 30, 2006, at B3.

18. Quoted in Daniel S. Levine, *Foundation Moves to Grab a Piece of Stem Cell Profits,* SAN FRANCISCO BUSINESS TIMES, Mar. 27, 2006; *available at* http://sanfrancisco.bizjournals.com/sanfrancisco/stories/2006/03/27/story2 .html.

19. Press release: *Wisconsin Alumni Research Foundation Changes Stem Cell Policies to Encourage Greater Academic, Industry Collaboration; available at* www.warf.org/news/news.jsp?news_id=209.

20. *Id.*

21. U.S. Patent Nos. 6,090,622 (filed Mar. 31, 1997) (issued July 18, 2000); 6,245,566 (filed Mar. 31, 1998) (issued June 12, 2001); 6,562,619 (filed Apr. 20, 2000) (issued May 13, 2003).

22. Joanne Cavanaugh Simpson, *Golden Opportunity—or Overwhelming Obstacle?* JOHNS HOPKINS MAGAZINE (Feb. 2001); *available at* http:// www.jhu.edu/~jhumag/0201web/patent.html.

23. *Quoted in id.*

24. R. H. Coase, *The Problem of Social Cost,* 3 JOURNAL OF LAW & ECONOMICS 1 (1960).

25. Edmund W. Kitch, *The Nature and Function of the Patent System,* 20 JOURNAL OF LAW & ECONOMICS 265, 271–79 (1977).

26. For a compelling defense of this claim, see Robert P. Merges & Richard R. Nelson, *On the Complex Economics of Patent Scope,* 90 COLUMBIA LAW REVIEW 839, 872–77 (1990); *see also* Hazuka, *supra* note 7, at 178, 190 (describing a range of reasons that upstream patents [for basic inventions] might not be efficiently licensed to downstream inventors [those who come up with applied inventions]); *cf.* Rebecca S. Eisenberg, *Bargaining over the Transfer of Proprietary Research Tools: Is This Market Failing or Emerging? in* EXPANDING THE BOUNDARIES OF INTELLECTUAL PROPERTY: INNOVATION POLICY FOR THE KNOWLEDGE SOCIETY 223, 225–26 (Rochelle Cooper Drey-

fuss et al. eds., 2001) (maintaining that friction in the licensing of biomedical patents is a serious obstacle to biomedical research). Rarely, a firm places some of its patents in the public domain to ward off real or perceived industry stagnation resulting from its patent rights. *See Survey of Patents and Technology: An Open Secret,* ECONOMIST, Oct. 22, 2005, at 12 (discussing IBM's pledge of five hundred software patents to the public domain).

27. *See* Wadman, *supra* note 14, at 272.

28. The only stem cell patents granted to Geron in the United Kingdom cover neural and hepatic cells produced through the differentiation of hESCs. U.K. Patents Nos. GB2379447 (filed May 16, 2001) (issued Nov. 30, 2004) and GB2380490 (filed Apr. 26, 2001) (issued Nov. 30, 2004).

29. European Patent Convention, *supra* note 6, art. 53(a).

30. *See id.,* art. 7.

31. European Group on Ethics in Science & New Technologies, Ethical Aspects of Patenting Inventions Involving Human Stem Cells, Opinion No. 16 (May 7, 2002); *available at* http://ec.europa.eu/european_group_ethics/docs/avis16_en.pdf.

32. U.K. Patent Office, Inventions Involving Human Embryonic Stem Cells, Apr. 2003; *available at* http://www.patent.gov.uk/patent/p-decision making/p-law/p-law-notice/p-law-notice-stemcells.htm.

33. 35 UNITED STATES CODE §§ 101–03, 112.

34. *Id.* § 102(b).

35. *See id.* § 101; U.S. Patent & Trademark Office, Department of Commerce, MANUAL OF PATENT EXAMINING PROCEDURE § 2107.01(I), (II) (8th ed., rev. Aug. 2006). Concerns of scientists and others that biotechnology patents had been issued for expressed sequence tags, single nucleotide polymorphisms, and full-length genes with no indication of the function or utility of the claimed gene products led the PTO to issue more stringent utility guidelines in January 2001. At that time, the PTO declared genes and gene products unpatentable without proof of function; before that, people could patent any isolated DNA or protein sequence. *See* Utility Examination Guidelines, 66 FEDERAL REGISTER 1092, 1093 (Jan. 5, 2001); *see generally* Molly A. Holman & Stephen R. Munzer, *Intellectual Property Rights in Genes and Gene Fragments: A Registration Solution for Expressed Sequence Tags,* 85 IOWA LAW REVIEW 735 (2000).

36. 35 UNITED STATES CODE § 103(a).

37. *Id.* § 112, paragraph 1.

38. *Id.* § 112.

39. *Funk Brothers Seed Co. v. Kalo Inoculant Co.,* 333 U.S. 127, 130 (1948).

40. *Laboratory Corporation of America Holdings v. Metabolite Labora-*

*tories, Inc.,* 548 U.S., 126 S. Ct. 2921, 2922 (2006) [hereinafter *LabCorp v. Metabolite*] (Breyer, J., dissenting from dismissal of writ of certiorari as improvidently granted).

41. *See American Fruit Growers, Inc. v. Brogdex Co.,* 283 U.S. 1, 11–12 (1931) (finding that an orange treated with borax and thereby rendered resistant to blue mold decay was not a "manufacture," or manufactured article, within the meaning of the patent statute); *Hartranft v. Wiegmann,* 121 U.S. 609, 614–15 (1887) (opining that cleaning and polishing a seashell did not transform the shell into a manufactured article).

42. For select cases in which claims of purified chemical elements were not patentable due to a lack of novelty, *see General Electric Co. v. De Forest Radio Co.,* 28 F.2d 641 (3d Cir. 1928) (tungsten); *In re Marden,* 47 F.2d 957 (C.C.P.A. 1931) (uranium); *id.* at 958 (vanadium).

43. *Funk Brothers,* 333 U.S. at 132 (stating bacterial product claims were not patentable because they were merely a discovery of the laws of nature in action and therefore lacked invention).

44. *Diamond v. Chakrabarty,* 447 U.S. 303 (1980); *see generally* U.S. Patent No. 4,259,444 (filed June 7, 1972) (issued Mar. 31, 1981).

45. *Chakrabarty,* 447 U.S. at 319–22 (Brennan, J., dissenting).

46. *See id.* at 309–10.

47. *Id.* at 309 (quoting Senate Report No. 82–1979, at 5 [1952]; House of Representatives Report No. 82–1923, at 6 [1952]); *see also J.E.M. Ag Supply, Inc. v. Pioneer Hi-Bred Int'l, Inc.,* 534 U.S. 124, 134 (2001) (upholding patent protection for genetically engineered plants).

48. *See Diamond v. Diehr,* 450 U.S. 175, 185 (1981) (stating that natural phenomena are unpatentable).

49. *Cf.* Sina A. Muscati, *"Some More Human Than Others": Assessing the Scope of Patentability Related to Human Embryonic Stem Cell Research,* 44 JURIMETRICS JOURNAL 201, 221 (2004) (arguing that unmodified stem cells are not inventive and that only process patents should be issued for techniques that isolate and culture them); Merges & Nelson, *supra* note 26, at 851 ("It can be argued that it is stretching the concept of inventing greatly to say that the [biotechnology] patentee [who purifies products that exist in nature] really invented the products. The true invention seems to be a way of producing those products in a desirable form").

50. Claim 1 of the '780 patent covers: "A purified preparation of primate embryonic stem cells which (i) is capable of proliferation in an in vitro culture for over one year, (ii) maintains a karyotype in which all the chromosomes characteristic of the primate species are present and not noticeably altered through prolonged culture, (iii) maintains the potential to differen-

tiate into derivatives of endoderm, mesoderm, and ectoderm tissues throughout the culture, and (iv) will not differentiate when cultured on a fibroblast feeder layer." U.S. Patent No. 5,843,780 (filed Jan. 18, 1996) (issued Dec. 1, 1998). The remaining composition of matter claims (2–8) in the '780 patent all claim a "preparation" or a "purified preparation." Claims 9 and 10 are for processes (methods). Claim 11 is a product-by-process claim, on which *see generally* Roger E. Schechter & John R. Thomas, PRINCIPLES OF PATENT LAW 213–15 (2004). The '806 patent contains similar language, save that in key places the word "human" replaces "primate." U.S. Patent No. 6,200,806 (filed June 26, 1998) (issued Mar. 13, 2001), claims 1, 3, 9.

51. *In re Bergy*, 563 F.2d 1031, 1035 (C.C.P.A. 1977).

52. The first such patent was U.S. Patent No. 5,004,681 (filed Nov. 12, 1987) (issued Apr. 2, 1991), granted to Edward Boyse, Hal Broxmeyer, and Gordon Douglas and assigned to a predecessor of PharmaStem Therapeutics, Inc. *See PharmaStem Therapeutics, Inc. v. Viacell, Inc.*, No. 02–148, 2004 U.S. Dist. LEXIS 18638 (D. Del. 2004) (holding that U.S. Patents Nos. 5,004,681 and 5,192,553, covering cryopreserved therapeutic compositions containing hematopoietic stem cells obtained from umbilical cord or placental blood of a newborn and methods pertaining to the therapeutic use of such compositions, are valid, despite several obviousness and anticipation challenges).

53. Patents granted to Johns Hopkins University relating to adult stem cells derived from bone marrow, including the very first adult stem cell patent, U.S. Patent No. 4,714,680 (filed Feb. 6, 1984) (issued Dec. 22, 1987), have been the subject of *Johns Hopkins Univ. v. CellPro, Inc.*, 152 F.3d 1342 (Fed. Cir. 1998), and *Nexell Therapeutics, Inc. v. Amcell Corp.*, 143 F.Supp.2d 407 (D. Del. 2001) (finding that U.S. Patent No. 4,714,680 survived all validity challenges).

54. *See, e.g., Amgen, Inc. v. Chugai Pharmaceutical Co. Ltd.*, 18 U.S.P.Q.2d 1016 (Fed. Cir. 1991) (upholding patent covering purified and isolated DNA encoding human erythropoietin); *see also* U.S. Patent No. 4,703,008 (issued Oct. 27, 1987).

55. Kyle Jensen & Fiona Murray, *Intellectual Property Landscape of the Human Genome,* 310 SCIENCE 239, 239 (2005); Lori Pressman et al., *The Licensing of DNA Patents by U.S. Academic Institutions: An Empirical Survey,* 24 NATURE BIOTECHNOLOGY. 31, 33 (2006).

56. Council Directive 98/44, Legal Protection of Biotechnological Inventions, article 3.2, 1998 OFFICIAL JOURNAL (L 213) 13, 18 (EC) (hereinafter EC Biotechnology Directive). A joint declaration of policy made in 1988 by the United States, European Union, and Japanese Patent Offices also supports the

position that a purification of a naturally existing product is sufficiently inventive for patent protection: "Purified natural products are not regarded . . . as products of nature or discoveries because they do not, in fact, exist in nature in a purified form. Rather, they are regarded for patent purposes as biologically active substances or chemical compounds and eligible for patenting on the same basis as other chemical compounds. . . . Microorganisms isolated from nature would qualify for patenting if the characteristic property or quality of the isolate is not expressed by the natural product, such as a biologically pure culture." *European Patent Office, Japanese Patent Office & United States Patent and Trademark Office*, 7 BIOTECHNOLOGY LAWYER REPORTS 159, 163 (1988).

57. *LabCorp v. Metabolite, supra* note 40.

58. *See* text accompanying notes 29–32, *supra.*

59. 12 F.Cas. 1018, 1018–19 (C.C.D. Mass. 1817) (No. 8568).

60. For a brief overview of the beneficial utility doctrine and its history, *see* Thomas A. Magnani, *The Patentability of Human-Animal Chimeras,* 14 BERKELEY TECHNOLOGY LAW JOURNAL 443, 451–54 (1999).

61. *See* Donald J. Quigg, U.S. Patent & Trademark Office, *Animals— Patentability,* 1077 OFFICIAL GAZETTE OF THE UNITED STATES PATENT & TRADEMARK OFFICE., PATENTS, OG 24 (Apr. 21, 1987) (warning that any "claim directed to or including within its scope a human being will not be considered patentable subject matter under 35 U.S.C. 101"). The commissioner thought the grant of even a time-limited property right in a human being would run afoul of the Thirteenth Amendment. *Id.*

62. Media Advisory, U.S. Patent & Trademark Office, *Facts on Patenting Life Forms Having a Relationship to Humans* (Apr. 1, 1998) (quoting *Tol-O-Matic, Inc. v. Proma Produkt–und Marketing Gesellschaft m.b.H.,* 945 F.2d 1546, 1553 (Fed. Cir. 1991) (citations omitted); *available at* http://www.uspto .gov/web/offices/com/speeches/98-06.htm.

63. *See, e.g.,* Kojo Yelpaala, *Owning the Secret of Life: Biotechnology and Property Rights Revisited,* 32 MCGEORGE LAW REVIEW 111, 205 (2000).

64. *Juicy Whip, Inc. v. Orange Bang, Inc.,* 185 F.3d 1364, 1366–67 (Fed. Cir. 1999).

65. *See* Utility Examination Guidelines, 66 FEDERAL REGISTER 1092, 1095 (Jan. 5, 2001).

66. Consolidated Appropriations Act, 2004, Public Law No. 108-199, § 634, 118 STATUTES AT LARGE 3, 101 (2004); Consolidated Appropriations Act, 2005, Public Law No. 108-447, § 626, 118 STATUTES AT LARGE 2809, 2920 (2005); Science, State, Justice, Commerce, and Related Agencies Act, 2006, Public Law No. 109-108, § 623, 119 STATUTES AT LARGE 2290, 2342 (2006).

67. European Group on Ethics in Science & New Technologies, *supra* note 31, at 15 (quoted in Muscati, *supra* note 49, at 218).

68. 35 UNITED STATES CODE § 112; *Invitrogen Corp. v. Clontech Laboratories, Inc.*, 429 F.3d 1052, 1070–71 (Fed. Cir. 2005) (discussing enablement in the context of biotechnology inventions).

69. *Vas-Cath, Inc. v. Mahurkar*, 935 F.2d 1555, 1563–64 (Fed. Cir. 1991) (emphasis omitted).

70. *See generally Warner-Jenkinson Co. v. Hilton Davis Chem. Co.*, 520 U.S. 17 (1997) (tracing the concept of equivalents in the court system); Martin J. Adelman & Gary L. Francione, *The Doctrine of Equivalents in Patent Law: Questions That* Pennwalt *Did Not Answer*, 137 UNIVERSITY OF PENNSYLVANIA LAW REVIEW 673 (1989) (discussing the "element-by-element" and "claim as a whole" approaches to judicial determinations of equivalence in the *Pennwalt* context). Limitations on the doctrine of equivalents include prior art, prosecution history estoppel, the all elements rule, and the public dedication doctrine, on which *see generally* Schechter & Thomas, *supra* note 50, at 310–26.

71. *O'Reilly v. Morse*, 56 U.S. (15 How.) 62, 86, 112 (1854).

72. *Id.*, 56 U.S. at 112–20.

73. *See, e.g., Schering Corp. v. Amgen, Inc.*, 222 F.3d 1347 (Fed. Cir. 2000); *Regents of the University of California v. Eli Lilly & Co.*, 119 F.3d 1559 (Fed. Cir. 1997); *Amgen, Inc. v. Chugai Pharmaceutical*, 927 F.2d 1200 (Fed. Cir. 1991). *See generally* Natasha N. Aljalian, *The Role of Patent Scope in Biopharmaceutical Patents*, 11 BOSTON UNIVERSITY JOURNAL OF SCIENCE & TECHNOLOGY LAW 1, 31 (2005); Dan L. Burk & Mark A. Lemley, *Policy Levers in Patent Law*, 89 VIRGINIA LAW REVIEW 1575, 1678–79 (2003).

74. Schechter & Thomas, *supra* note 50, at 188.

75. *See* Amy Rachel Davis, *Patented Embryonic Stem Cells: The Quintessential "Essential Facility"?* 94 GEORGETOWN LAW JOURNAL 205, 216 (2006) (tracing the history of gene-related patents).

76. Technically, FTCR sought *ex parte* reexamination of the '780 and '806 patents and *inter partes* reexamination of the '913 patent. For a description of the differences between these processes, see 35 UNITED STATES CODE §§ 301–07, 311–18 (2000). For able commentary, see Mark D. Janis, *Rethinking Reexamination: Toward a Viable Administrative Revocation System for U.S. Patent Law*, 11 HARVARD JOURNAL OF LAW & TECHNOLOGY 1 (1997); Mark D. Janis, *Inter Partes Patent Reexamination*, 10 FORDHAM INTELLECTUAL PROPERTY MEDIA & ENTERTAINMENT LAW JOURNAL 481 (2000).

77. *See* Schechter & Thomas, *supra* note 50, at 74 (distinguishing novelty and nonobviousness).

78. The patents are: U.S. Patent No. 5,166,065 (filed Aug. 3, 1989) (issued Nov. 24, 1992) ("In Vitro Propagation of Embryonic Stem Cells"); U.S. Patent No. 5,453,357 (filed Oct. 9, 1992) (issued Sept. 16, 1995) ("Pluripotential Embryonic Cells and Methods of Making Same"). The articles are: E. J. Robertson et al., *Isolation, Properties, and Karyotype Analysis of Pluripotential (EK) Cell Lines from Normal and Parthenogenetic Embryos*, 10 TERATOCARCINOMA STEM CELLS 647 (Lee M. Silver, Gail R. Martin, & Sidney Strickland eds., 1983); Elizabeth J. Robertson, *Embryo-Derived Stem Cell Lines*, in TERATOCARCINOMAS AND EMBRYONIC STEM CELLS 71–112 (1987); J. Piedrahita et al., *On the Isolation of Embryonic Stem Cells: Comparative Behavior of Murine, Porcine and Ovine Embryos*, 34 THERIOGENOLOGY 879 (1990); Ariff Bongso et al., *Isolation and Culture of Inner Cell Mass Cells from Human Blastocysts*, 9 HUMAN REPRODUCTION 2110 (1994).

79. Office Action from *Ex Parte* Reexamination No. 90/008,102, Mar. 30, 2007; Office Action from *Ex Parte* Reexamination No. 90/008,139, Mar. 30, 2007; Office Action from *Inter Partes* Reexamination No. 95/000,154, Mar. 30, 2007.

80. 35 UNITED STATES CODE § 134.

81. *Id.* § 141.

82. U.S. Patent No. 5,166,065 (filed Aug. 3, 1989) (issued Nov. 24, 1992); U.S. Patent No. 5,453,357 (filed Oct. 9, 1992) (issued Sept. 16, 1995).

83. Bongso et al., *supra* note 78.

84. *See* FTCR Request for *Ex Parte* Reexamination of Patent No. 5,843,780 (July 18, 2006) (Declaration of Dr. Jeanne F. Loring, Ph.D., paragraphs 7–8).

85. *See Standard Oil Co. v. American Cyanamid Co.*, 774 F.2d 448, 454 (Fed. Cir. 1985) ("A person of ordinary skill in the art is . . . presumed to be one who thinks along the line of conventional wisdom in the art and is not one who undertakes to innovate, whether by patient . . . systematic research or by extraordinary insights, it makes no difference which"). *See also* Rebecca S. Eisenberg, *Obvious to Whom? Evaluating Inventions from the Perspective of PHOSITA*, 19 BERKELEY TECHNOLOGY LAW JOURNAL 885, 889–897 (2004) (criticizing the Federal Circuit for assuming limited ability of ordinarily skilled practitioners).

86. *In re Eli Lilly & Co.*, 902 F.2d 943 (Fed. Cir. 1990); *In re O'Farrell*, 853 F.2d 894 (Fed. Cir. 1988).

87. *See generally* Schechter & Thomas, *supra* note 50, at 163–68.

88. 35 UNITED STATES CODE § 271(e)(1). This section, as amended, is the safe harbor provision of the Drug Price Competition and Patent Term Restoration Act (generally referred to as the Hatch-Waxman Act), Public Law No. 98–417, § 202, 98 STATUTES AT LARGE 1585, 1603 (1984).

89. Congress passed the Hatch-Waxman Act to overrule legislatively

*Roche Prods., Inc. v. Bolar Pharm. Co.*, 733 F.2d 858 (Fed. Cir. 1984), in which the court ruled that generic drug makers could not perform any tests on name-brand drugs until their patents expired. *See* House of Representatives Report No. 98–847, at 45–46 (1984).

90. 21 UNITED STATES CODE §301 *et seq.*, especially § 355(a).

91. *See Eli Lilly & Co. v. Medtronic, Inc.*, 496 U.S. 661, 669–70 (1990).

92. *Merck*, 545 U.S. 193, 200 (2005).

93. *Id.* at 208.

94. *Id.* at 206–208.

95. The FDA approach to regulating treatments derived from hESCs and hASCs is discussed in detail in Chapter 9.

96. The FDA has sought investigational new drug applications for work on ooplasm transfer, which most techniques of SCNT employ. The resulting stem cells would have the nuclear DNA of the patient donor but the mitochondrial DNA of the oocyte donor; in virtually all cases the two donors will be different individuals. This result raises questions about germ line gene therapy, over which the FDA has claimed jurisdiction. *See* Lawrence B. Ebert, *Lessons to Be Learned from the Hwang Matter: Analyzing Innovation the Right Way*, 88 JOURNAL OF THE PATENT & TRADEMARK OFFICE SOCIETY 239, 253–54 (2006); Margaret Foster Riley & Richard A. Merrill, *Regulating Reproductive Genetics: A Review of American Bioethics Commissions and Comparison to the British Human Fertilisation and Embryology Authority*, 6 COLUMBIA SCIENCE & TECHNOLOGY LAW REVIEW 1, 5 nn.16–18 (2005); *see also* Justin C. St. John et al., *The Potential Risks of Abnormal Transmission of mtDNA through Assisted Reproductive Technologies*, 8 REPRODUCTIVE BIOMEDICINE ONLINE 34 (2004), *available at* www.rbmonline.com/Article/1080.

97. *Merck*, 545 U.S. at 205 fn. 7.

# Chapter 5.
## The Taxpayers' Stake in Stem Cell Profits

1. *California Stem Cell Research and Cures Initiative* § 2–3; *available at* http://vote2004.ss.ca.gov/voterguide/propositions/prop71text.pdf.

2. *Id.* § 5 (proposing the addition of § 125290.30[h] to chapter 3, article 1, of the California Health and Safety Code).

3. *CIRM Intellectual Property Policy for Non-Profit Organizations* (approved Feb. 10, 2006); *available at* http://www.crim.ca.gov/policies/pdf/IPPNPO.pdf [hereinafter *CIRM Non-Profit Policy*]; CALIFORNIA CODE OF REGULATIONS § 100308(b).

4. *CIRM Policy for For-Profit Organizations* (Dec. 7, 2006); *available at*

www.cirm.ca.gov/policies/pdf/ForProfitOrg.pdf [hereinafter *CIRM For-Profit Policy*].

5. For a clear and concise history of this debate, see Rebecca Eisenberg, *Public Research and Private Development: Patents and Technology Transfer in Government-Sponsored Research,* 82 VIRGINIA LAW REVIEW 1663, 1671–91 (1996).

6. 35 UNITED STATES CODE §§ 200–11 (2000).

7. *Id.* § 210(c) (2000); Exec. Order No. 12,591, 52 FEDERAL REGISTER 13,414 (Apr. 10, 1987) (amended by Exec. Order No. 12,618, 52 FEDERAL REGISTER 48,661 [Dec. 22, 1987]).

8. 35 UNITED STATES CODE § 202 (2000); 37 CODE OF FEDERAL REGULATIONS § 401.4(b)(3) (2006).

9. *See* Peter S. Arno & Michael H. Davis, *Why Don't We Enforce Existing Drug Price Controls? The Unrecognized and Unenforced Reasonable Pricing Requirements Imposed upon Patents Deriving in Whole or in Part from Federally Funded Research,* 75 TULANE LAW REVIEW 631, 659 (2001).

10. 35 UNITED STATES CODE § 203.

11. Rebecca Eisenberg and Arti Rai argue that the threat of exercising "march-in" rights helped the government to negotiate reasonable hESC licenses from WARF for government-sponsored researchers. Rebecca S. Eisenberg & Arti K. Rai, *Proprietary Considerations, in* 1 HANDBOOK OF STEM CELLS 793 (Robert Lanza et al. eds., 2004).

12. For a review and criticism of the evidence presented to Congress, *see* Eisenberg, *supra* note 5, at 1702–4 and sources cited in footnotes 159–166.

13. 35 UNITED STATES CODE § 200.

14. According to a recent survey conducted by the Association of University Technology Managers, more than 3,800 patents were granted to American universities in 2004, compared to 250 in 1980. *AUTM U.S. Licensing Survey: FY 2004* (Ashley J. Stevens ed., 2004), *available at* http://www .autm.net/events/File/04AUTMSurveySum-USpublic.pdf. *See also* David C. Mowery et al., *The Growth of Patenting and Licensing by U.S. Universities: An Assessment of the Effects of the Bayh-Dole Act of 1980,* 30 RESEARCH POLICY 99, 104 (2001).

15. *See* Jerry G. Thursby & Sukanya Kemp, *Growth and Productive Efficiency of University Intellectual Property Licensing,* 31 RESEARCH POLICY 109, 110 (2002).

16. *See* University Research: Controlling Inappropriate Access to Federally Funded Research Results, GAO/RCED-92–104, at 11 (U.S. Gen. Accounting Office, May 1992); *available at* http://archive.gao.gov/d32t10/ 146696.pdf (documenting the increase in technology transfer offices among major research universities).

17. Thursby & Kemp, *supra* note 15, at 121.

18. The figures are provided by the *AUTM U.S. Licensing Survey: FY 2004, supra* note 14, at 3, 14, 24.

19. *Innovation's Golden Goose,* ECONOMIST, Dec. 14, 2002, at 3, 3.

20. The most exhaustive of the revisionist critiques is David C. Mowery et al., IVORY TOWER AND INDUSTRIAL INNOVATION: UNIVERSITY-INDUSTRY TECHNOLOGY TRANSFER BEFORE AND AFTER THE BAYH-DOLE ACT IN THE UNITED STATES (2004); *see also* Eisenberg, *supra* note 5; Arti K. Rai & Rebecca S. Eisenberg, *Bayh-Dole Reform and the Progress of Biomedicine,* 66 LAW & CONTEMPORARY PROBLEMS. 289 (Winter/Spring 2003). In 1954, 80 percent of federal funding for academic research went to defense-related projects; in 2001, more than 60 percent of federal funding for academic research came from the NIH and only 8.7 percent from the Defense Department. Mowery et al., IVORY TOWER AND INDUSTRIAL INNOVATION, *supra* note 20, at 24–25 & tbl. 2.2.

21. *See* Mowery et al., IVORY TOWER AND INDUSTRIAL INNOVATION, *supra* note 20, at 35–57, 99–128.

22. *See* Rai & Eisenberg, *supra* note 20, at 295–96 (arguing that this rationale for patent protection fails to hold up when inventions can be disseminated without substantial investment).

23. *See id.* at 297.

24. *See* Michael A. Heller & Rebecca S. Eisenberg, *Can Patents Deter Innovation? The Anticommons in Biomedical Research,* 280 SCIENCE 698, 699 (1988).

25. 35 UNITED STATES CODE § 102(b).

26. On the importance of "priority" in academic science, which promotes a race to publication, *see* Paula E. Stephan, *The Economics of Science,* 34 JOURNAL OF ECONOMIC LITERATURE 1199, 1208 (1996).

27. Jeremy M. Grushcow, *Measuring Secrecy: A Cost of the Patent System Revealed,* 33 JOURNAL OF LEGAL STUDIES 59 (2004).

28. Jerry Thursby et al., Objectives, Characteristics, and Outcomes of University Licensing: A Survey of Major Universities (unpublished manuscript, July 2000); *cited in* Rai & Eisenberg, *supra* note 20, at 306 n. 83.

29. *See* Gary Pulsinelli, *Share and Share Alike: Increasing Access to Government-Funded Inventions under the Bayh-Dole Act,* 7 MINNESOTA JOURNAL OF LAW SCIENCE & TECHNOLOGY 393, 440–41 (2006).

30. Most researchers credit the increase in licensing activity post–Bayh-Dole to increased faculty disclosure of inventions and increased university initiatives in patenting and licensing rather than to significant changes in faculty research. *See* Mowery et al., IVORY TOWER AND INDUS-

TRIAL INNOVATION, *supra* note 20, at 117–26; Jerry G. Thursby & Marie C. Thursby, *University Licensing and the Bayh-Dole Act*, 301 SCIENCE 1052, 1052 (2003); Jerry G. Thursby & Marie C. Thursby, *Who Is Selling the Ivory Tower? Sources of Growth in University Licensing*, 48 MANAGEMENT SCIENCE 90, 101–2 (2002).

31. For an interesting review of the literature on the reward structure of science, *see* Stephan, *supra* note 26, at 1200–1203 (1996).

32. *CIRM Non-Profit Policy, supra* note 3, at 35.

33. *Id.* at 37; 17 CALIFORNIA CODE OF REGULATIONS § 100306(a). The *CIRM For-Profit Policy* does not include this requirement.

34. Eisenberg, *supra* note 5, at 1701.

35. Eisenberg & Rai, *supra* note 11, at 794.

36. *AUTM U.S. Licensing Survey: FY 2004, supra* note 14, at 2.

37. *See generally* Roger G. Noll, *Designing an Effective Program of State-Sponsored Human Embryonic Stem Cell Research*, 21 BERKELEY TECHNOLOGY LAW JOURNAL 1143, 1153–54 (2006) (arguing that an efficient public R&D policy "should focus on projects that researchers otherwise would not pursue").

38. Richard J. Gilbert, *Dollars for Genes: Revenue Generation by the California Institute for Regenerative Medicine*, 21 BERKELEY TECHNOLOGY LAW JOURNAL 1107, 1113–14 (2006).

39. The Bayh-Dole Act requires nonprofit organizations to share revenues generated by government-funded inventions with the inventor, but it does not specify in what amount. 35 UNITED STATES CODE sec. 202(c)(7)(B). CIRM policy mimics this requirement. *CIRM Non-Profit Policy, supra* note 3, at 36. CIRM estimates that the inventor's share is typically 30–40 percent. *CIRM For-Profit Policy, supra* note 4, at 34. The University of California's policy allocates 35 percent of net licensing income to the inventor. Gilbert, *supra* note 38, at 1112.

40. 17 CALIFORNIA CODE OF REGULATIONS § 100306(d); *id.* § 100406 (d) (draft, March 16, 2007).

# Chapter 6.
## Autonomy and Informed Consent

1. *See* James H. Jones, BAD BLOOD: THE TUSKEGEE SYPHILIS EXPERIMENT (2d ed. 1993) (especially chapters 1, 8, and 9).

2. Jean Heller, *Syphilis Victims in U.S. Study Went Untreated for 40 Years*, NEW YORK TIMES, July 26, 1972, at 1.

3. TRIALS OF WAR CRIMINALS BEFORE THE NUREMBERG MILITARY TRIBUNALS UNDER CONTROL COUNCIL LAW NO. 10, Vol. 2, 181–82 (U.S. Govt. Printing Office, 1946–49).

4. 45 CODE OF FEDERAL REGULATIONS §§ 46.103(b), 46.109, 46.119 (2005). The common rule also applies to institutions that have signed assurances with the federal government that they will follow the rule even when conducting research that is not federally funded, and similar FDA regulations apply to research involving any FDA-regulated drugs or devices. *See* 21 CODE OF FEDERAL REGULATIONS §§ 56.103, 312.66,

5. 45 CODE OF FEDERAL REGULATIONS § 46.111(a)(1)-(2).

6. *Id.* § 46.111(a)(4)-(5).

7. *Id.* § 46.116; *see also* Daniel S. Strouse, *Informed Consent to Genetic Research on Banked Human Tissue,* 45 JURIMETRICS JOURNAL 135, 138 (2005) ("The cardinal value advanced by informed consent to research is regard for autonomy").

8. 45 CODE OF FEDERAL REGULATIONS § 46.116(a).

9. *Id.* § 46.109(b).

10. 105 N.E. 92, 93 (N.Y. 1914).

11. 317 P.2d 170 (Cal.App. 1957).

12. *Id.* at 181 (quoting jury instructions).

13. *See, e.g., Natanson v. Kline,* 350 P.2d 1093, 1106 (Kan. 1960), and *Canterbury v. Spence,* 464 F.2d 772, 786–87 (D.C. Cir. 1972).

14. Peter H. Schuck, *Rethinking Informed Consent,* 103 YALE LAW JOURNAL 899, 916–17 (1994).

15. *See* Jesse A. Goldner, *An Overview of Legal Controls on Human Experimentation and the Regulatory Implications of Taking Professor Katz Seriously,* 38 ST. LOUIS UNIVERSITY LAW JOURNAL 63, 80–87 (1993) (reviewing cases in the context of "therapeutic" clinical research).

16. *See* 45 CODE OF FEDERAL REGULATIONS § 46.101; 21 CODE OF FEDERAL REGULATIONS pt. 50. *See also* Jocelyn Kaiser, *ScienceScope,* 275 SCIENCE 605 (1997) (noting that the common rule does not apply to "state-funded studies or research by private institutions not receiving federal funds").

17. *See* Strouse, *supra* note 7, at 136 n.2.

18. *See* California Institute of Regenerative Medicine, *Third Revised Medical and Ethics Standards Regulations; available at* www.cirm.ca.gov/laws/pdf/stds_publ_cmt.pdf.

19. Over the last decade bills have been introduced in Congress that would effectively apply the common rule to all research, not just research sponsored by the federal government, but none have made it to the floor for

a vote. *See, e.g.,* Human Research Subject Protections Act of 1997, S. 193, 105th Congress (1997); Human Research Subject Protections Act of 2002, H.R. 4697, 107th Congress (2002).

20. 637 F.Supp. 1463 (M.D.N.C. 1986), *affirmed,* 829 F. 2d 1340 (4th Cir. 1987).

21. *Id.* at 1468.

22. 782 A.2d 807, 846–47 (Md. 2001). The *Grimes* court did find that researchers had a duty to obtain informed consent in a context it labeled nontherapeutic, but only because federal funds supported the research and the common rule thus applied.

23. 264 F.Supp. 2d 1064, 1066 (S.D. Fla. 2003).

24. *Id.*

25. *Id.* at 1067.

26. *Id.*

27. U.S. Patent No. 5,679,635 (filed Sept. 9, 1994) (issued Oct. 21, 1997).

28. *Greenberg,* 264 F.Supp.2d at 1067.

29. *Id.* at 1068.

30. *Id.* at 1069.

31. *See id.*

32. 793 P.2d 479 (Cal. 1990).

33. *Id.* at 481.

34. *Id.*

35. U.S. Patent No. 4,438,032 (filed Jan. 6, 1983) (issued Mar. 20, 1984).

36. *Moore,* 793 P.2d at 483.

37. *Id.*

38. *Id.* at 485.

39. *Id.* at 483–84.

40. *Id.* at 486.

41. *Greenberg,* 264 F.Supp.2d at 1070.

42. *Id.* at. 1070–71.

43. *Cf.* National Commission for the Protection of Human Subjects of Biomedical & Behavioral Research, The Belmont Report: Ethical Principles and Guidelines for the Protection of Human Subjects of Research 11 (1978) ("the research subject, being in essence a volunteer, may wish to know considerably more about risks gratuitously undertaken than do patients who deliver themselves into the hand of a clinician for needed care").

44. *Accord* Strouse, *supra* note 7, at 141 n.28.

45. *See* Office of Inspector General, Department of Health & Human Services, Recruiting Human Subjects: Pressures in Industry Spon-

SORED CLINICAL RESEARCH 17–20 (2000); *reprinted in* Carl H. Coleman et al., THE ETHICS AND REGULATION OF RESEARCH WITH HUMAN SUBJECTS 371–75 (2005).

46. Ethics Committee of the American Society for Reproductive Medicine, *Donating Spare Embryos for Embryonic Stem-Cell Research,* 78 FERTILITY & STERILITY 957, 959–60 (2002) (calling for "someone other than the treating infertility specialist [to] make requests for embryos for research purposes"); *but see* Bernard Lo et al., *Informed Consent in Human Oocyte, Embryo, and Embryonic Stem Cell Research,* 82 FERTILITY & STERILITY 559, 562 (2004) (claiming there is no reason for concern if the treating physician is not involved in the research project).

47. *See* Coleman et al., *supra* note 45, at 376 (citing the opposition of "several professional organizations," including the American College of Physicians).

48. Quite a different issue is whether egg donors, and research subjects generally, should be offered financial incentives. *See, e.g.,* James A. Anderson and Charles Weijer, *The Research Subject as Wage Earner,* 23 THEORETICAL MEDICINE AND BIOETHICS 359 (2002); Neal Dickert et al., *Paying Research Subjects: An Analysis of Current Policies,* 136 ANNALS OF INTERNAL MEDICINE 368 (2002); Ethics Committee of the American Society for Reproductive Medicine, *Financial Incentives in Recruitment of Oocyte Donors,* 74 FERTILITY & STERILITY 216 (2000);

49. 45 CODE OF FEDERAL REGULATIONS § 46.102(f).

50. *Id.*

51. *Id.*

52. Office for Human Research Protections, Department of Health & Human Services, Guidance on Research Involving Coded Private Information or Biological Specimens 3 (Aug. 10, 2004); *available at* www.hhs.gov/ohrp/humansubjects/guidance/cdebiol.pdf (last visited Nov. 15, 2006).

53. 45 CODE OF FEDERAL REGULATIONS § 46.101(b)(4).

54. *See* Coleman et al., *supra* note 45, at 706–7.

55. 45 CODE OF FEDERAL REGULATIONS § 46.116(d).

56. *Id.* 46.102(f) (defining "human subject" as "a living individual").

57. *See* Strouse, *supra* note 7, at 140. When unusual genetic material is tied to demographic information, it often would be possible for a persistent researcher to identify an individual even if the data are technically deidentified. *See* Isaac S. Kohane & Russ B. Altman, *Health-Information Altruists: A Potentially Critical Resource,* 353 NEW ENGLAND JOURNAL OF MEDICINE 2074 (2005) (describing the ease of reidentifying deidentified data).

58. 437 F.Supp.2d 985 (E.D. Mo. 2006).

59. *Id.* at 999.

60. Committee on Guidelines for Human Embryonic Stem Cell Research, National Research Council, GUIDELINES FOR HUMAN EMBRYONIC STEM CELL RESEARCH 83 (2005) [hereinafter NRC GUIDELINES]; *cf.* Lori B. Andrews, *Harnessing the Benefits of Biobanks,* 33 JOURNAL OF LAW, MEDICINE & ETHICS 22, 27–28 (2005) (arguing that informed consent should be required before banked tissue samples are used in research and that blanket consent for all future research is not sufficient for this purpose).

61. *See, e.g.,* Henry T. Greely, *Breaking the Stalemate: A Prospective Regulatory Framework for Unforeseen Research Uses of Human Tissue Samples and Health Information,* 34 WAKE FOREST LAW REVIEW 737, 758 (1999); Strouse, *supra* note 7, at 142–43.

62. Greely calls such blanket consent for future research "permission" rather than "informed consent" since such broad consent cannot be fully informed. *See* Greely, *supra* note 61, at 754, 758–59.

63. 696 N.E.2d 174 (N.Y. 1998).

64. *Id.* at 176–77.

65. *Davis v. Davis,* 842 S.W.2d 588 (Tenn. 1992) (no preexisting agreement); *A.Z. v. B.Z.,* 725 N.E.2d 1051 (Mass. 2000) (preexisting agreement to donate was of uncertain duration and outweighed by public policy supporting the man's desire not to become a parent); *J.B. v. M.B.,* 783 A.2d 707 (N.J. 2001) (preexisting agreement unenforceable if one party changes his or her mind before donation is made). For an analysis of the reasoning in these cases, see Judith F. Daar, *Frozen Embryo Disputes Revisited: A Trilogy of Procreation-Avoidance Approaches,* 29 JOURNAL OF LAW, MEDICINE & ETHICS 197 (2001). The Israeli Supreme Court awarded the frozen embryos of a separated couple to the wife for implantation over the husband's objections where a subsequent hysterectomy meant the embryos represented the wife's only opportunity to have biological children. Joel Greenberg, *Israeli Court Gives Wife the Right to Her Embryos,* NEW YORK TIMES, Sept. 13, 1996, at A4.

66. NRC GUIDELINES, *supra* note 60, at 83; Ethics Committee of the American Society for Reproductive Medicine, *Donating Spare Embryos for Embryonic Stem-Cell Research,* 82 FERTILITY & STERILITY S224 (2004) (Supp. 1) [hereinafter *ASRM 2004 Guidelines*].

67. *Id.* at S226. The American Academy of Pediatrics is in agreement. *See* Committee on Pediatric Research & Committee on Bioethics, American Academy of Pediatrics, *Human Embryo Research* 813, 815 (2001).

68. *See ASRM* 2004 *Guidelines, supra* note 66, at S226.

69. CALIFORNIA HEALTH & SAFETY CODE § 125315(b).

70. *See* Andrea D. Gurmankin et al., *Embryo Disposal Practices in IVF Clinics in the United States*, POLITICS & LIFE SCIENCES, Aug. 9, 2004, at 4, 6.

71. 45 CODE OF FEDERAL REGULATIONS § 46.116(a)(8).

# Chapter 7.
# Buying and Selling Human Tissues

1. Committee on Guidelines for Human Embryonic Stem Cell Research, National Research Council, GUIDELINES FOR HUMAN EMBRYONIC STEM CELL RESEARCH 85 (2005) [hereinafter NRC GUIDELINES] (Recommendation 15).

2. *Id.* at 87 (Recommendation 16).

3. National Institutes of Health Guidelines for Research Using Human Pluripotent Stem Cells and Notification of Request for Emergency Clearance, 65 FEDERAL REGISTER 51,976, at 51,979 (Aug. 25, 2000); *available at* http://stemcells.nih.gov/staticresources/news/newsArchives/NIHSguideline 2000.pdf.

4. American Association of Pediatrics, *Human Embryo Research*, 108 PEDIATRICS 813, 815 (2001).

5. Notice of Criteria for Federal Funding of Research on Existing Human Embryonic Stem Cells and Establishment of NIH Human Embryonic Stem Cell Registry (Nov. 7, 2001); *available at* http://grants.nih.gov/ grants/guide/notice-files/NOT-OD-02–005.html.

6. Stem Cell Research Enhancement Act of 2005, H.R. 810, 105th Congress § 1: "(a) In General. Notwithstanding any other provision of law (including any regulation or guidance), the Secretary shall conduct and support research that utilizes human embryonic stem cells in accordance with this section (regardless of the date on which the stem cells were derived from a human embryo) . . . [provided] (3) The individuals seeking fertility treatment donated the embryos with written informed consent and without receiving any financial or other inducements to make the donation."

7. CALIFORNIA HEALTH & SAFETY CODE § 125290.35(b)(3).

8. *Id.* § 125350, 125355.

9. See Massachusetts General Laws chapter 111L § 8 (embryos, gametes, and cadaveric tissue); New Jersey Statutes § 26:2Z-1 (embryonic and cadaveric tissues); Maryland Code §§ 5-2B-10, 5-2B-12 (embryos); Connecticut General Statutes Annotated 05-149 § 1(c)3.

10. MISSOURI CONSTITUTION article III, § 38(d) (2006).

11. 42 UNITED STATES CODE § 274e(c)(1).

12. The legislative history of the NOTA specifically states that that statute's prohibition of sales "is not meant to include blood and blood derivatives, which can be replenished and whose donation does not compromise the health of the donor." Senate Report No. 98–382 at 3982 (1984). *See generally* Charles M. Jordan, Jr. & Casey J. Price, *First Moore, Then Hecht: Isn't It Time We Recognize a Property Interest in Tissues, Cells, and Gametes?* 37 REAL PROPERTY, PROBATE & TRUST JOURNAL 151, 173 (2002).

13. 42 UNITED STATES CODE § 274e(a).

14. *Accord* Radhika Rao, *Property, Privacy, and the Human Body,* 80 BOSTON UNIVERSITY LAW REVIEW 359, 376 (1999). It is less clear whether, if regenerative medicine achieves its full potential and stem cells are used directly as therapeutic agent, NOTA will prohibit the sale of tissues for the purpose of creating therapeutic stem cells.

15. All fifty states and the District of Columbia adopted the 1968 version of the UAGA. A minority of states subsequently adopted the 1987 revised version. For a complete list of statutory citations, see Eric B. Seeney, Moore *10 years Later—Still Trying to Fill the Gap: Creating a Personal Property Right in Genetic Material,* 32 NEW ENGLAND LAW REVIEW 1131, 1153–54 n.204 (1998).

16. Uniform Anatomical Gift Act § 6(a) (1987).

17. *Id.,* § 10(a).

18. *Id.,* § 10(a) & cmt.

19. 18 UNITED STATES CODE § 1122(a).

20. 42 UNITED STATES CODE 289g-2(a).

21. FLORIDA STATUTES § 873.01; GEORGIA CODE ANNOTATED § 16–12–160; 720 ILLINOIS COMPILED STATUTES § 5/12–20; MARYLAND CODE ANNOTATED, HEALTH-GENERAL I § 5–408; MASSACHUSETTS GENERAL LAWS chapter 111l, § 8; MICHIGAN COMPILED LAWS § 333.10204; MINNESOTA STATUTES § 145.422; TEXAS PENAL CODE ANNOTATED § 48.02; VIRGINIA CODE ANNOTATED § 32.1–289.1.

22. *See, e.g.,* CALIFORNIA PENAL CODE § 367f (defining "human organ" to exclude plasma and sperm); 720 ILLINOIS COMPILED STATUTES § 5/12–20 (permitting the purchase or sale of blood and "other self-replicating body fluids"); MICHIGAN COMPILED LAWS § 333.10204 (same).

23. VIRGINIA CODE ANNOTATED § 32.1–289.1 (excepting "hair, ova, blood, and other self-replicating body fluids").

24. *See, e.g.,* Emily Jackson, REGULATING REPRODUCTION: LAW, TECHNOLOGY AND AUTONOMY 165–66 (2001); Christopher Thomas Scott, STEM

Cell Now: From the Experiment that Shook the World to the New Politics of Life 24–25 (2006).

25. Louisiana's ban on organ sales is limited to sales for transplantation purposes. *See* Louisiana Revised Statutes Annotated § 14:101.1.

26. *See Id.§* 9:122 (West 2006) (prohibiting sale of human ova).

27. *See, e.g.,* Robert Steinbrook, *Egg Donation and Human Embryonic Stem Cell Research,* 354 New England Journal of Medicine 324, 324 (2006).

28. *See, e.g.,* California Health & Safety Code § 125320; Connecticut General Statutes § 19a–32d ; Florida Statutes § 873.05 ; 720 Illinois Compiled Statutes 510/6; Indiana Code § 35–46–5–3; Louisiana Revised Statutes Annotated § 9:122; Massachusetts General Laws chapter 111l, § 8; Michigan Compiled Laws § 333.2690; Minnesota Statutes § 145.422 ; New Jersey Statutes Annotated § 26:2Z-2 ; North Dakota Century Code § 14–02.2–02 ; Rhode Island General Laws § 11–54–1; South Dakota Codified Laws § 34–14–17.

29. *See, e.g.,* California Penal Code § 367f(c)(2) ; NOTA, 42 United States Code § 274e(c)(2).

30. NRC Guidelines, *supra* note 1, at 70–72 (Recommendation 16).

31. American Society for Reproductive Medicine, *2002 Guidelines for Gamete and Embryo Donation,* 77 Fertility & Sterility S1, S8 (Supp. 5 2002) [hereinafter *ASRM 2002 Guidelines*] (supporting "levels of compensation that [minimize] the possibility of undue inducement of donors").

32. *See, e.g.,* Kenneth Baum, *Golden Eggs: Towards the Rational Regulation of Oocyte Donation,* 2001 B.Y.U. Law Review 107, 146–47.

33. *See generally* Alan Wertheimer, Coercion 204 (1987).

34. In an arrangement known as egg sharing, some fertility clinics charge women seeking IVF treatment a lower fee—sometimes as much as 50 percent lower—in exchange for their donating eggs to other women. *See* Ethics Committee of the American Society for Reproductive Medicine, *Financial Incentives in the Recruitment of Oocyte Donors,* 74 Fertility & Sterility 216, 219 (2000). *See* Kari L. Karsjens, *Boutique Egg Donations: A New Form of Racism and Patriarchy,* 5 DePaul Journal of Health Care Law 57, 83 (2002) (arguing that nineteen- or twenty-year-old college women cannot fully appreciate the inherent risks of egg donation).

35. NRC Guidelines, *supra* note 1, at 86.

36. *Accord* Julia D. Mahoney, *The Market for Human Tissue,* 86 Virginia Law Review 163, 213 (2000); James A. Anderson & Charles Weijer, *The Research Subject as Wage Earner,* 23 Theoretical Medicine & Bioethics 359, 364–65 (reviewing the history of worker protection statutes).

37. Margaret Jane Radin, *Market-Inalienability,* 100 HARVARD LAW REVIEW 1849, 1911 (1987).

38. Robert M. Veatch, *Why Liberals Should Accept Financial Incentives for Organ Procurement,* 13 KENNEDY INSTITUTE OF ETHICS JOURNAL 19, 32 (2003).

39. See Rick Weiss, *S. Korean Stem Cell Team Paid Women for Eggs,* WASHINGTON POST, Nov. 22, 2005, at A21.

40. James Brooke, *Korean Leaves Cloning Center in Ethics Furor,* NEW YORK TIMES, Nov. 25, 2005, at A1.

41. *See, e.g.,* Baum, *supra* note 32, at 134–36; Charlotte H. Harrison, *Neither* Moore *nor the Market: Alternative Models for Compensating Contributors of Human Tissue,* 28 AMERICAN JOURNAL OF LAW & MEDICINE 77, 89 (2002). This argument was made in a concurring opinion in *Moore,* when Justice Arabian complained that John Moore "entreats us to regard the human vessel—the single most venerated and protected subject in any civilized society—as equal with the basest commercial commodity. He urges us to commingle the sacred with the profane." *Moore,* 793 P.2d 479, 497 (Cal. 1990) (Arabian, J., concurring).

42. Radin, *supra* note 37, at 1912.

43. Leon R. Kass, *Organs for Sale? Propriety, Property, and the Price of Progress,* 107 PUBLIC INTEREST 65, 83 (1992) (arguing against the commodification of the human body).

44. Radin, *supra* note 37, at 1925–26; *see also* Note, *The Price of Everything, The Value of Nothing: Reframing the Commodification Debate,* 117 HARVARD LAW REVIEW 689, 692 (2003) (explaining the argument as follows: "exchanging children for money corrupts the value of children because money and children belong in different spheres of valuation").

45. *Cf.* David B. Resnik, *Regulating the Market for Human Eggs,* 15 BIOETHICS 1, 6 (2001) ("One problem with [the] deontological argument against commodification [of human eggs is that] most people would not hold that human eggs have the same moral worth as children, adults, or even embryos").

46. See notes 21–28 and accompanying text, *supra.*

47. *Id.*

48. *See* Anna Mulrine, *Making Babies,* U.S. NEWS & WORLD REPORT, Sept. 27, 2004, at 60 (stating that IVF insurance coverage is "a rarity in the United States, where 85 percent of insured Americans have policies that will not cover that treatment").

49. *See* Cynthia B. Cohen, *Selling Bits and Pieces of Humans to Make Babies: The Gift of the Magi Revisited,* 24 JOURNAL OF MEDICINE & PHILOSOPHY 288, 296 (1999).

50. Centers for Disease Control & Prevention, *2003 Assisted Reproductive Technology Success Rates*, § 4; *available at* www.cdc.gov/ART/ART2003/section4.htm.

51. Search conducted on November 6, 2006.

52. *See, e.g.,* Kerry Howley, *Ova for Sale: The Art of the Deal in the Gray Market for Human Eggs*, 38 REASON 19, 21 (2006) (reporting the author's inclusion in catalogue of donors listing heights, weights, ages, prices, SAT scores, and academic degrees).

53. Richard M. Titmuss, THE GIFT RELATIONSHIP: FROM HUMAN BLOOD TO SOCIAL POLICY 242 (1971).

54. A comment to the Uniform Anatomical Gift Act provides: "Altruism and a desire to benefit other members of the community are important moral reasons which motivate many to donate. Any perception on the part of the public that transplantation unfairly benefits those outside the community, those who are wealthy enough to afford transplantation, or that it is undertaken primarily with an eye toward profit rather than therapy will severely imperil the moral foundations, and thus the efficacy of the system." Uniform Anatomical Gift Act § 10.

55. *See* Kieran Healy, *Embedded Altruism: Blood Collection Regimes and the European Union's Donor Population*, 105 AMERICAN JOURNAL OF SOCIOLOGY 1633, 1637 (2000).

56. Ana M. Sanchez et al., *The Potential Impact of Incentives on Future Blood Donation Behavior*, 41 TRANSFUSION 172, 175 tbl. 3 (2001).

57. Philippa Howden-Chapman et al., *Blood Money: Blood Donors' Attitudes to Changes in the New Zealand Blood Transfusion Service*, 312 BRITISH MEDICAL JOURNAL 1131, tbl. 1 (1996).

58. Nicholas Wade, *2 New Efforts to Develop Stem Cell Line for Study*, NEW YORK TIMES, June 7, 2006, at A18.

59. *See* Baum, *supra* note 32, at 139. On black markets, *see, e.g.,* Clair Weaver, *Women Illegally Trade in Eggs*, SUNDAY TELEGRAPH (Australia), June 4, 2006, at Local 14; Louis Matheieu Gagne, *Life for Sale*, TORONTO SUN, Mar. 5, 2006, at News: 5.

60. *See* Mary Braid, *The Price of Eggs*, INDEPENDENT ON SUNDAY (London), Mar. 26, 2006, at 58 (citing the Human Fertilisation and Embryology Authority).

61. 793 P.2d 479 (Cal. 1990).

62. *Id.* at 495.

63. *See, e.g.,* Donna M. Gitter, *Ownership of Human Tissue: A Proposal for Federal Recognition of Human Research Participants' Property Rights in Their Biological Material*, 61 WASHINGTON & LEE LAW REVIEW 257, 279–80

(2004); Thomas P. Dillon, *Source Compensation for Tissues and Cells Used in Biotechnical Research: Why a Source Shouldn't Share in the Profits,* 64 NOTRE DAME LAW REVIEW 628, 633–34 (1989).

64. Informed consent documents that specify rights and responsibilities of subjects and researchers have the legal force of contract. See *Dahl v. HEM Pharms. Corp.,* 7 F.3d 1399, 1405 (9th Cir. 1993) (finding that informed consent documents between researchers and subjects are contracts); *Grimes v. Kennedy Krieger Inst., Inc.,* 782 A.2d 807, 843–44 (2001) (same).

65. *See, e.g.,* Gitter, *supra* note 63, at 279; Dillon, *supra* note 63, at 638–39.

66. For a description of both the risks and the pain involved with retrieving ova from a woman's ovaries, see Ellen A. Waldman, *Disputing over Embryos: Of Contracts and Consents,* 32 ARIZONA STATE LAW JOURNAL 897, 903–04 (2000).

67. *See* notes 11–28, *supra.*

68. *ASRM 2002 Guidelines, supra* note 31, at 218–19.

69. New York State Task Force on Life and the Law, ASSISTED REPRODUCTIVE TECHNOLOGIES: ANALYSIS AND RECOMMENDATIONS FOR PUBLIC POLICY 237 (1998).

70. *See, e.g.,* Resnik, *supra* note 45.

71. *See, e.g.,* Braid, *supra* note 60.

72. *See The Authority Decision: HFEA Policy Statement on Eggs for Research* (Feb. 2007); *available at* www.hfea.gov.uk/en/1506.html.

73. *See* Sanchez et al., *supra* note 56 (reporting that 56 percent of survey participants received an incentive for their last blood donation).

74. *Id.; see also* Ronald G. Strauss, *Blood Donations, Safety, and Incentives,* 41 TRANSFUSION 165, 165 (2001) (identifying the U.S. Postal Service and Boeing).

75. *See* Department of Health & Human Services, Food & Drug Administration & Center for Biologics Evaluation & Research, *Recruiting Blood Donors: Successful Practices* (July 7, 2000); *available at* http://www.fda.gov/cber/minutes/rctbld0707p2.pdf (workshop acknowledging that "There were, and still are, some blood-credit programs available where, if you donate blood, there are certain 'insurance-type' programs that people in your family . . . will be able to get blood at no cost").

76. *See* Gitter, *supra* note 63, at 315–19; Jon F. Merz, *Discoveries: Are There Limits on What May Be Patented, in* WHO OWNS LIFE? 99, 112 (David Magnus et al. eds., 2002).

77. The United Network for Organ Sharing (UNOS) keeps an up-to-the-minute count of people on the waiting list on its Web site, www.unos.org.

78. *See* Russell Korobkin, *Sell an Organ, Save a Life,* Los Angeles Times, Oct. 20, 2005, at M5.

## Chapter 8.
## Default Rules for Tissue Donations

1. The precise facts underlying the Moore case were never fully developed in the judicial record because the litigation concerned whether the lower court had properly granted the defendant's motion to dismiss. The factual description here is cobbled together from a number of sources that often disagree as to some of the specifics.

2. The IPO price of the Genetics Institute stock was $29.75 per share. *See Financing Business: Genetics Institute, Inc.,* Wall Street Journal, May 21, 1986.

3. *Moore v. Regents of the University of California,* 793 P.2d 488-92 (Cal. 1990).

4. *See, e.g.,* Mary J. Hildebrand et al., *Toward a Unified Approach to Protection of Genetic Information,* 22 Biotechnology Law Report 602, 604 (2003) (asserting *Moore* "held that an individual does not retain a protectable property interest in his excised cells"); Radhika Rao, *Property, Privacy, and the Human Body,* 80 Boston University Law Review 359, 373 (1999) (citing *Moore* for the proposition that "spleen cells are not considered to be the property of the person from whose body they were withdrawn"); Eric B. Seeney, Moore *10 Years Later—Still Trying to Fill the Gap: Creating a Personal Property Right in Genetic Material,* 32 New England Law Review 1131, 1165 (1998) (California court would not "[grant] Moore property rights in genetic materials").

5. *See generally* Stephen R. Munzer, A Theory of Property 22–23 (1990).

6. For a full discussion, see Chapter 7.

7. *McFall v. Shimp,* 10 Pa. D.&C.3d 90 (1978); *see also Curran v. Bosze,* 566 N.E.2d 1319 (Ill. 1990).

8. Uniform Anatomical Gift Act § 2 (1987).

9. *See Hall v. Fertility Institute of New Orleans,* 647 So.2d 1348 (La. Ct.App. 1994); *Hecht v. Superior Ct.,* 59 Cal.Rptr.2d 222 (Cal. Ct.App. 1996).

10. National Organ Transplant Act of 1984, 42 United States Code §§ 273, 274 (2005).

11. *See Davis v. Davis,* 842 S.W.2d 588 (Tenn. 1992); *Kass v. Kass,* 696 N.E.2d 174 (N.Y. 1998).

12. 793 P.2d at 501 (Broussard, J., dissenting).

13. *United States v. Arora,* 860 F.Supp. 1091 (D. Md. 1994).

14. *See* Dorothy Nelkin & Lori Andrews, *Homo Economicus: Commercialization of Body Tissue in the Age of Biotechnology,* 28 HASTINGS CENTER REPORT 30, 35 (1998).

15. Rebecca Skloot, *Taking the Least of You,* NEW YORK TIMES MAGAZINE, April 16, 2006, at 38, 44.

16. 20 Cal.Rptr.2d 275 (Ct.App. 1993).

17. *Hecht,* 20 Cal.Rptr.2d at 281–84.

18. 264 F.Supp.2d 1064 (S.D. Fla. 2003).

19. *Greenberg,* 264 F.Supp.2d at 1066–67.

20. *Id.* at 1067 (quoting plaintiffs' complaint).

21. 264 F.Supp.2d at 1075.

22 *Id.* at 1072 (emphasis added).

23. *Id.* at 1072–73.

24. The parties subsequently settled the case, and no trial on the unjust enrichment claim occurred. *See* http://www.canavanfoundation.org/news/09–03_miami.php.

25. 45 CODE OF FEDERAL REGULATIONS § 46.116.

26. *See* Carl H. Coleman et al., THE ETHICS AND REGULATION OF RESEARCH WITH HUMAN SUBJECTS 739–40 (2005). At least one court has refused to grant any legal effect to the OHRP guidance where plaintiffs asserted that their informed consent to make a tissue donation was invalid because the consent form stated, "I give up any property rights I may have in . . . tissue samples." *The Washington University v. Catalona,* 437 F.Supp.2d 985, 992, 998 (E.D. Mo. 2006).

27. *See* Ian Ayres, *Preliminary Thoughts on Optimal Tailoring of Contractual Rules,* 3 SOUTHERN CALIFORNIA INTERDISCIPLINARY LAW JOURNAL 1, 5 (1993).

28. *See* Charles J. Goetz & Robert E. Scott, *The Mitigation Principle: Toward a General Theory of Contractual Obligation,* 69 VIRGINIA LAW REVIEW 967, 971 (1983).

29. *See generally* Russell Korobkin, *The Status Quo Bias and Contract Default Rules,* 83 CORNELL LAW REVIEW 608, 613–17 (1998).

30. *Cf.* Charlotte H. Harrison, *Neither Moore nor the Market: Alternative Models for Compensating Contributors of Human Tissue,* 28 AMERICAN JOURNAL OF LAW & MEDICINE 77, 92 (2002) (noting that donors often give tissue because they wish to promote research on a particular disease).

31. *See* Ian Ayres & Robert Gertner, *Filling Gaps in Incomplete Contracts: An Economic Theory of Default Rules,* 99 YALE LAW JOURNAL 87, 97–99 (1989).

32. *Cf.* Harrison, *supra* note 30.

33. *Cf.* Ian Ayres & Robert Gertner, *Majoritarian vs. Minoritarian De-*

*faults,* 51 STANFORD LAW REVIEW 1591, 1599–1600 (1999) ("ceteris paribus . . . defaults that produce positive externalities should be favored").

34. *Cf.* Korobkin, *Status Quo Bias, supra* note 29, at 623–625 (1998) (explaining the "preference-exogeneity assumption" of law and economic analysis).

35. *See* Russell Korobkin, *The Endowment Effect and Legal Analysis,* 97 NORTHWESTERN UNIVERSITY LAW REVIEW 1227, 1228–29 (2003).

36. William Samuelson & Richard Zeckhauser, *Status Quo Bias in Decision Making,* 1 JOURNAL OF RISK & UNCERTAINTY 7, 17 (1988).

37. *See* David Cohen & Jack L. Knetsch, *Judicial Choice and Disparities between Measures of Economic Values,* 30 OSGOODE HALL LAW JOURNAL 737, 747 (1992).

38. Brigette C. Mandrian & Dennis F. Shea, *The Power of Suggestion: Inertia in 401(k) Participation and Savings Behavior,* 116 QUARTERLY JOURNAL OF ECONOMICS. 1149 (2001).

39. Korobkin, *Status Quo Bias, supra* note 29, at 633–47.

40. People who share a common disease are increasingly banding together to create more power vis-à-vis researchers. As noted in Chapter 7, in 2001, a group representing patients with PXE did so. *See* Donna M. Gitter, *Ownership of Human Tissue: A Proposal for Federal Recognition of Human Research Participants' Property Rights in Their Biological Material,* 61 WASHINGTON & LEE LAW REVIEW 257, 315–19 (2004).

41. *Cf.* Harrison, *supra* note 30, at 79 (noting that donors of valuable tissues often report "feeling misled and betrayed when they discovered too late that researchers and companies expected to profit from what the contributors had offered with no strings attached").

42. 45 CODE OF FEDERAL REGULATIONS § 46.111(a)(4)–(5), § 46.116(a).

43. Elisa Eiseman & Jasen J. Castillo, HANDBOOK OF HUMAN TISSUE SOURCES: A NATIONAL RESOURCE OF HUMAN TISSUE SAMPLES at 141 (Appendix B).

44. *Cf.* R. Alta Charo, *Body of Research: Ownership and Use of Human Tissues,* 355 NEW ENGLAND JOURNAL OF MEDICINE 1517, 1519 (2006) (discussing scientists' fears that expanding conceptions of property rights could interfere with the use of banked tissues).

45. *Moore,* 793 P.2d at 493.

46. One possible objection is that even researchers who make no representations that could reasonably be interpreted as promises of compensation could be dragged into litigation by donors who claim that verbal representations were made and that such allegations would be sufficient to avoid summary judgment. But if researchers include in their consent documents

clear statements that no compensation will be forthcoming, allegations of inconsistent verbal statements should be inadmissible under the parol evidence rule and thus insufficient to avoid a motion for summary judgment.

    47. *Moore,* 793 P.2d at 495–96.

## Chapter 9.
## Looking Forward

    1. *See* A. D. Auerbach et al., *Prenatal Identification of Potential Donors for Umbilical Cord Blood Transplantation for Fanconi Anemia,* 30 TRANSFUSION 682, 682–83 (1990).

    2. On the medical advantages of an HLA-matched sibling donor, *see* John E. Wagner & Margaret L. MacMillan, *Unrelated Donor Hematopoietic Cell Transplantation, in* FANCONI ANEMIA: STANDARDS FOR CLINICAL CARE 109, 109–10 (2003).

    3. A detailed account of the Nashes' story can be found in Lisa Belkin, *The Made-to-Order Savior,* NEW YORK TIMES MAGAZINE, July 1, 2001, at 36.

    4. *Id.* at 111.

    5. Susan M. Wolf et al., *Using Preimplantation Genetic Diagnosis to Create a Stem Cell Donor: Issues, Guidelines, and Limits,* 31 JOURNAL OF LAW MEDICINE & ETHICS 327, 328 (2003).

    6. *Id.*

    7. Donna M. Gitter, *Am I My Brother's Keeper? The Use of Preimplantation Genetic Diagnosis to Create a Donor of Transplantable Stem Cells for an Older Sibling Suffering from a Genetic Disorder,* 13 GEORGE MASON LAW REVIEW 975, 976 (2006); Wolf et al., *supra* note 5.

    8. *R (on the application of Quintavalle) v. Human Fertilisation and Embryology Auth.,* [2005] UKHL 28 (House of Lords 2005).

    9. On the Hashmi and Whitaker cases, *see* Gitter, *supra* note 7, at 911–1009. After the Whitaker case, the HFEA reversed its position and permitted another family with a child afflicted with Diamond-Blackfan Anemia to use PGD to identify embryos that would be HLA-compatible with the sick child. *Id.* at 1009–11.

    10. Scholars disagree on whether the Kantian imperative, properly understood, prohibits the use of a child for the benefit of a sibling if the child is otherwise treated and valued as an end in itself. *See* Ronald M. Green et al., *Case Commentary,* 6 CAMBRIDGE QUARTERLY OF HEALTHCARE ETHICS 101, 103 (1997). The version of the Kantian imperative that would distinguish the

Whitaker and Hashmi cases—what I refer to here as the "strict" version—would prohibit the use of a person solely as a means to an end in any one instance, even if the person is otherwise valued as an end.

11. *See* John A. Robertson et al., *Conception to Obtain Hematopoietic Stem Cells,* 32 HASTINGS CENTER REPORT 34, 36 (2002).

12. *Cf.* Bruce Gordon et al., *The Use of Normal Children as Participants in Research on Therapy,* 18 I.R.B. 5, 7 (1996) (reporting that an IRB approved the use of child peripheral blood donors in research on the effectiveness of such treatment on siblings with leukemia based on the reasoning that the psychological benefits of donation to the donors outweighed the risks).

13. *See* Wolf et al., *supra* note 5, at 334.

14. John Rawls, A THEORY OF JUSTICE 12 (1971).

15. For a more general argument as to why the propriety of assigning "rights" to health care services is best judged from this perspective, *see* Russell Korobkin, *Determining Health Care Rights from behind a Veil of Ignorance,* 1998 UNIVERSITY OF ILLINOIS LAW REVIEW 801.

16. *See, e.g., Hart v. Brown,* 289 A.2d 386 (Ct. Super. Ct. 1972) (citing psychological benefits and deference to parents); *Strunk v. Strunk,* 445 S.W.2d 145 (Ky. 1969) (psychological benefit of saving brother would exceed physical trauma of surgery); *Little v. Little,* 576 S.W.2d 493 (Tex. Civ.App. 1979) (citing psychological benefit resulting from close relationship between donor and recipient).

17. *See, e.g., In re Guardianship of Pescinski,* 226 N.W.2d 180 (Wis. 1975); *In re Richardson,* 284 So.2d 185 (La. App. 1973); *Curran v. Bosze,* 566 N.E.2d 1319 (Ill. 1990).

18. 21 UNITED STATES CODE § 355(d).

19. 21 CODE OF FEDERAL REGULATIONS § 312.21.

20. 21 UNITED STATES CODE § 321(g)(1).

21. 42 UNITED STATES CODE § 262(i).

22. J. A. DiMasi et al., *The Price of Innovation: New Estimates of Drug Development Costs,* 22 JOURNAL OF HEALTH ECONOMICS 151, 165–66 (2003). The authors studied the period ending in the year 2000. The costs today are probably significantly higher.

23. *Abigail Alliance v. Von Eschenbach,* 445 F.3d 470 (D.C. Cir. 2006).

24. 21 CODE OF FEDERAL REGULATIONS § 312.34.

25. *See* Gina Kolata & Kurt Eichenwald, *Business Thrives on Unproven Care, Leaving Science Behind,* NEW YORK TIMES, Oct. 3, 1999, at A1.

26. See Patricia C. Kuszler, *Financing Clinical Research and Experimental Therapies: Payment Due, but from Whom?* 3 DEPAUL JOURNAL OF HEALTH CARE LAW 441, 457–62 (2000).

27. 21 CODE OF FEDERAL REGULATIONS § 1271.10.

28. The FDA has specifically advised the cord blood industry that cord blood products intended for use in persons *unrelated* to the donor are considered both drugs and biological products and as such require premarket approval. Center for Biologics Evaluation and Research, *Guidance for Industry: Minimally Manipulated, Unrelated, Allogenic Placental/Umbilical Cord Blood Intended for Hematopoietic Reconstitution in Patients with Hematological Malignancies* 5 (Dec. 2006); *available at* www.fda.gov/cber/guidelines .htm. (The guidance concedes that the same products "for autologous use, or use in a first- or second-degree blood relative . . . may not require premarket review." *Id.* at 2.) Because the FDA has determined from the literature and clinical data that the use of hematopoietic stem cells from cord blood for hematopoietic reconstitution is safe and effective, however, the agency has determined that individual manufacturers need not provide clinical data of safety and effectiveness for this treatment in order to obtain approval. *Id.* at 5. However, under the agency's policy, new stem cell treatments would require an IND, followed by clinical proof of safety and effectiveness, in order to obtain approval.

29. 21 CODE OF FEDERAL REGULATIONS § 1271.150.

30. *See generally* Lars Noah, *Ambivalent Commitments to Federalism in Controlling the Practice of Medicine,* 53 UNIVERSITY OF KANSAS LAW REVIEW 149, 172–76 (2004).

31. *See, e.g.,* David G. Owen, PRODUCTS LIABILITY LAW 492–515 (2005) (describing how courts apply variants of the dominant "risk-utility" test).

32. *Id.* at 606. Courts have not been uniform in how they define when behavior is unreasonable, and thus "design defect" liability attaches in the context of prescription drugs. Following the general law of products liability, some courts have determined that liability is appropriate if the technology was available to make the drug safer without reducing its functionality. *See, e.g., Feldman v. Lederle Laboratories,* 479 A.2d 374 (N.J. 1984). Others have been more protective of the pharmaceutical industry. *See, e.g., Brown v. Superior Ct.,* 751 P.2d 470 (Cal. 1988). In its latest policy statement on the subject, the American Law Institute proposes that design defect liability be assessed against makers of prescription drugs only when there is no class of patients for whom the drug's benefits would exceed its foreseeable risks such that reasonable physicians would prescribe it. RESTATEMENT (THIRD) OF TORTS: PRODUCTS LIABILITY § 6(c).

33. *See, e.g.,* James M. Wood et al., *Product Liability Protection for Stem Cell Research and Therapies: A Proposal,* 18 HEALTH LAWYER 1 (2005).

34. House of Representatives Report No. 99–908, at 4; *reprinted in*

1986 UNITED STATES CODE, CONGRESSIONAL AND ADMINISTRATIVE NEWS 6344, 6345; *Schafer v. Am. Cyanamid Co.*, 310 F.3d 1, 4 (1st Cir. 1994) (noting the act's purpose of "free[ing] manufacturers from the specter of large, uncertain tort liability"). For a brief history of the act, see Victor E. Schwartz and Liberty Mahshigian, *National Childhood Vaccine Injury Act of 1986: An Ad Hoc Remedy of a Window for the Future?* 48 OHIO STATE LAW JOURNAL 387 (1987). On the deterioration of the litigation climate in the context of vaccines, see Gary L. Freed et al., *Safety of Vaccinations: Miss America, the Media, and Public Health,* 276 JOURNAL OF THE AMERICAN MEDICAL ASSOCIATION 1869, 1870 (1996).

35. 42 UNITED STATES CODE §§ 300aa-1–300aa-34.

36. *Id.* § 300aa-11(a)(2)(A), 42 UNITED STATES CODE § 300aa-14(a); Senate Report No. 99–380; *reprinted in* 1986 UNITED STATES CODE, CONGRESSIONAL AND ADMINISTRATIVE NEWS 6287, 6353.

37. 26 UNITED STATES CODE § 9510(b)(1); 26 UNITED STATES CODE § 4131(b)(1).

38. 42 UNITED STATES CODE § 300aa-22(c) and § 300aa-23(d)(2).

39. CDC National Vaccine Program Office: Vaccine Fact Sheets, *National Vaccine Injury Compensation Program; available at* www.hhs.gov/nvpo/factsheets/fs_tableIV_doc1.htm.

40. *See, e.g.,* Coenraad F. M. Hendriksen, *Refinement, Reduction and Replacement of Animal Use for Regulatory Testing: Current Best Scientific Practices for the Evaluation of Safety and Potency of Biologicals,* 43 ILAR JOURNAL s43 (2002) (discussing quality control problems unique to vaccines and other "biologicals"); *cf. Campagna ex rel. Greco v. American Cyanamid Co.,* 767 A.2d 996 (N.J.Super.A.D., 2001) (concerning polio virus that did not meet FDA manufacturing standards).

41. According to the National Vaccine Information Center, it had compensated only approximately two thousand families. National Vaccine Information Center, *Vaccination Decisions; available at* www.nvic.org/Issues/Intro-Message.htm.

42. Health Resources and Services Administration, U.S. Department of Health and Human Services, *National Vaccine Injury Compensation Program (VICP): Frequently Asked Questions; available at* www.hrsa.gov/vaccine compensation/.

43. Precise requirements vary from state to state. *See, e.g.,* CALIFORNIA HEALTH & SAFETY CODE § 120335.

44. Jason L. Williams, *Patient Safety or Profit: What Incentives Are Blood Shield Laws and FDA Regulations Creating for the Tissue Banking Industry?* 2 INDIANA HEALTH LAW REVIEW 295, 304 (2005).

45. Institute of Medicine, HIV AND THE BLOOD SUPPLY: AN ANALYSIS OF CRISIS DECISION MAKING 93–95 (Lauren B. Leveton et al. eds., 1995).

46. *Id.* at 5.

47. *See, e.g.,* George W. Conk, *Is There a Design Defect in the Restatement (Third) of Torts: Products Liability?* 109 YALE LAW JOURNAL 1087, 1100–1101 (2000) (arguing that blood shield laws, by removing the incentive to pursue research and development of pasteurization techniques, allowed the blood products industry to make products that were avoidably unsafe).

48. 21 UNITED STATES CODE § 360k(a); *Horn v. Thoratec Corp.,* 376 F.3d 163 (3d. Cir. 2004) (finding state law design defect claims are preempted by the provision of the Food, Drug, and Cosmetics Act dealing with medical devices when the devices have gone through the premarket approval process). Richard Epstein has argued that this rule should be extended to prescription drugs. Richard A. Epstein, OVERDOSE: HOW EXCESSIVE GOVERNMENT REGULATION STIFLES PHARMACEUTICAL INNOVATION 197–201 (2006).

49. *See* Institute of Medicine, THE FUTURE OF DRUG SAFETY: PROMOTING AND PROTECTING THE HEALTH OF THE PUBLIC S-3 (Alina Baciu et al. eds. 2006) (uncorrected prepublication copy); Catherine T. Struve, *The FDA and the Tort System: Postmarketing Surveillance, Compensation, and the Role of Litigation,* 5 YALE JOURNAL OF HEALTH POLICY, LAW & ETHICS 587, 597 (2005).

50. *Id.* at 600–606, 612.

# Index